PRAYERS O[...]

WHO BY FIRE, WHO BY WATER

Un'taneh Tokef

Edited by
Rabbi Lawrence A. Hoffman, PhD

JEWISH LIGHTS Publishing
Woodstock, Vermont

Who by Fire, Who by Water–Un'taneh Tokef

2013 Quality Paperback Edition, First Printing

Library of Congress Cataloging-in-Publication Data
Who by fire, who by water—unetaneh tokef / edited by Lawrence A. Hoffman. — 2010 hardcover ed.
p. cm.
Includes bibliographical references.
ISBN 978-1-58023-424-5 (hardcover)
1. U-netanneh tokef. 2. High Holidays—Liturgy. 3. Judaism—Liturgy. 4. Judgment of God. I. Hoffman, Lawrence A., 1942–
BM670.U25H64 2010
 296.4'53—dc22

                                                                2010004067

10 9 8 7 6 5 4 3 2 1

Manufactured in the United States of America
Cover Design: Tim Holtz
Cover Art: © Renovatio/Fotolia

Published by Jewish Lights Publishing
A Division of LongHill Partners, Inc.
Sunset Farm Offices, Route 4, P.O. Box 237
Woodstock, VT 05091
Tel: (802) 457-4000   Fax: (802) 457-4004
www.jewishlights.com

Contents

Acknowledgments vii

Prayers of Awe, Intuitions of Wonder 1
Rabbi Lawrence A. Hoffman, PhD

Un'taneh Tokef as Poetry and Legend 13
Rabbi Lawrence A. Hoffman, PhD

The Legend of Rabbi Amnon 26
Translated by Rabbi Lawrence A. Hoffman, PhD

Un'taneh Tokef: Translation 29
Dr. Joel M. Hoffman

Un'taneh Tokef: Behind the Translation 33
Dr. Joel M. Hoffman

PART I THE MORAL CHALLENGE OF *UN'TANEH TOKEF:*
CAN THE PRAYER EVEN BE SALVAGED?

1. The Exodus and the Elephant 51
   Rabbi Tony Bayfield, DD

2. Awe-full Thoughts on Words a Melody Cannot Save 55
   Rabbi Andrew Goldstein, PhD

3. Is *Un'taneh Tokef* Palatable? 60
   Rabbi Delphine Horvilleur

4. From Text to Life to Text: The *Un'taneh Tokef*
   Feedback Loop 63
   Rabbi Noa Kushner

5. A Rationalist's View 67
   Rabbi Charles H. Middleburgh, PhD

6. Universalism versus Martyrdom: *Un'taneh Tokef*
   and Its Frame Narrative   72
   Rabbi Marc Saperstein, PhD

7. Somehow Linked to God   77
   Rabbi Daniel G. Zemel

PART II REINTERPRETING *UN'TANEH TOKEF*
   FOR OUR TIME

8. A Biblical Perspective   83
   Dr. Marc Brettler

9. God as the Ultimate Writer   88
   Dr. Erica Brown

10. "How Was Your Flight?"   93
    Dr. Joel M. Hoffman

11. Passing before God: The Literary Theme
    of *Un'taneh Tokef*   98
    Rabbi Elie Kaunfer

12. The Poetics of Prayer: How *Un'taneh Tokef* Means
    What It Means   103
    Dr. Reuven Kimelman

13. Death without Dying   109
    Rabbi Lawrence Kushner

14. Laminated in the Book of Life?   113
    Rabbi Ruth Langer, PhD

15. *Un'taneh Tokef* through Israeli Eyes   117
    Rabbi Dalia Marx, PhD

16. The Litmus Test of Belief   122
    Rabbi Rachel Nussbaum

17. Meditations on the Poetry of *Un'taneh Tokef*   126
    Rabbi Margaret Moers Wenig, DD

18. Who by Fire: Contemporary Personal
    and Literary Reflections   131
    Dr. Wendy Zierler

PART III *Un'taneh Tokef* and the Limitations of the Human Condition

19. Stark and Inescapable   139
   Merri Lovinger Arian

20. At the Edge of the Abyss   142
   Rabbi Sharon Brous

21. The Answer Is "Me!"   145
   Rabbi Edward Feinstein

22. The Dance between Fate and Destiny   151
   Rabbi Karyn D. Kedar

23. Empowering Human Beings to Challenge Fate   155
   Rabbi Asher Lopatin

24. Who by Common Trial   160
   Catherine Madsen

25. A Text in Context   164
   Rabbi Jonathan Magonet, PhD

26. The Power of Vulnerability   169
   Rabbi Or N. Rose

27. Mortal Matters: The Faith of *Un'taneh Tokef*   172
   Rabbi David Stern

28. Turning Fate into Destiny   177
   Rabbi Avraham Weiss

29. Death Rehearsal   182
   Rabbi David J. Wolpe

PART IV *Un'taneh Tokef* and Its Call for Sanctity, Transformation, and Renewal

30. The Power of the Thin Whisper of Silence   187
   Rabbi Ruth Durchslag, PsyD

31. Evoking Fear, Prescribing Hope:
   From Suffering to Service   191
   Rabbi Elyse D. Frishman

32. The Four Holinesses of *Un'taneh Tokef*:
 A Halakhic Understanding   196
 Rabbi Daniel Landes

33. Trembling with Angels: The Power of Rehearsal   201
 Liz Lerman

34. The Eternal and the Ephemeral:
 The Stark Contrasts of *Un'taneh Tokef*   206
 Rabbi Aaron Panken, PhD

35. Theology or Anthropology?   211
 Rabbi Sandy Eisenberg Sasso

36. "How Awesome and Dreadful:
 God Is Enthroned and Rules with Love"   216
 Rabbi Jonathan P. Slater, DMin

37. God's Hands   221
 Rabbi Brent Chaim Spodek and Ruth Messinger

38. The Call to Turn Inward   225
 Rabbi David A. Teutsch, PhD

39. Shattered Pottery—Unshattered Hope   229
 Rabbi Gordon Tucker, PhD

40. Everything Has Consequences   232
 Dr. Ellen M. Umansky

41. The Seven Questions You're Asked in Heaven   235
 Dr. Ron Wolfson

Notes   240
Glossary   247

Acknowledgments

Acknowledgments begin with the many High Holy Day worshipers for whom *Un'taneh Tokef* has proved important. Knowing me as a liturgist, they have written me numerous letters over the years, calling this poem everything from creative, brilliant, and moving to banal, outmoded, and troubling. Either way, it is clear that *Un'taneh Tokef* has entered the popular liturgical canon alongside such familiar staples as *Adon Olam*, Psalm 23, and *Shehecheyanu*. But with a passion! I begin by admiring this Jewish passion—the insistence that our prayers say something that matters, and that what they say be taken seriously as a guide to God and the human condition.

To these worshipers in general, I add the many colleagues, artists, composers, poets, philosophers, theologians, and critics who added more technical voices to the conversation. Many of them are included here. To them—to all the contributors whose commentaries found their way into this volume—I am grateful.

Particular thanks go to Dr. Joel M. Hoffman, whose expertise in translation became more and more evident with every line of *Un'taneh Tokef.* He has been part of my liturgical partnership with Jewish Lights throughout the award-winning pilot series *My People's Prayer Book: Traditional Prayers, Modern Commentaries* and then again with *My People's Passover Haggadah: Traditional Texts, Modern Commentaries.* Particularly here, with this singular poem of enormous complexity, we are dependent on his linguistic competence. I also consulted with him at times in translating parts of the legend of Rabbi Amnon, although this translation (unlike *Un'taneh Tokef*) is my own, so that any errors in translating it are mine, not his.

I was blessed with colleagues who knew much more than I did about *Un'taneh Tokef.* First and foremost, Dr. Susan Einbinder, master medievalist, directed me to relevant literature. Dr. Sharon Koren too shared her expertise in medieval history with me. Dr. Wendy Zierler drew my attention to *Un'taneh Tokef* in Hebrew literature. Rabbi Margaret Moers Wenig has taught a class in High Holy Day liturgy for many years and shared her mastery of it with me. Others, who had already composed articles on the subject, are included as contributors here, and at least a partial list of scholars whose work I consulted (those writing in English) is represented in my bibliography.

In addition, I was blessed by conversations with prayer-book editors, who had faced the challenge of deciding what to do with *Un'taneh Tokef*—Rabbis Andrew Goldstein, Jonathan Magonet, and Charles Middleburgh: they too are among the contributors here. For background on Christian liturgical parallels, I was able to communicate with Drs. Robert Taft and Stefanos Alexopoulos, who directed me to relevant sources.

Throughout the months of extensive research, I benefited from the work of student rabbi Rachel Shafran Steiner, my research assistant. Soon-to-be Rabbi Shafran Steiner was sufficiently moved by the material that she has since embarked on her own study, as a rabbinic thesis.

And of course, as always, there is my ongoing gratitude to Jewish Lights Publishing. Publisher Stuart M. Matlins first approached me with the idea, as suggested to him by Dan Adler in response to a High Holy Day program developed by Rob Eshman, editor in chief of *The Jewish Journal of Greater Los Angeles*. I was delighted to continue my long and warm relationship with Stuart, who shares my passion for Jewish liturgy and my insistence that it be presented to a reading public with the professional competence and personal commitment that it deserves. Emily Wichland, vice president of Editorial and Production, remains the very best editor with whom to work—profound thanks, as always, go to Emily for her abundant wisdom, skill, patience, and perseverance. For her copyediting, my thanks go to Debra Corman; and for proofreading, Miriam Aronin. I happily include as well all the others at Jewish Lights, especially Tim Holtz, director of Production, who designed the cover for this book; and Kristi Menter, who typeset the English text.

Prayers of Awe, Intuitions of Wonder

Rabbi Lawrence A. Hoffman, PhD

Unsettling Choices

Unsettling choices make up part of every prayer book—most especially the *machzor* for the High Holy Days. The word *machzor* denotes holiday liturgy in general, as opposed to the *siddur,* the daily and Shabbat prayer book. *Siddur* means "order," indicating the intentional organization of the worship service into a carefully choreographed whole. A *machzor* is a *siddur* that has been specially adapted to holidays, not just Rosh Hashanah and Yom Kippur (the *Yamim Nora'im,* the "Days of Awe"), but also the three harvest festivals of the Bible (Passover, Shavuot, and Sukkot), when pilgrims flocked to the Temple to celebrate God's bounty. Literally, *machzor* means "cycle," from the root *ch.z.r.,* "to return," signifying the specific versions of Jewish prayer that are recited cyclically, as the earth rotates around the sun and we find ourselves at familiar times of the year again and again—the harvest seasons, on one hand, and the awe-inspiring days of judgment, on the other.

Originally, even before it was applied to the kind of comprehensive prayer book that we have now, *machzor* denoted a collection of synagogue poetry called *piyyutim,* which were penned by liturgical geniuses in the Land of Israel somewhere around the fifth to the seventh centuries. These were highly elaborated poems, usually with many parts, intended for singular occasions in the year, not just holidays but specific Shabbatot (Sabbaths) as well. The most common kind was composed with the specific Torah and *haftarah* readings in mind and then divided into parts

1

that could be allocated among the various blessings of the central synagogue prayer, the *Amidah*.

The extent of this early period of creativity can be appreciated only by realizing that the Torah was then completed in a triennial reading, not an annual one, as today. Even "triennial," however, is a misnomer, since when holidays fell on Shabbat, the normal Sabbath reading was postponed a week, so that, in actuality, it took more like three and a half years or so to complete an entire Torah cycle from Genesis through Deuteronomy. These early Palestinian poets actually wrote *piyyutim* for every single reading in this triennial cycle, not just for the annual one. Any one of these poems is likely to warrant our holding the poet in high regard—all the more so hundreds of them, sometimes several for each specific reading in the cycle. A *machzor*, then, was a collection of such poetry intended for insertion into the standard service—*Machzor Yannai*, for instance, the set of poems composed by the poet Yannai, who lived somewhere around the fifth century in the Land of Israel.

Our earliest prayer books were just called *siddur* or *seder* (the same thing, in effect) and were all-inclusive, doubling as *machzor* and *siddur*. Both *Seder Rav Amram* (c. 860) and *Siddur Saadiah* (c. 920), for example, our first two comprehensive prayer books, contained prayers for every occasion (including the Passover Haggadah). The same is true of the eleventh-century *Machzor Vitry*, our first prayer book from western Europe, which specifically addresses the concept of an annual cycle (hence its name, *machzor*) but contains prayers for every day of the year, not just holidays.

As time went on, the contents kept on growing, particularly because the art of the *piyyut* continued for centuries after its golden age in Palestine, and norms of piety dictated that new poems never eliminate old ones, but instead just be added. Eventually, people complained that it was becoming impossible to carry the entire volume to synagogue and back—in this age before printing, prayer books were usually handwritten on heavy folio-sized pages, sometimes with gold-leaf illustrations that really added to the weight of the thing! Only then did Ashkenazi Jews separate *machzor* from *siddur* as two separate genres of prayer book. In time, the home prayer book for the Passover seder, the Haggadah, was further split off as its own composition. Today, most Sephardim, too, follow that usage.

Prayer books in general—*siddur,* Haggadah, *machzor*—can be unsettling. Their contents derive from centuries past when people thought much differently about such things as sin and punishment, life and death; when war was rampant, disease seemed heaven-sent, and interreligious harmony was impossible even to imagine. It is not easy for modern worshipers to make their way through a traditional book of prayer without being challenged by at least some of its content.

Not that content is necessarily what counts most in prayer. Prayer is a mode of public recitation that neither demands nor, sometimes, even rewards careful attention to literal meaning. The words may have been chosen centuries ago for reasons that have nothing to do with their cognitive message. Sometimes they were selected for their poetic impact or even their potential to function as a meaning*less* mantra. At other times, they served as allusions to biblical or rabbinic teachings. Or they may have just fulfilled a demand in Jewish law that a given prayer include certain words or exclude others. Regular worshipers who use fully traditional prayer books treat prayer as poetry, song, historical reminiscence, a link to tradition, halakhic obligation, or Hebrew recitation that is simply *davened* through by habit or by custom. In any case, they have learned not to worry about the literal meaning of each and every word, phrase, or even sentence. Liberal prayer books do their best to eliminate or reinterpret bothersome contents. But even so, prayer is necessarily challenging on occasion. It reminds us of our finitude, our frailty, and our moral responsibility. It holds us accountable.

All the more is this true with the *machzor,* especially the one for the High Holy Days. To begin with, the solemnity of the occasion has prompted readings (especially *piyyutim*) that push human imagination to its limits—how else does one address such imponderables as life and death, sin and punishment, and our moral nakedness before the divine? Also, even people who rarely attend daily and Shabbat services come for the High Holy Days.

These occasional worshipers are less likely to have internalized the artistry of the prayer service as a whole. They do not know how to *daven* it through without concern for Hebrew meaning. If the prayers are translated, they are not likely to treat content as secondary to other concerns. Even regulars are apt to be caught up short when High Holy Day prayers that are not part of their daily or weekly routine make claims that strain the imagination or seem morally offensive to modern sensitivities.

Fiction, Non-Fiction, or Something Else?

The problem with prayer-book content emerged when modern consciousness taught us that the most basic literary distinction is between fiction and non-fiction. Prayers can hardly be fiction, we imagine, so they must be non-fiction, in which case they should be judged on the basis of "true or false," like scientific accounts of nature or of history. Talk about God or the universe is expected to be amenable to demonstrable scientific proof. If we cannot affirm its contents, we judge it false and prefer not saying it.

Liberal worshipers faced this dilemma in ways that traditional ones did not: because their prayer books delivered prayers in translation, they suddenly discovered what they had been saying for many years but had never known it. Prayer-book editors responded with a number of strategies. They changed the Hebrew, so that the English would come out "decently"; they purposefully mistranslated the originals to avoid ideas that ancient authors had no trouble with but that modern worshipers found horrifying; they composed alternative prayers in the vernacular—prayers on the same theme as the original, but saying what modern people were likely to appreciate; they called for the prayer to be sung, so no one would pay much attention to the words; or they omitted the troublesome prayers altogether.

But there are limits to each of these strategies. People object to being bamboozled by false translations; they want to know what they are saying. And the liturgy has its own integrity—some prayers are so entrenched in tradition that it is virtually impossible to take them out. Regulars, especially, want to honor the tradition and are willing to pay the price of having a prayer here or there that disturbs them. In their regular attendance, they have spent many hours discussing such prayers and have learned to reinterpret the words or simply to shrug them off. They may even say that the whole point is the cognitive challenge; prayer is not supposed to satisfy us. It is intended to get us in touch with centuries past, minds that are not our own, and attitudes that we may find difficult, but that should not on that account be trashed as if they must obviously be less cogent than what we, nowadays, take for granted.

High Holy Days, however, attract a preponderance of people who are not regulars. But they are hardly illiterates; they object to people telling them that the old-time religion is good and proper, just because it is old-time. To the claim that if they were regulars they would have less difficulty with prayer, they are likely to respond that the chain of causation is just the other way around. If they weren't so honest about the need for prayers to speak truths, they would have become regulars a long time ago. It is precisely because they have trouble with the liturgy that they stay away. Their problem is that although they have given up on daily and Shabbat attendance at services, they would rather not have to do so on the most solemn days of the Jewish year.

And precisely on these days the problems of prayer proliferate because of the preponderance of *piyyutim*, poems that are hard to understand and that were composed long before the time when contemporary sensibilities came into being. How could their authors possibly have predicted the way people think today? It is easy to forget that they didn't know they were "medieval." (Who knows what people a thousand years hence will say about us "moderns"?) In any event, they, like us, responded to the only world they knew, and in their case, that world was supersaturated with war, not as the absence of a state of normalcy called peace, but as the daily state of events at which no one should be much surprised. They suffered poverty and plague as a matter of course, knew nothing of medical realities, and confused what meager science they had with popular superstition. They died of elementary abscessed wounds, thought the mentally ill were possessed by demons, accepted torture as an everyday practice, and had never heard of such concepts as "insurance," "contractual guarantees," and "human rights." It would never have occurred to them that they might be relatively secure against the floods and fires of nature, or the rape and pillage of armies that regularly passed through town on military missions no one understood, much less predicted. Should we be surprised to find that the High Holy Days particularly, with their accent on the tenuousness of life and the moral insolvency of the natural order, should evoke prayerful cries for divine vengeance? Or the hope that repentance might annul the horrors that every adult either knew firsthand or had heard about from parents and grandparents who were lucky just to survive?

Writ large, these are our concerns too. It is still quite astonishing that any of us is here at all and that those of us who are do not die sooner than we do. That is why we come to High Holy Day services, despite their tedious length, baffling organization, and problematic prayers in translation. That too is why the prayers are problems to begin with. We know what they are supposed to remind us of: our mortality, moral defects, and aspirations to be better than what we are. When they sound so medieval as to miss the point, or when their outmoded imagery gets in the way, we are doubly angered: first, because we have to put up with them; and second, because we wish they did for us what they must have done for generations past.

Complicating matters is our still very poor understanding of our ancestors, whom we envision as humorless saints who did not have to suffer the problems with prayer that plague us. But what if they were more like us than we think? Did the same prayers that bother us bother them—an all-powerful, all-good, and all-knowing God who lets innocent children die, for example? When they encountered these liturgical claims, did they take them literally? Or had they already come to terms with the inexpressibility of the profound? Did they have to await modern literary criticism to develop what we now call "readership strategies"—or did they already know enough to read the way we do, recognizing the poetics of simile, hyperbole, personification, and the rest? That they lived in medieval times makes them neither childishly naïve nor mentally incompetent, after all. Some of them were geniuses like Maimonides, who denied God's corporeality and anticipated our unease with prayers that treat God as if God were an all-too-human judge requiring pacification by prayer and petition. But was Maimonides the only one who thought such "heresies," or was he just a particularly prominent person who dared say them out loud? Great writers do not always provide ideas that no one has ever entertained so much as they couch them in words that evoke knowing nods from readers who more or less suspected these truths anyway but had no way of expressing them.

What shall we say, similarly, about the authors of these prayers? How would we know if they wrote ironically, rather than literally, for example? Their Hebrew was unvocalized, leaving us, the readers, to guess at punctuation like commas and periods, but also exclamation points for intensity, question marks to denote rhetorical uncertainties, and quotation marks to warn against a literal understanding of what they bracket. What if we have been getting all this wrong? We can see, for example, how frequently they cited the Bible; but if their primary concern was quoting, how would we know if they intended the quotes as literal truths? We quote Shakespeare's "seven ages of man" to get across the idea of human development, but not to say that there are specifically seven such ages that "men," say, but not women, go through. If someone writes "divinely," we do not mean they really write like God. What if our most gifted writers of prayer almost never took their writing literally? What if they were gifted the way writers are today—able to stretch language imaginatively enough to convey what ordinary conceptual thought will never quite arrive at?

Why don't we give them the same benefit of the doubt that we do poets like William Blake, who describes the "Tyger tyger, burning bright," and asks,

> When the stars threw down their spears,
> And water'd heaven with their tears,
> Did He smile His work to see?
> Did He who made the lamb make thee?

No one objects that tigers do not burn or that stars neither throw down spears nor cry. Why, then, do we attribute banality to poems in the liturgy?

By mistakenly treating prayer books as scientific textbooks, worshipers were led either to denounce or to defend their prayers as they found them, rather than to subject them to the attention they would need to survive the litmus test of rational understanding. A minority of supporters offered a sophisticated defense of what religion is all about, but by and large, when Enlightenment critics declared it hopeless, the majority went into fundamentalist retreat, reiterating all the old sureties, but louder, as if insistent use alone would rescue them from attack. It is easy to assume, therefore, that religious believers have escaped ordinary intelligence—as if science speaks truths, art suggests them, and religion trashes them. We will never find our way through the complexities of prayer if we do not grant that its writers were souls like us, who marveled at nature's grandeur, questioned the persistence of evil, and held out for a God of ultimate meaning—even when the world seemed mired in the muck of desperation.

Philosopher Paul Ricoeur described the elemental religious mentality as a "first naivete." There comes a time when most of us learn to question childish views of God, the universe, and the human aspiration to control our fate by magic, incantation, and even heartfelt prayer—which do not (as a rule) appear to be effective. The process of entertaining doubt about the things we value most evokes what he called a "hermeneutic of suspicion,"—"hermeneutic" being the philosophical term to describe modes of understanding that guide our efforts to interpret reality. When doubt first assails us, we are apt to become dubious about everything—a state of mind that is usually associated with adolescence. So far so good. Religiously speaking, we have all pretty much gone through adolescence. But Ricoeur predicted a stage beyond wholesale skepticism: the reapplication of thought, newly sophisticated, to everything we came to doubt and the formation of a more mature understanding of religion. He called this the "second naivete."

Healthy people achieve a second naivete. From utterly trashing our parents, we grow to understand them and put our faith in them in different ways than we did as children. When we discover life's disappointments, pains, and tragedies, we do not quickly abandon hope, promise, love, and the search for goodness. We reapply those aspirations in deeper, more nuanced ways.

Take science, as another example of this move from first to second naivete. When old pictures of reality prove groundless, scientists do not abandon the search for descriptions, even though they know they will never find adequate words to fully capture what their mathematics demonstrate. The famous image of atoms as electrons circling a nucleus is pure metaphor. It is just a better metaphor than the ones we used before. Second naivete is the adult way of maintaining our engagement with essential matters that elude easy comprehension, exchanging childish understandings of them for better ones that more adequately do them justice. We need a second naivete regarding prayer.

This series, *Prayers of Awe*, seeks such a second naivete, a way of finding depth in what our first naivete once took literally but that subsequently became subject to suspicion. Beginning with *Who by Fire, Who by Water—Un'taneh Tokef,* we will explore the prayer-book issues that defy easy understanding but may yet yield precious insights if exposed to the kind of mature analysis that we apply to music, philosophy, literature, and all the other expressions of thought and feeling that we refuse to call worthless. To arrive at possible readings of these prayers, we have invited a series of perspectives from scholars, artists, musicians, scientists, and everyday worshipers—all of whom take prayer seriously and think deeply about it before dismissing it. We prejudice no particular viewpoint, as long as it is informed by a thoughtful second naivete.

Contributors to this volume were asked to comment on *Un'taneh Tokef* but not necessarily to address their remarks to any particular concern. Nonetheless, their commentaries fall into four broad categories, each one reflecting a different theme relevant to the High Holy Days:

- The Moral Challenge of *Un'taneh Tokef:* Can the Prayer Even Be Salvaged?
- Reinterpreting *Un'taneh Tokef* for Our Time
- *Un'taneh Tokef* and the Limitations of the Human Condition
- *Un'taneh Tokef* and Its Call for Sanctity, Transformation, and Renewal

To be sure, this categorization is somewhat arbitrary; I do not mean to pigeonhole our authors, who, I know, range well beyond any specific topic. But some organization seemed desireable, if only to focus readers' attention on areas of concern that whole synagogues might wish to explore as they prepare for the High Holy Day season. The first topic suggests that *Un'taneh Tokef,* as we have it, may be unsalvageable because of the depth of moral ambivalence that it suggests. The second suggests new interpretations that address that ambivalence. The third raises ultimate issues of human mortality. And the fourth focuses on the specifically human need to experience the holy and to engage in transformation and renewal as a necessary outcome of the High Holy Day message.

We have grouped the commentaries into these four categories, then, to provide thought-provoking and inspiring discussions that a simple alphabetical listing of contributions would not have permitted.

Are There Limits?

The prayer book is liturgy, not literature, just as prayer is not study and the sanctuary not a classroom. It may not be enough to recognize literary technique and poetic understanding in prayers that we once thought futile. Even if sophisticated study will eventually inject difficult prayers with spiritual insight, it may yet be true that the amount of liturgical education required is more than we can expect worshipers to have. The damage done by the obvious meaning of a prayer may be too large a price to pay.

Take, for example, one of the final lines of the Grace after Meals (*Birkat Hamazon*): "I have been young and am now old, but I have never seen the righteous abandoned, and their children seeking bread." The line is biblical, Psalm 37:25. Somehow, over time, it became part of the *Birkat Hamazon,* where it functions still, even though it is patently untrue, at least on the face of it. In our first naivete, we imagine a world where good people get rewarded and live happily ever after. When we subsequently discover righteous people dying of poverty all over the world, the hermeneutic of suspicion sets in; "How dare the psalmist say such a thing? What stupidity!" we think.

With further maturity, we reclaim the prayer and recycle it through our imagination. The Rabbis read lines like this midrashically, supplying different punctuation, perhaps, to invite creative interpretation. What if we read it as "I have been young and am now old, but I have never looked! The righteous are abandoned, and their children seek bread." Now it is a brilliant end to meals; it is a call to stop and look at what the world really is—how many people will never have half the meal that we have just consumed!

But can we count on the average worshiper to develop such a reading strategy? In study, possibly; in prayer, hardly. When we pray, the line accosts us; it comes and goes with such rapidity that we are apt to get stuck on it. "How dare our liturgy say such a thing!" we probably conclude. The existence of this single line threatens to throw prayer in general into disarray. We may be so offended that we will never recite the *Birkat Hamazon* again.

Seeing liturgy this baldly is not just a function of liberal religion, which has made all sorts of liturgical changes, including some that traditionalists abhor. The students of no less a personage than the Vilna Gaon credit their master with preferring that we not say the line in question—not aloud, at any rate. The prayer book they assembled after his death prints the line in tiny type and without punctuation, as if to suggest that it would not be so bad if people skipped over it.

So, too, with the various troublesome prayers that our series addresses. That they have some enlightened meaning will become evident to anyone who reads the commentaries. That they should all remain without emendation (or even if they should remain at all) is a judgment call that transcends whatever meanings an in-depth analysis reveals. Much more is at stake than how much a prayer disturbs us and how well we can allay that disturbance. Disturbing us may be precisely the point. Then too, Jewish law, tradition, and custom make their own precedential demands upon us, and however much Jews differ on what those demands are, we all agree that there is no absence of demand. This book takes no position on a single specific meaning that any given prayer must have, and it makes no final determination as to how this or that congregation of

Jews should choose to handle the prayer in question. Should they include it as is? Include it with commentary? Keep the Hebrew intact but translate it "creatively"? Emend the Hebrew to accord with the creative translation? Omit translation altogether? Provide alternative readings in the vernacular? Omit the prayer even in the Hebrew original? All of these are strategies that one or another congregation or tradition has attempted at one time or other.

This series, Prayers of Awe, begins with an admission and a commitment: we admit the legitimacy of worshipers finding prayer passages troublesome; we commit ourselves to engage such passages as the sophisticated works of art they are, before either dismissing them out of hand or retaining them out of habit. "Awe" after all, has a dual sense—it evokes both wonderment and dread. The High Holy Days with just one or the other can only be "halfway" Days of Awe. The dread seems evident to worshipers who find a prayer shocking. The wonder is less easily attained. Although we cannot determine here what everyone should do with the prayers that we discuss, we can provide intuitions of wonder that should go into the decision.

In the end, these are prayers, after all, not stories, articles, or even collections of poetry that we buy off the stand and read at our leisure. The best analogy is to drama—liturgy is sacred drama. But it is drama with a twist. Tragedy, said Aristotle, is a portrayal of terrible acts that command our sympathy. We properly cry at the tragic hero's end. But we experience the event at a distance, knowing we have seen a depiction, not the real thing. Seeing the victim murdered on stage, we do not hurry out to call the police. Instead, we step back and consider the human condition of which this tragedy is expressive.

Prayer allows us no such distance. The drama of prayer invites us in as part of the cast: we read the lines, sing the songs, dress for the occasion, and obey the choreography of standing, sitting, following the Torah around the room, and so on. We sympathize with Hamlet but never become part of his Danish court. We pray as part of the people Israel with just the opposite expectation. When we leave the service, its lines should be truly our own, as if written just for us, for this very moment. We should be moved, but not at a distance. If it is the High Holy Days, we are to leave with the conviction that we are indeed mortal beings; that we do balance good and evil, sometimes giving in to the latter at the expense of the former; that there is indeed a divine presence before whom we stand; and that we can, with proper repentance and resolve, wipe the slate clean and begin anew with all the promise of a world re-created, a child reborn, a mind reformed, and a conscience reawakened. This series aims at such a liturgical reawakening.

Un'taneh Tokef as Poetry and Legend

Rabbi Lawrence A. Hoffman, PhD

O ne of the most fascinating yet baffling aspects of High Holy Day services is their *piyyutim*, their "poetry." At least half the traditional liturgy is made up of *piyyutim*, some going back to late antiquity, others composed in the Middle Ages. As much as any other factor, it is the choice of *piyyutim* that differentiates one holiday from another. *Un'taneh Tokef* is a *piyyut*.

Every other day, it seems, new *piyyutim* turn up in the treasure trove of genizah fragments housed at Cambridge University or among the manuscripts that the Hebrew University, in particular, has amassed over its years of becoming the central holder of everything Jewish. So we know a great deal about these *piyyutim* by now.[1] At the same time, some very basic questions remain a quandary.

The *Piyyut* in Jewish Liturgy

When and why, for example, did *piyyutim* get started in the first place? We do not know even that for sure. The earliest great poets (*payyetanim*), Yose ben Yose, Yannai, and Eliezer Kallir, lived in the Land of Israel, but their exact dates elude us. They are mentioned first in medieval documents that were written centuries later, by authors who had no historical consciousness. Kallir, the greatest of the three (and probably the greatest Jewish poet who ever lived), was at first considered to be one of the Tannaim, the Rabbis who laid the foundation for Judaism in the first and second centuries CE. But that traditional date is highly unlikely, since, among other things, the liturgy had not developed sufficiently by the

13

second century to allow for the complex poetry that Kallir produced, and we have no indication whatsoever that the art of the *piyyut* was even around that far back. At the other extreme, some early scholars from the nineteenth century placed him as late as the ninth or tenth century. But their view is equally improbable. It is colored by their general dislike of *piyyutim*, because their flowery language and complex poetic style made them hard to understand. Believing that early developments in Jewish culture were more authentic than later elaborations, they found it convenient to imagine *piyyutim* as a late accretion that could be discarded in the interest of liturgical reform.

The most likely date for Kallir is no later than the conquest of Palestine by Islam in 635, since his poetry alludes to the destruction wrought by earlier Christian rulers but has nothing to say about the Muslims who replaced them. The second most illustrious poet of the time, Yannai, who is described as Kallir's teacher, must have lived just before that. The third great innovator, Yose ben Yose, preceded Yannai and is usually dated somewhere in the fourth or fifth century. So *piyyutim* probably arose between the fourth and the seventh centuries, a time of great ferment in Jewish life.

By the end of the fourth century, the Roman Empire had become Christianized, with a "branch office" (as it were) in beleaguered Rome and the central administration established farther to the east, in Constantinople. Churches were replacing pagan temples, and Christian liturgy, relocated within them, was being outfitted to reflect the fusion of official religion with imperial pomp and ceremony. Synagogues had begun as more of a meeting place than a locus for prayer, but by the fourth century, they were becoming religious and liturgical centers akin to the new churches—albeit without the monetary means to compete for architectural and artistic splendor. Liturgical authors, however, were the artistic equals of their Christian parallels and were just as caught up in the poetic aesthetics of the time. By then, the basic prayers of church and synagogue were well established, but room was being made within them for elaborative poetry. Jews called that poetry *piyyutim*.

Like poetry in most times and places, the message was often secondary to the form. The advanced poetry of Kallir, especially, obeys rules of composition that make the poetic content exceptionally hard to decipher—hence the opposition to it among scholars in the nineteenth century. And they were not the first to complain. The best-known objection, perhaps, comes from Abraham ibn Ezra (1089–1164), the famous Spanish grammarian and biblical commentator. In response to the advice by Ecclesiastes to "keep your mouth from being rash and let not your throat be quick to bring forth speech before God" (5:1), he unleashes a lengthy diatribe in which he adjures his readers to be careful about what they say in prayer:

> When we pray, it is forbidden to inject into our prayers *piyyutim*, the basic meaning of which we do not understand. We should not rely on the goodwill of the author, since there is no one who does not sin, and whose sin might not be continued by copyists. Take, for example, the poetry of Eliezer Kallir, who illustrates four problems. First, most of his poems are riddles and analogical allusions [which permit so many interpretations that one never knows exactly what one is saying]. Second, he mixes the language of the Talmud into his poems, and everyone knows that there are many languages within the Talmud that are not holy.... Why should we pray in the language of the Medes, the Persians, the Edomites, and the Ishmaelites? Third, even his Hebrew words are riddled with errors. The fourth problem is that his poetry is filled with midrashic lore, and our Sages said that Scripture should always be presented according to its true meaning. It follows that we should pray only with the true meaning of the text in mind, not according to some esoteric or analogical understanding.... [The analysis continues for an entire page of closely worded argument, after which Ibn Ezra concludes.] I have not been able to elucidate even one in a thousand errors that these poets display.

Ibn Ezra is only one of many great rabbis who despised *piyyutim* in general and the poetry of Kallir in particular. The list of opponents through the ages reads like a Who's Who of rabbinic leadership. "Even the angels do not understand these *piyyutim*," said one commentator! Yet *piyyutim* survived, Kallir's examples first among them.

Another enigma, then, is just how that happened, given how difficult they are to understand, even by us, who have scientific editions of the texts—not to mention multiple translations and scholarly aids to alert us to the many new words the poet made up and to his regular allusions to the Bible and Rabbinic literature. How in the world earlier generations put up with such opaque creative masterpieces is hard to imagine. Were earlier generations so Jewishly literate that they followed the poems as they were recited? Was it the music to which the poetry was set that people enjoyed? Was the poetry added specifically because the wording of the regular service was becoming so predictable that people demanded something more interesting to keep their minds occupied—a sort of verbal crossword puzzle? Did they tune out for the regular prayers but tune back in for the challenge of hearing an altogether new poem? We just do not know.

Whatever the case, *piyyutim* continued for centuries. New schools of poetic composition arose in medieval Sephardi (Spanish) and Ashkenazi (German) communities, each with its own aesthetic preferences. The Spanish poets came first, part of a golden age under Islam that was evident as early as the tenth century. Since they were still ruled by an Islamic regime, they borrowed Muslim styles of poetic rhythm based on the highly developed nature of poetic Arabic. Ashkenazi poets, who lived in Christian lands, knew nothing of Muslim style, so they adopted their own patterns of poetic composition. Sometimes authors wove their names into acrostics formed by combining the letters that introduce each line or verse. Sometimes we know the authors because of oral traditions that link them to their work. Often we have the poems but no clue to who wrote them.

There are different kinds of *piyyutim*, which can be classified according to content, style, and placement in the liturgy. As to content, for example, a *s'lichah* is a poem that deals with forgiveness; the High Holy Day liturgy has a great number of *s'lichot*. In terms of style, a *sh'lishiyah* (from the root *sh.l.sh.*, meaning "three") is a short poetic piece with three lines in it. Poems placed in the *Amidah* are generally called *k'rovot* (singular: *k'rovah*), from the root *k.r.v.*, meaning "to draw close in order to make an offering." A related word, *korban*, means "offering, a sacrifice to God." In a sense, a *k'rovah* is a poetic offering to God.

K'rovot are exceptionally long poems divided into stanzas that appear throughout the *Amidah*. Different stanzas take different poetic shape and content, depending on their placement. The stanzas of a particular kind of *k'rovah*, the most common one we have (called a *k'dushta*), are apportioned among the first three blessings alone. Its climactic ninth stanza, which comes just before the refrain *kadosh, kadosh, kadosh* ("Holy, holy, holy") is called a *silluk. Un'taneh Tokef* is a *silluk* composed for the first day of Rosh Hashanah. By now, it has become so famous that it is commonplace to recite it on both days of Rosh Hashanah and on Yom Kippur as well.

Ashkenazim say it as part of the reader's repetition of the *Musaf Amidah*, since *Musaf*, the extra service that follows the morning service (*Shacharit*) on Shabbat and holy days, is traditionally associated with extra sacrifices offered to God. What better place, then, to insert *k'rovot*, our poetic offerings? Reform Jews long ago shortened their service by eliminating *Musaf*—they objected to its petitions to restore the sacrificial cult, and they considered it largely redundant to what had gone before in any event. *Un'taneh Tokef* is so important, however, that they transferred it to the morning (*Shacharit*) service that still remained. The poem is Ashkenazi in origin, so Sephardim either do not say it at all or recite it prior to *Musaf*, with less energy than is allotted in Ashkenazi services, where it is a highlight of the day. That highlighted role emerged because, ever since the thirteenth century or so, *Un'taneh Tokef* has been associated with a legend about a famous rabbi in Ashkenaz, Rabbi Amnon of Mainz by name.

Rabbi Amnon, the Faithful

Many service goers will recall growing up with the legend of Amnon ringing in their ears. Rabbis would customarily rehearse it as an annual introduction to *Un'taneh Tokef*. If the words, the melody, and the hush in the room during the moment of the *piyyut's* recitation were not enough to command a child's attention, the story connected with it certainly was.

The story derives from a thirteenth-century work called *Or Zarua*, written by Rabbi Isaac of Vienna—often known, from his work, as Isaac Or Zarua. It appears twice after that in variant versions: first (1586/87) in a work called *Shalshelet Hakabbalah* ("Chain of Tradition") by a Sephardi Jew named Gedalyah ibn Yachya; then (1602), in a Yiddish book of tales and legends called the *Mayse Buch* (literally, "Story Book"). The latter is especially interesting. The story probably originated well before Isaac Or Zarua's day, appearing first in the popular Jewish dialect of Yiddish; it was then translated into Hebrew for *Or Zarua* and *Shalshelet Hakabbalah* and then translated back into more literary Yiddish for the *Mayse Buch*. This is genuinely a story of the people.

Rabbinic education customarily includes study of a series of important books that come from medieval Germany, including *Or Zarua*. Most
rabbis today, then, have either come across the tale as Isaac relates it or,
knowing it from their youth or from contemporaries and teachers, have
looked it up, in one form or another. So revered is it that they have sometimes felt the need to relay it to their congregants. Here and there, one
finds a traditional *machzor* that includes it in full; many others refer to it
at least obliquely. The versions that we get from the various sources differ
somewhat, but essentially, here is a synopsis of the tale—not for the faint-
hearted. (See pp. 26–28 for the actual translation.)

Rabbi Amnon is approached by the local bishop, who asks him to
convert. He puts the bishop off, saying he will think about it and return
word in three days. Almost immediately, however, consumed with
remorse for even suggesting that he might apostacize, he refuses to appear
when the three days are over. Perturbed by the sleight, the bishop dis-
patches soldiers to bring him to the castle by force. When asked why he
failed to appear of his own free will, Amnon explains that he should never
have promised to come in the first place. Even saying he would is a griev-
ous enough sin to deserve punishment, which he is perfectly willing, even
anxious, to undergo. Since it is his tongue that sinned, his tongue should
be cut from his mouth. The bishop, however, maintains that the sin was
performed by Amnon's feet, which he did not use to carry him to the
palace as he had promised. He thereupon orders that Amnon's toes and
fingers be hacked off.

What is left of Amnon is then carried on a knight's shield back to
the Jewish quarter. When Rosh Hashanah next arrives, Amnon asks to be
delivered to the synagogue, where he is placed next to the prayer leader,
alongside his amputated parts. As the leader is about to recite the
K'dushah—the prayer specifying God's sanctity—Amnon asks him to
wait a minute while he, Amnon, "sanctifies God's name."

"And so, let holiness rise up to You," he begins, after which he recites
Un'taneh Tokef, a prayer no one has ever heard before. When he finishes, he
disappears from before the congregation, somehow taken by God from this
world. Three days later, he reappears in a dream to "Rabbi Kalonymus, ben
Meshullam, ben Kalonymus, ben Moshe, ben Kalonymus" to teach him
the prayer and instruct him to publicize it far and wide throughout the
diaspora as a witness and testimonial to what he has done.

What do we make of such a story?

It could, of course, be absolutely true, but if so, it is rather strange that we have no confirming information from any other source about a Rabbi Amnon who lived in Mainz. One would expect that a rabbi of such fame would be well enough known to turn up elsewhere in Ashkenazi writings. But he doesn't. Then too, the details of the story seem patently to be composed of bits and pieces of other tales, a combination of folk motifs from elsewhere. An eleventh-century Italian chronicle called *M'gillat Ahima'az*, for instance, knows of someone whose hands and feet are cut off by the authorities and who mysteriously disappears, as if taken up by God, on Yom Kippur. Some of these motifs go back to the biblical Joseph, who becomes a medieval model of a Jew who withstands temptation. The Amnon tale even borrows the biblical description of Joseph in its presentation of its hero—Amnon is "well built and handsome," just like Joseph (Genesis 39:6). Unlike Joseph, however, who steadfastly refuses the overtures of Potiphar's wife, Amnon expresses doubt in the face of temptation. Apostasy to Christianity is like whoring after the powers that be, and Amnon almost fails the test. No wonder he is so grief-stricken as to demand that his tongue be severed for his crime. Isn't it likely, then, that instead of an actual historical event being portrayed here, we have a morality tale, a reflection of a difficult period in Jewish history when persecution was the order of the day and Jews might well have considered abandoning Judaism to save themselves and their children?

Still, there may be some reliable historical core below the patently fictional detail. Another school of thought, therefore, searches for the kernel of historical truth on which the legend, if it is that, has been constructed. The most likely reconstruction to emerge from this camp locates not one but several Rabbi Amnons—in Italy.

The original Amnon is a biblical figure, King David's oldest son, who is remembered most for raping his half-sister Tamar and being killed for it by her avenging brother Absalom. Italian Jews customarily named their children after biblical personalities, especially people associated with King David—even those with an unsavory biblical reputation, like Amnon. There was no Amnon of Mainz, but there was an Amnon of Oria in southern Italy who is described by Italian sources as having been martyred in 925. Another Italian Amnon is the father of a tenth-century synagogue poet named Chananel. Moreover, as we shall see, *Un'taneh Tokef* is an old *piyyut* that was already in use in Italy.

Perhaps, then, the Amnon of Mainz is really an Amnon of Italy who suffered persecution and passed along an old *piyyut* that made its way from Italy into Germany as part of the general transmission of Jewish culture from the Mediterranean world to the German communities in the Rhineland.

Well, maybe. Who can say? But even so, Rabbi Amnon of Mainz is an invention, as is the story that surrounds him. That story, as we have it, is indeed a pious tale about martyrdom, the stuff of legend, rooted in the catastrophic era of the First and Second Crusades.

In 1095, Pope Urban II came to Clermont, France, to declare a Crusade against the Muslims who had occupied the Holy Land. While regular armies were being assembled, a ragtag army of peasant populists took to the highways, anxious to leave immediately. When they arrived in the Rhineland, the center of German Jewry, they took out their hatred on the Jews, massacring them in large numbers. It was the first wholesale murder Jews had experienced. Later tales told of mothers and fathers slaughtering their own children rather than letting them fall into the clutches of the Crusaders, who would torture, maim, and murder them in ways too horrid to imagine. It was our medieval forebears' equivalent to what the Shoah is for us.

The survivors, like survivors in our time, sought to come to terms with the massive deaths of the innocent as best they could. Among their explanations was the idea that God had required them to be martyrs for God's own glory, *al kiddush hashem* (as they put it), "to sanctify the name of God." Stories of martyrdom circulated widely throughout the next several generations.

The official armies of the First Crusade that followed the peasants reached their destination and enjoyed military success. They established the Latin Kingdom of Jerusalem throughout current-day Israel and extended their dominion under a variety of other Christian kingdoms spread out northward along the Mediterranean coast. The kingdom of Jerusalem lasted almost a century—it was lost to Saladin the Great in 1187—but not without a Second Crusade proclaimed in 1145. The year before (1144), European Christians had received the frightening news that a Muslim counteroffensive had taken the far-north Crusader city of Edessa, part of modern Turkey. In 1146, Crusaders again marched through the Rhineland and again massacred Jewish inhabitants. Word of the carnage comes from *Sefer Z'chirah*, "The Book of Memory," compiled by Rabbi Ephraim of Bonn some time afterward, probably as late as 1177. The slaughter was so great, he says, that "the day after, the bishop ordered the remains of all the slaughtered saints to be loaded onto wagons" along with "all their severed limbs, hips, shoulders, fingers, and toes" and be buried. The bishop had come to the Jews' aid, but too late, and was now, at least, permitting a proper burial.

Ephraim's "Book of Memory" collects tales of Jewish martyrdom, which the author saw as a particularly beautiful way to serve God with the most ultimate thing we own: our lives. By 1177, word had spread of a newly outfitted Muslim army ready to engage the Crusaders in a final military showdown, a course of events that Ephraim interpreted as the beginning of the long-awaited era of Jewish redemption. His recitation of all that Jewish martyrs had suffered was a plea to God to hasten the end and grant Jews the reward that was so greatly owed them. He may also have feared another round of massacres as new Crusader armies passed through on their way to battle, in which case he would have enshrined the death of future martyrs in a plea to God that if not now, then someday, at least, final deliverance might dawn.

Most scholars think the legend of Amnon, as we know it, originated with Ephraim and was then passed down through the generations to Isaac Or Zarua of Vienna—who, in fact, personally attributes it to Ephraim. Like the sainted Amnon of Mainz, the Jews of Ephraim's day were killed for the sanctification of God's name; like him, too, they were hacked to pieces.

Amnon served Ephraim as a sermonic model; whatever history there may have been (if there was any) was secondary. At the point where the legend describes his faithful martyrdom, it informs us, "That is why his name is Rabbi *Amnon* [Rabbi 'Faithful']—because *he'emin*, 'he had faith,' in the living God, and because of his faith, he suffered horrendous torment out of love, just on account of something that crossed his lips."

The author is drawing our attention to a Hebrew pun. The Hebrew word for "faith" is *emunah*; "faithful" is *ne'eman*. But Hebrew is written without vowels, allowing rabbis to play with alternative vowel combinations to provide additional layers of meaning. *Ne'eMaN* has been rearranged as *aMNoN*, who emerges as the medieval personification of that extreme degree of faith that resulted in so many deaths under the hands of the Crusaders. Amnon epitomizes those who died *al kiddush hashem*, "to sanctify the name of God."

Whether he lived or not, however, may be beside the point. If he didn't die for his faith, countless others did. The Amnon story was not the only tale circulating at the time. Numerous others had been composed as well—"martyr stories" had become a genre of folk literature among the Jews of Crusader Europe. Ephraim of Bonn did not so much make up this story as he adapted it from many similar accounts with which he was familiar. He probably intended it as an explanation for *Un'taneh Tokef*, a prayer that had reached him and that seemed like the kind of thing a martyr would have written. In his story, he correctly describes it as a *silluk*, the last and climactic stanza of a *k'dushta*. As a poet himself, he had written his own *piyyutim* and knew the structure of a classical *k'dushta*. Knowing that a *silluk* is customarily introduced by the words "And so, let holiness rise up to You" (*uv'khen l'kha ta'aleh k'dushah*), he has Amnon begin his deathbed poem that way. The genius of the legend is that, unlike the others of its kind, this one has Amnon not simply dying but disappearing into heaven, like the prophet Elijah, whom Jewish tradition expects to return at the end of time. We are put on notice that Amnon too will make another appearance, as indeed he does—in a dream to "Kalonymus, ben M'shullam, ben Kalonymus, ben Moshe, ben Kalonymus." German Jewry knew many by the name Kalonymus, obviously, all of them members of the Kalonymide family, the founding dynasty of Italian Jews who crossed the Alps and founded the German Rhineland communities in the first place. Amnon's poem is thus linked to German Jewry's founding family, who are said to have instituted it upon Amnon's own request, made in a dream.

In a double entendre, both Amnon (in his death) and the poem that he is said to have written (and that gets said every Rosh Hashanah and Yom Kippur) exemplify holiness. It is the quintessential martyr's prayer offered up to God by the most famous medieval martyr—who died as a willing sacrificial offering to God in order to "sanctify God's name." But it is also what we say every single year—as a *silluk* to a *k'dushta*, which is itself a subcategory of a *k'rovah*, meaning "offering."

The fact that *Un'taneh Tokef* is a *silluk* provides yet another bit of poetic irony. *Silluk* comes from the root *s.l.k.*, meaning "go up," the idea being that the final stanza of the poem arises like sacrificial smoke to God. In the Amnon story, more than the *silluk* rises to God that way. So too does Amnon himself, who simply disappears like Elijah. The verb is *niStaLeK*, a play on words with *SiLluK*.

But if there was no Amnon to write *Un'taneh Tokef,* who did author it? We do not know for sure. It could not have been Ephraim; had he been its composer, it would have resembled other German *piyyutim* of his time—the way (that is) that Amnon himself would have written it—and Ephraim knew what those *piyyutim* looked like because he was himself a poet who wrote them. But it doesn't look at all like medieval German poetry, and we know it was already being recited in eleventh-century Italy.

Even before our knowledge of Italian liturgy that contained it, it was assumed to have been written prior to the rise of German Jewry, possibly by an unknown author from the classic era of Jewish poetry mentioned above—someone familiar, moreover, with the poetry of the Byzantine Church. That claim was made in 1959 by the late Professor Eric Werner, whose name deserves mention as the founder of Jewish musicology in America. He had arrived here as one of several scholars whom the Hebrew Union College rescued from Nazi Germany.

Werner's European education outfitted him not just with what was then known regarding the history of Jewish music, but also with competence in the classics—Hebrew, of course, but also Greek and Latin. His linguistic skill allowed him to make use of earlier studies that suggested a similarity between *Un'taneh Tokef* and a poem by a famous Byzantine poet known as Romanos the Melodist. Romanos had penned poetry for Christian liturgy in a style called *kontakion,* and indeed, at least one parallel-sounding *kontakion* does exist; it celebrates the awesome nature of the second coming of Jesus as suggested by Christian interpretation of Scripture, especially the Book of Revelation.

Scholars today believe Werner's link between Romanos and the unknown author of *Un'taneh Tokef* is incorrect. Among other things, both church and synagogue poets drew on common biblical citations in their work. That both Romanos and the mysterious author of *Un'taneh Tokef* wrote poetry that sounded similar because of shared biblical paradigms does not mean that either one borrowed directly from the other or even that they knew of each other's existence. But Werner was not altogether in error. His general dating is accurate enough, and indeed, recent finds have revealed what looks like an earlier version of *Un'taneh Tokef* from that very era—by none other than Yannai.

Yannai was enormously prolific. Most of his poetry has not reached us in prayer-book form—that is, we would never know of his poems were it not for independent collections of his work preserved in manuscripts.

These circulated in the Middle Ages, and one of them does indeed look very much like our *Un'taneh Tokef.* Presumably, it existed in various versions, in part because it was passed down orally, and in part because of several extant scribal variations that developed, each with its own understanding of what the original words were. One of those versions became the *Un'taneh Tokef* that we have as the capstone "ninth" section of the main *piyyut* for our High Holy Days.

The other sections that we customarily use come from Kallir. Kallir himself seems to have been familiar with a version of *Un'taneh Tokef,* which he cites within his own work for the High Holy Days, the way one poet refers back to another or a composer writes "variations" on the work of a respected predecessor. He had composed his own nine-part poem for the Days of Awe. We even know what the ninth one (the *silluk*) was. It was recited as late as the eleventh century by Jews in France and was commonplace in Italy much earlier—a magnificent description of the heavenly court trying not just individuals universally, but the entire people of Israel and pardoning them.

If this reconstruction is correct, we would have to say that at some point, someone dropped the *silluk* by Kallir in favor of the parallel composition by Yannai. It has been suggested that German Jews inherited the Yannai version and worried that the French original would replace it. If so, the purpose of the Amnon myth was to enshrine *Un'taneh Tokef* as a poem that absolutely had to be retained. Alternatively, German congregations, like their French equivalents, were used to saying the entire Kallir poem. But the Yannai *silluk*, with its accent on the fateful deaths of individuals, fit the historical circumstances in Germany, with its rash of martyrdom at the hands of Crusaders. It was then that it replaced Kallir's original. Ephraim of Bonn would have inherited this relatively recent tradition of saying *Un'taneh Tokef* and, in order to explain it, decided to append an explanation of the poem's origin in terms of a story that he adapted from the surrounding cluster of folk motifs: the story of Amnon of Mainz. The story ends, after all, with the dream in which Amnon orders the leading family of Ashkenazi Jewry to include his poem forever.

Un'taneh Tokef Today

It is almost impossible now to separate the poem from the legend. The latter lay buried in medieval books ever since Isaac Or Zarua's day, certainly. But average people did not necessarily know about it. We do not even hear of rabbis regularly and as a matter of course, throughout the centuries, drumming its message home the way rabbis in the 1950s (and after) did. That is because it reminded them of the Holocaust, our own version of dying *al kiddush hashem.* The story was therefore revived with particular vigor after World War II—and possibly before that, in other places where Jews suffered the results of modern anti-Semitism. Whatever the case, the story is well enough known today for us to have to struggle with what to do with it. That is the question that this book poses—not just what to do with a poem whose theology we may have trouble living with, but what to do with it especially in the light of its association with martyrdom.

For some, the poem is of such sublime poetic beauty that it would be criminal to expunge it. Others cringe at its message and would gladly do away with at least some of it as a piece of liturgy, even though it would remain as a poem outside the prayer book to be studied like other poetic compositions from the past. Yet others find the Amnon story compelling, if not as a historical set of facts, then as a witness to Jews who truly did die *al kiddush hashem*; still others would prefer jettisoning the poem because of its association with martyrdom and a theology of martyrdom that we have difficulty maintaining today. However the matter turns out, the decision should be made knowledgeably, taking into account the weight of history, literary criticism, poetic aesthetics, and contemporary concern for a liturgy that offers modern meaning to modern Jews. This book offers that background.

The Legend of Rabbi Amnon

Translated by Rabbi Lawrence A. Hoffman, PhD

[The following is the original story, translated from *Sefer Or Zarua*, a twelfth-century work by Rabbi Isaac of Vienna.]

The story of Rabbi Amnon of Mainz, who was the greatest of his generation, wealthy, of fine lineage, well built, and handsome: The nobles and the bishop began asking him to apostacize to their mistaken way, and he refused to listen to them. When they [continually] spoke to him day after day, and he didn't listen to them, the bishop badgered him. One day they took hold of him, and he said, "I want to seek advice and think the matter through for three days" [he said this just to put them off]. But the minute he took leave of the bishop, what he had said sunk in—how an expression of doubt had left his lips, as if there were a possibility that some kind of advice or thought process would lead him to deny the living God. He went home unable to eat or drink. All his relatives and friends came to console him, but he refused to be comforted and said, "Because of what I said, I will go to my grave in grief." He wept in his sorrow.

On the third day, while Amnon was still pained and anxious, the bishop sent for him, and he replied, "I won't go." The evil one sent princes, more numerous and of greater standing than at first, and he still refused to go. So the bishop said, "Have Amnon come here hurriedly, against his will," and they quickly brought him.

He asked, "What's this, Amnon, why didn't you come to me as you stipulated—that you would take counsel and get back to me and do what I asked?"

Amnon replied, "Let me adjudicate my own case. The tongue that lied to you should be sentenced to be cut off" [Amnon wanted to sanctify the name of God because of what he said].

"No," the bishop responded. "It is not your tongue that I will cut off, for it spoke well. Rather it is your legs that did not come to me, as you promised, that I will chop off, and the rest of your body that I will torment."

The evil one commanded that the joints of his fingers and toes be hacked off. At each joint, they would ask him, "Amnon, now do you want to convert to our faith?" and he would say, "No!"

When they finished hacking, the evil one commanded that Rabbi Amnon be laid on a shield with his fingers and toes beside him and be sent home. That is why his name is Rabbi *Amnon* [Rabbi "Faithful"]— because *he'emin*, "he had faith," in the living God, and because of his faith, he suffered horrendous torment out of love, just on account of something that crossed his lips.

The time eventually rolled around for Rosh Hashanah to arrive and he asked his relatives to take him to the synagogue (along with all the joints, which had been preserved) and to lay him next to the prayer leader. They did so, and when the prayer leader got to [a particular *piyyut* in] the *K'dushah*, Rabbi Amnon said, "Wait, while I sanctify the name of God." In a loud voice, he then responded, "And so, let holiness rise up to You," as if to say, "I have sanctified your name, with regard to your sovereignty and your unity." Then he recited, "And let us acknowledge the power of this day's holiness [*un'taneh tokef k'dushat hayom*]," and said, "Truly, You are judge and prosecutor," in order to accept the verdict—how they sacrificed his fingers and toes, and so forth. Then he mentioned, "Everyone's signature is in it ... and You will record all living beings," since that was what was decreed for him on Rosh Hashanah. When he had completed the final part of the poem [the *silluk*] he was taken up [*nistallek*] and in the sight of everyone, he disappeared from the world, and was no more, because God took him. Of him it is said, "How much goodness You have stored up for those who love You ..." (Psalm 31:20).

After the words [that Amnon spoke] and the truth [that he recounted], on account of which Rabbi Amnon was taken up, he was invited into the yeshivah on high. On the third day after his purification [the ritualized cleansing that is performed on everyone who dies], he appeared in a night vision to our Rabbi Kalonymos, son of Rabbi M'shulam, son of Rabbi Kalonymos, son of Rabbi Moshe, son of Rabbi

Kalonymos, and taught him that very *piyyut*: *Un'taneh tokef k'dushat hayom*; and he commanded him to distribute it throughout the far reaches of the Exile, that it might be a witness and memorial to him—and the *gaon* [the sage] did so.

Un'taneh Tokef
TRANSLATION

Dr. Joel M. Hoffman

And so let holiness rise up to you,
For you are our God, king.

וּבְכֵן לְךָ תַעֲלֶה קְדֻשָׁה
כִּי אַתָּה אֱלֹהֵינוּ מֶלֶךְ

[1] And let us acknowledge the power
of this day's holiness,
For it is full of awe and dread.

[2] And on it your kingdom will be
exalted
And your throne will be established
in love.

[3] And You will reign from it in truth.
Truly You are judge

[4] And prosecutor and litigant and
witness
And author and sealer, and recorder
and recounter.

[5] And You will remember everything
that has been forgotten
And You will open the book of
memories

[6] And it will be read from:
Everyone's signature is in it.

[7] And a great shofar will be sounded
And a thin whisper of a sound will
be heard.

[1]וּנְתַנֶּה תֹקֶף קְדֻשַּׁת הַיּוֹם
כִּי הוּא נוֹרָא וְאָים
[2]וּבוֹ תִנָּשֵׂא מַלְכוּתֶךָ
וְיִכּוֹן בְּחֶסֶד כִּסְאֶךָ
[3]וְתֵשֵׁב עָלָיו בֶּאֱמֶת
אֱמֶת כִּי אַתָּה הוּא דַיָּן
[4]וּמוֹכִיחַ וְיוֹדֵעַ וָעֵד
וְכוֹתֵב וְחוֹתֵם וְסוֹפֵר וּמוֹנֶה
[5]וְתִזְכֹּר כָּל הַנִּשְׁכָּחוֹת
וְתִפְתַּח סֵפֶר הַזִּכְרוֹנוֹת
[6]וּמֵאֵלָיו יִקָּרֵא
וְחוֹתַם יַד כָּל אָדָם בּוֹ
[7]וּבְשׁוֹפָר גָּדוֹל יִתָּקַע
וְקוֹל דְּמָמָה דַקָּה יִשָּׁמַע

29

⁸And angels will recoil
And be gripped by shaking and
trembling

⁹And they will say, "This is the day of
judgment,"
For reviewing the hosts on high in
judgment.

¹⁰For they will not be innocent when
You judge them.
And all who enter the world will
pass before You like sheep.

¹¹As a shepherd searches for his flock
And has his sheep pass under his
staff

¹²So too will You record and recount
And review all living beings as You
have them pass by.

¹³And You will decide the end of all
creatures
And write down their sentence.

¹⁴On Rosh Hashanah they will be
written down
And on Yom Kippur they will be
sealed:

¹⁵How many will pass on and how
many will be created,
Who will live and who will die,

¹⁶Who at their end and who not at
their end,
Who by fire and who by water,

¹⁷Who by warfare and who by
wildlife,
Who by hunger and who by thirst,

⁸וּמַלְאָכִים יֵחָפֵזוּן

וְחִיל וּרְעָדָה יֹאחֵזוּן

⁹וְיֹאמְרוּ הִנֵּה יוֹם הַדִּין

לִפְקוֹד עַל־צְבָא־מָרוֹם בַּדִּין

¹⁰כִּי־לֹא־יִזְכּוּ בְעֵינֶיךָ בַּדִּין

וְכָל־בָּאֵי־עוֹלָם יַעַבְרוּן לְפָנֶיךָ

כִּבְנֵי־מָרוֹן

¹¹כְּבַקָּרַת רוֹעֶה עֶדְרוֹ

מַעֲבִיר צֹאנוֹ תַּחַת־שִׁבְטוֹ

¹²כֵּן־תַּעֲבִיר וְתִסְפֹּר וְתִמְנֶה

וְתִפְקֹד נֶפֶשׁ כָּל־חַי

¹³וְתַחְתֹּךְ קִצְבָּה לְכָל־בְּרִיָּה

וְתִכְתֹּב אֶת־גְּזַר דִּינָם

¹⁴בְּרֹאשׁ הַשָּׁנָה יִכָּתֵבוּן

וּבְיוֹם צוֹם כִּפּוּר יֵחָתֵמוּן

¹⁵כַּמָּה יַעַבְרוּן וְכַמָּה יִבָּרֵאוּן

מִי יִחְיֶה וּמִי יָמוּת

¹⁶מִי בְקִצּוֹ וּמִי לֹא־בְקִצּוֹ

מִי בָאֵשׁ וּמִי בַמַּיִם

¹⁷מִי בַחֶרֶב וּמִי בַחַיָּה

מִי בָרָעָב וּמִי בַצָּמָא

¹⁸Who by earthquake and who by plague,
Who by strangling and who by stoning,

¹⁹Who will rest and who will wander,
Who will be tranquil and who will be troubled,

²⁰Who will be calm, and who will be tormented,
Who will be exalted and who humbled,
Who will be rich and who will be poor?

²¹And repentance, prayer, and charity
Help the hardship of the decree pass.

²²For your glory is like your name,
Slow to anger, quick to forgive.

²³For You do not want the dead to die,
But for them to turn from their path and live.

²⁴You wait until the day they die,
Accepting them immediately if they return.

²⁵Truly You are their creator
And You know their nature

²⁶For they are flesh and blood.

²⁷Their origin is from dust
And their end is to dust:

²⁸At their peril gathering food,
They are like shattered pottery,

מִי בָרַעַשׁ וּמִי בַמַּגֵּפָה ¹⁸

מִי בַחֲנִיקָה וּמִי בַסְּקִילָה

מִי יָנוּחַ וּמִי יָנוּעַ ¹⁹

מִי יַשְׁקִיט וּמִי יִטָּרֵף

מִי יִשָּׁלֵו וּמִי יִתְיַסָּר ²⁰

מִי יָרוּם וּמִי יִשָּׁפֵל

מִי יַעֲשִׁיר וּמִי יֵעָנִי

וּתְשׁוּבָה וּתְפִלָּה וּצְדָקָה ²¹

מַעֲבִירִין אֶת־רֹעַ הַגְּזֵרָה

כִּי כְּשִׁמְךָ כֵּן תְּהִלָּתֶךָ ²²

קָשֶׁה לִכְעֹס וְנוֹחַ לִרְצוֹת

כִּי לֹא תַחְפֹּץ בְּמוֹת הַמֵּת ²³

כִּי אִם בְּשׁוּבוֹ מִדַּרְכּוֹ וְחָיָה

וְעַד יוֹם מוֹתוֹ תְּחַכֶּה־לּוֹ ²⁴

אִם יָשׁוּב מִיַּד תְּקַבְּלוֹ

אֱמֶת כִּי אַתָּה הוּא יוֹצְרָם ²⁵

וְיוֹדֵעַ יִצְרָם

כִּי הֵם בָּשָׂר וָדָם ²⁶

אָדָם יְסוֹדוֹ מֵעָפָר ²⁷

וְסוֹפוֹ לֶעָפָר

בְּנַפְשׁוֹ יָבִיא לַחְמוֹ ²⁸

מָשׁוּל כַּחֶרֶס הַנִּשְׁבָּר

²⁹ Like withered grass and like a faded
blossom,
Like a passing shadow and like a
vanishing cloud,

³⁰ And like blowing wind and like
sprouting dust
And like a dream that will fly away.

³¹ But You are king,
The living and everlasting God.

³² Your years are boundless
And the length of your days is
endless.

³³ Your glorious chariots are priceless
And the eternity of your name is
limitless.

³⁴ Your name suits You
And You suit your name.

³⁵ You named us after You;
Act for the sake of your name.

³⁶ And sanctify your name
Through those who declare the
sanctity of your name

³⁷ For the glory of your name,
Honored and sanctified,

³⁸ As the utterances of the assembly of
holy seraphim,
Who sanctify your name with "holy,"

³⁹ Inhabitants above with inhabitants
below
Thrice call out the trio of holiness
with "holy."

כְּחָצִיר יָבֵשׁ וּכְצִיץ נוֹבֵל ²⁹
כְּצֵל עוֹבֵר וּכְעָנָן כָּלָה
וּכְרוּחַ נוֹשָׁבֶת וּכְאָבָק פּוֹרֵחַ ³⁰
וְכַחֲלוֹם יָעוּף
וְאַתָּה הוּא מֶלֶךְ ³¹
אֵל חַי וְקַיָּם
אֵין קִצְבָה לִשְׁנוֹתֶיךָ ³²
וְאֵין קֵץ לְאֹרֶךְ יָמֶיךָ
וְאֵין שִׁעוּר לְמַרְכְּבוֹת כְּבוֹדֶךָ ³³
וְאֵין פֵּרוּשׁ לְעֵילוֹם שְׁמֶךָ
שִׁמְךָ נָאֶה לְךָ ³⁴
וְאַתָּה נָאֶה לִשְׁמֶךָ
וּשְׁמֵנוּ קָרָאתָ בִּשְׁמֶךָ ³⁵
עֲשֵׂה לְמַעַן שְׁמֶךָ
וְקַדֵּשׁ אֶת שִׁמְךָ ³⁶
עַל מַקְדִּישֵׁי שְׁמֶךָ
בַּעֲבוּר כְּבוֹד שִׁמְךָ ³⁷
הַנַּעֲרָץ וְהַנִּקְדָּשׁ
כְּסוֹד שִׂיחַ שַׂרְפֵי קֹדֶשׁ ³⁸
הַמַּקְדִּישִׁים שִׁמְךָ בַּקֹּדֶשׁ
דָּרֵי מַעְלָה עִם דָּרֵי מַטָּה ³⁹
קוֹרְאִים וּמְשַׁלְּשִׁים בְּשִׁלּוּשׁ
קְדֻשָּׁה בַּקֹּדֶשׁ

Un'taneh Tokef
BEHIND THE TRANSLATION

Dr. Joel M. Hoffman

[1] And let us acknowledge the power
of this day's holiness,
For it is full of awe and dread.

[2] And on it your kingdom will be
exalted
And your throne will be established
in love.

¹וּנְתַנֶּה תֹּקֶף קְדֻשַּׁת הַיּוֹם

כִּי הוּא נוֹרָא וְאָיֹם

²וּבוֹ תִּנָּשֵׂא מַלְכוּתֶךָ

וְיִכּוֹן בְּחֶסֶד כִּסְאֶךָ

[1] *And:* The first nine lines of the poem begin in Hebrew with *v'*, "and." The Hebrew *v'* is both more commonly used and more general in intent than the English "and," variously representing "because," "so," "then," and other meanings. Still, to maintain the poetic effect, we start the poem in English with "and" here and repeat the word until line 10.

The introductory line, "And so, let holiness ..." also begins with "and" but is technically not part of the poem. *Un'taneh Tokef* is an example of a *silluk*, the last of nine sections that make up a standard kind of poetic addition to the liturgy called a *k'dushta* (see pp. 16–17). "And so, let holiness ..." is the regular introduction that announces the beginning of the *silluk*.

[1] *Acknowledge:* Literally, "give," but the Hebrew verb is commonly used in the sense of "allow" or "permit" (as in Psalm 66:9, where God does not "give" [that is, "allow"] our feet to slip).

[1] *Power of this day's holiness:* Or, "this day's holy power." Due to a quirk of Hebrew grammar, the original is ambiguous. In one case, this

33

day has particular holiness, and the holiness has power. In another possible, but less likely, scenario, the day has power, and that power is holy (in which case it would mean, "the holiness of this day's power").

The word for "power" here, *tokef,* may refer more specifically to the kind of power that comes from authority. (We find the word in Esther 9:29, where it seems to have this nuance.) If so, the impact of the opening is similar to "Let us defer to the authority of this day's holiness...."

[1] *It:* Presumably "the day," but perhaps "the power." For grammatical reasons, the masculine "it" in Hebrew cannot refer back to the feminine "holiness."

[1] *Is full of awe and dread:* We have two adjectives in Hebrew. The common translations "awful" or "awesome" for the first (*nora*) and "dreadful" for the second (*ayom*) rely upon nearly archaic usages of those words. Originally, "awe" was a combination of fear and appreciation, the sort of reaction one might have to nearby powerful lightning. But "awful" in modern English has only a negative connotation, and "awesome" only a positive one. "Awe-inspiring" is the right idea. (Because the "High Holy Days" are called the "*nora* days" in Hebrew, the allusion here is similar to "it is full of high holiness.")

[2] *Kingdom will be exalted:* This line is reminiscent of Numbers 24:7 ("His [God's] kingdom will be exalted"), where the phrase forms part of Balaam's third blessing of the people of Israel. Normally kings, not kingdoms, are exalted. In Numbers 24:7, we find both: "His king will be higher than [King] Agag, and His kingdom will be exalted."

[2] *Established in love:* The Hebrew for "love" here is *chesed.* "Mercy" is another option. English speakers have difficulty agreeing on the precise meanings of those words and of words like them (for example, "pity" or "kindness"). It is considerably more difficult to establish what the older Hebrew word means. Proverbs (16:12 and 25:5) uses what seems to be similar language, contrasting wickedness with a throne established in *tz'dakah* or *tzedek* ("justice"). Perhaps the point here is that "love" will replace or augment "justice."

³ And You will reign from it in truth.
Truly You are judge

⁴ And prosecutor and litigant and
    witness

And author and sealer, and recorder
    and recounter.

וְתֵשֵׁב עָלָיו בֶּאֱמֶת³

אֱמֶת כִּי אַתָּה הוּא דַיָּן

וּמוֹכִיחַ וְיוֹדֵעַ וָעֵד⁴

וְכוֹתֵב וְחוֹתֵם וְסוֹפֵר וּמוֹנֶה

³ *Reign from it:* Literally, "sit on it." Hebrew doesn't have special kingship terms like "throne" and "reign," using the common "chair" and "sit" instead. But in English a "king's chair" is not a "chair," but rather a "throne," so we use that word above. And a king doesn't merely "sit"; he "reigns." But he also doesn't reign "on" a chair; he reigns from it. This line, beginning with "your throne will be established in love" (line 2), is based on Isaiah 16:5, "A throne will be established in love and [a ruler who seeks justice] will reign from it [literally, 'sit on it'] in truth."

³ *In truth. Truly:* We try to capture the Hebrew assonance, where *be'emet* ("in truth") is followed by *emet* (literally, "truth"). The pattern of starting a phrase with the same word that ended the previous one is common in the liturgy. Here we have to make do with the near match between "in truth" and "truly."

⁴ *Prosecutor:* Though the Hebrew here, *mochi'ach*, is broader than our English "prosecutor," we assume that all of these Hebrew words refer to roles in a court, so we try to find similar roles in English, even where the differences between our modern courts and older courts make it impossible to find an exact match.

⁴ *Litigant:* Literally, "knower." Perhaps "expert witness" is the point. The language is reminiscent of *Pirkei Avot* 4:22, where in the time to come, those who have been born and who have died will be born again, to know and make known and let it be known that "God understands, is judge, is witness, and is appellant...."

The central image in *Un'taneh Tokef* is that God simultaneously plays all of the roles of the court. (The American Reform *Gates of Repentance*, "judge, arbiter, counsel, and witness," and the British Liberal *Gate of Repentance*, "Judge, Arbiter, Expert, and Witness" convey essentially the same point. The American Conservative *Mahzor for Rosh Hashanah and Yom Kippur* offers, "You judge and prosecute, discern motives and bear witness.")

⁵ And You will remember everything
that has been forgotten
And You will open the book of
memories

⁶ And it will be read from:
Everyone's signature is in it.

⁷ And a great shofar will be sounded
And a thin whisper of a sound will
be heard.

⁵וְתִזְכֹּר כָּל הַנִּשְׁכָּחוֹת

וְתִפְתַּח סֵפֶר הַזִּכְרוֹנוֹת

⁶וּמֵאֵלָיו יִקָּרֵא

וְחוֹתָם יַד כָּל אָדָם בּוֹ

⁷וּבְשׁוֹפָר גָּדוֹל יִתָּקַע

וְקוֹל דְּמָמָה דַקָּה יִשָּׁמַע

⁵ *Everything that has been forgotten:* Literally, "all the forgottens." The Hebrew word *nishkachot* is in the feminine plural (ending in -*ot*), which is usually used for events, as opposed to the masculine plural (ending in -*im*), usually for people. Similarly, from the word *rishon* ("first") we get the *rishonim*, "people from a long time ago" (used to designate the first great rabbis after the Talmud was completed), and the *rishonot*, "events from a long time ago."

⁵ *Book of memories:* In Esther 6:1, King Ahasuerus, too, has a "book of memories." The act of reading from this book prompts the king to honor Mordecai and, eventually, prevents the destruction of the Jews.

⁶ *It will be read from:* The odd language here is reminiscent of Esther 6:2. Some translations—recognizing the passive verb here—suggest that the book "speaks for itself."

⁶ *Everyone's signature is in it:* The Hebrew we translate as "signature" is, literally, "hand print," and the word for "print" comes from the same root as "seal" (line 4). Perhaps the point is, "everyone's fingerprints are all over it." The language may reflect Job 37:7, where God takes the elements (snow, rain, etc.) and signs them on every person's hand. The British Reform *Forms of Prayer* suggests, "every man has signed it by his life."

The Hebrew reads, "and everyone's...." We omit the word "and" because of the oddity of connecting a future tense verb ("it *will be read* from") and a present tense verb ("*is* in it") that way in English.

⁷ *And a great shofar will be sounded:* Based on Isaiah 27:13, "On that day a great shofar will be sounded and" the lost and exiled "will bow down before Adonai on the holy mountain in Jerusalem."

⁸ And angels will recoil
And be gripped by shaking and
   trembling
⁹ And they will say, "This is the day of
   judgment,"
For reviewing the hosts on high in
   judgment.

⁸וּמַלְאָכִים יֵחָפֵזוּן

וְחִיל וּרְעָדָה יֹאחֵזוּן

⁹וְיֹאמְרוּ הִנֵּה יוֹם הַדִּין

לִפְקֹד עַל־צְבָא־מָרוֹם בַּדִּין

⁷ *A thin whisper of a sound:* Commonly, "still, small voice," for the Hebrew *kol d'mamah dakah.* The Hebrew *kol,* which literally means "voice," was regularly used more generally to mean "sound." We don't know for sure what *d'mamah,* translated here as "whisper," means. The text is from 1 Kings 19:12, where Elijah finds God not in the mighty wind, earthquake, or fire (perhaps a volcano), but rather in a thin whisper of a sound. Similarly, in Job 4:16, we find *d'mamah* and *kol* juxtaposed: "I heard a whisper and a sound."

⁸ *And angels will recoil:* In the line above ("a thin whisper of a sound") we saw an oblique reference to Job 4:16. Job 4:18 has angels, as does this line. Literally reading between the lines, we find the connecting thought in Job 4:17: "Can humans be acquitted by God, cleared by their maker?" The image there is probably of standing in judgment in God's cosmic court. We don't know for sure what the verb *yeichafeizun* means here. "Recoil" is a good guess.

⁸ *Be gripped by shaking and trembling:* In Psalm 48:7, we similarly find "gripped," "shaking," and "trembling." There, the image is "trembling like a woman in labor."

⁹ *For reviewing the hosts on high in judgment:* The language is similar to Isaiah 24:21, where God "reviews the hosts on high on high, and kings of the earth on the earth." Perhaps not coincidentally, the preceding line there, Isaiah 24:20, describes how the earth will shake (like *yeichafeizun,* "recoil"), though the verbs are not the ones we just saw here. The verb we translate as "review," *pakad,* is more commonly translated here and in Isaiah as "punish," because the result of failing the review is punishment. The verb is actually much more general, and in other contexts translations of it run from "remember" to "visit" to "oversee" and more. Finally, the odd English phrase "for reviewing" matches the odd Hebrew grammar here.

¹⁰For they will not be innocent when
You judge them.
And all who enter the world will
pass before You like sheep.

¹¹As a shepherd searches for his flock
And has his sheep pass under his
staff

¹⁰כִּי־לֹא־יִזְכּוּ בְעֵינֶיךָ בַּדִּין
וְכָל־בָּאֵי־עוֹלָם יַעַבְרוּן לְפָנֶיךָ
כִּבְנֵי־מָרוֹן
¹¹כְּבַקָּרַת רוֹעֶה עֶדְרוֹ
מַעֲבִיר צֹאנוֹ תַּחַת־שִׁבְטוֹ

¹⁰*For:* As in the Hebrew, this is the first line that doesn't begin with "and."

¹⁰*When You judge them:* Literally, "in your eyes in judgment," a phrase that makes almost no sense in English. The point, though, is clear. The line seems to be based on Job 15:15, "He [God] puts no trust in his holy ones; The heavens are not guiltless in his sight" (JPS); that is, "He doesn't trust his holy ones, and even the heavens are not found innocent by Him."

¹⁰*All who enter ... will pass:* We translate literally, rather than, for example, "all who dwell on earth" (American Reform *Gates of Repentance*), or simply "everyone," so that we can maintain the progression from "enter" to "pass." The line is from Mishnah Rosh Hashanah 1:2, where the context is as follows: "On four occasions is the world judged: On Passover, for produce; on Sh'mini Atzeret [the last day of Sukkot], for fruit and trees; on Rosh Hashanah, all who enter the world pass before him like soldiers [or sheep]—as [in Psalm 33:15], 'The One who makes everyone's hearts and minds understand everything they do'—and on Sukkot, they are judged for water."

The image in Hebrew is that people pass before God *kivnei maron*. The prefix *k'* (or *ki-*) means "like," so *kivnei maron* means "like *b'nei maron*" (the *b* changes to a *v* for complicated grammatical reasons). *B'nei* means "sons of," "children of," or more generally, "members of." To the Hebrew- and Aramaic-speaking ear, *maron* sounds like the Aramaic *amarna*, "lamb." So *b'nei maron* means "members of the flock," "lambs," or—because "son of" is sometimes used to express the gender of animals—"male lambs" (which, like male goats, we call "rams" in English). Taken with the prefix *ki-*, "like," *kivnei maron*, therefore, means "like sheep."

However, the phrase is widely regarded to have originated from the Late Greek word *noumeron* (literally, "number," but technically "military formation"). The Hebrew prefix *b'* (or *v'*) means "in," so *kiv-* means "like in," and *kivnumeron* means "like in military formation." The difference in Hebrew between "like members of the flock" and "like in military formation," then, is simply a *vav* (long line) versus a *yod* (short line). It's not hard to imagine a scribe getting that wrong. So while our text reads, "like members of the flock," the original intent may have been, "like in military formation."

[10] *Pass:* This is the first of several times we find the word "pass." Here the image is physical movement. Below, we will find a progression in the imagery from physical passing to more metaphoric movement.

[10] *Sheep:* See above, "all who enter ... will pass."

[11] *As a shepherd searches for his flock:* From Ezekiel 34:12. The context there is that the sheep have gone astray and the shepherd will find them. Similarly, Ezekiel continues, "So too will I [God] search for my sheep and save them from every place to which they have been scattered." However, the image of shepherds and sheep is misleading to modern readers.[1] Shepherds of antiquity were strong, brave, valiant protectors of the weak, while now they are scrawny, solitary, marginal members of society. (Write "shepherd" where it says "previous occupation" on a job application and see what happens.) So even though we understand all of the words in "a shepherd searches for his flock," and even though we have no better translation, we should be clear that the original metaphor was one of a mighty savior protecting the weak from predators.

[11] *And has his sheep pass under his staff:* From Leviticus 27:32, where "everything that passes under the staff" is used to mean "any herd- or flock-animal of any sort," such as "cattle and sheep." In English and in Hebrew, cattle come in herds and sheep in flocks, but in English goats are usually like cattle in that they form herds, while in Hebrew they form flocks. The two Hebrew words *eder* ("flock," here) and *tzon* ("sheep") are frequently interchangeable.

¹²כֵּן־תַּעֲבִיר וְתִסְפּוֹר וְתִמְנֶה

וְתִפְקֹד נֶפֶשׁ כָּל־חַי

¹³וְתַחְתֹּךְ קִצְבָה לְכָל־בְּרִיָּה

וְתִכְתֹּב אֶת־גְּזַר דִּינָם

¹⁴בְּרֹאשׁ הַשָּׁנָה יִכָּתֵבוּן

וּבְיוֹם צוֹם כִּפּוּר יֵחָתֵמוּן

¹⁵כַּמָּה יַעַבְרוּן וְכַמָּה יִבָּרֵאוּן

מִי יִחְיֶה וּמִי יָמוּת

¹⁶מִי בְקִצּוֹ וּמִי לֹא־בְקִצּוֹ

מִי בָאֵשׁ וּמִי בַמַּיִם

¹²So too will You record and recount
And review all living beings as You have them pass by.

¹³And You will decide the end of all creatures
And write down their sentence.

¹⁴On Rosh Hashanah they will be written down
And on Yom Kippur they will be sealed:

¹⁵How many will pass on and how many will be created,
Who will live and who will die,

¹⁶Who at their end and who not at their end,
Who by fire and who by water,

¹²*Review:* This is the same verb *pakad* that we saw in line 9. Here, "punish" clearly does not work.

¹²*As You have them pass by:* This is the same image of "passing" that runs throughout the poem. The original is a single word that means "cause to pass," instead of our phrase ("as You have them pass by"). The first and last phrases in a sentence are both points of emphasis, so even though we move "pass" from the beginning to the end, we maintain the emphasis on the uniting theme of the poem.

¹³*Their:* We prefer the plural here to avoid "his," "her," or "his/her." The Hebrew is clearly inclusive.

¹⁵*Pass on:* We are fortunate that our English expression from the verb "pass" means the same thing as the Hebrew expression from the parallel *avar* (which we translate throughout the poem as "pass").

¹⁶*Who by fire and who by water:* We find the juxtaposition of the Hebrew *ba'eish* and *bamayim* in Psalm 66:12, where the words mean "through fire and water." Some editions of *Un'taneh Tokef* reverse the order ("water … fire").

¹⁷Who by warfare and who by
   wildlife,
   Who by hunger and who by thirst,
¹⁸Who by earthquake and who by
   plague,
   Who by strangling and who by
   stoning,

¹⁷מִי בַחֶרֶב וּמִי בַחַיָּה

מִי בָרָעָב וּמִי בַצָּמָא

¹⁸מִי בָרַעַשׁ וּמִי בַמַּגֵּפָה

מִי בַחֲנִיקָה וּמִי בַסְּקִילָה

¹⁶*By water:* Or "in water." We prefer "by" so we can maintain the poetic structure throughout the translation below.

¹⁷*Who by warfare and who by wildlife:* Literally, who by "the sword" and who by "[wild] animal." The translation problem is twofold. Most importantly, both swords and animals presented real dangers to life when the poem was written. A community hearing the poem would probably have lost members to both "the sword" and "the wild animal," while the same cannot be said for us now. Secondly, we have poetic alliteration in the Hebrew, with *cherev* ("sword") and *chayah* ("animal"). Our translation of "warfare … wildlife" preserves the poetic effect.

While death by wildlife is uncommon, it is less rare than death by actual wild animals, which most readers never even encounter. The point of the line was probably to juxtapose violence from human sources and violence from natural sources. (British Reform *Forms of Prayer* spells out the imagery here: "by the violence of man or the beast.") Ezekiel 5:17 combines these various calamities: God will send "hunger [famine] and evil beasts," "plague and blood will pass though you," and God will bring "the sword upon you." The verb there, "pass," is probably not coincidental.

¹⁷*Hunger:* Or "famine." But we don't have a complement to "famine" the way we have "thirst" to match "hunger."

¹⁸*Plague:* "Pandemic" might be better. The Hebrew word here is the general one for a plague-like outbreak, as opposed to the word we saw in Ezekiel 5:17, which is a specific kind of plague. In English, "plague" functions either way.

¹⁸*Stoning:* Even when this was written, stoning was an antiquated notion, so we translate literally.

¹⁹Who will rest and who will wander,
    Who will be tranquil and who will
        be troubled,

¹⁹מִי יָנוּחַ וּמִי יָנוּעַ

מִי יַשְׁקִיט וּמִי יִטָּרֵף

¹⁹ *Who will rest and who will wander:* This pair is exceedingly difficult to translate. The two Hebrew words, *yanu'ach* and *yanu'a*, literally mean "stay/rest" and "move about/wander," as we have translated. But they sound almost the same in Hebrew, the similarity in Hebrew being even more pronounced than the English transliteration might suggest. They are also recognized as opposites, appearing not just here, but also, for example, as technical terms in Hebrew grammar: there are two kinds of the Hebrew vowel *sh'va*, and they are named *nach*, akin to *yanu'ach*, and *na*, akin to *yanu'a*. (The English translations "quiescent" and "mobile" for those grammatical terms hardly work for our current purposes.) A similar euphonic effect is seen in the English pair "stay" and "stray," but that translation, while coming very close to what we want, doesn't work here because the Hebrew verb *yanu'ach* is most commonly associated with Shabbat, where it means "rest," not "stay." (The verb also appears in Job 3:13, as part of why Job wishes he had died. See below, "tranquil and who will be troubled.") We have no pair of words that means the same thing as the Hebrew and that also imparts the same poetic impact. Because these words set the stage for the pairs that follow, we opt to translate literally, missing the poetry but capturing the meaning.

¹⁹ *Tranquil and who will be troubled:* We use "tranquil" and "troubled" because they most accurately convey the individual Hebrew words, just as we used "rest" and "wander" above. And once again, we miss the Hebrew poetry—in this case, because the Hebrew words are quite different and the English somewhat the same. (ArtScroll's "who will live in harmony and who will be harried" is similarly an attempt to capture the poetic nature of the Hebrew pair.) The first word, *yashkit*, is a third-person Hebrew verb that is similar in form and means essentially the same thing as the third-person *yishkot*, which appears in the first person (*eshkot*), rather than third, in Job 3:13. The context is Job cursing the day he was born. Had he died at birth, he laments, he would be quiet (*yishkot/yashkit*) and he would rest (like *yanu'ach*, which we just saw). In our prayer here, rest and quiet represent the good side of living, while in Job, they are the good side of dying.

²⁰Who will be calm, and who will be
   tormented,
   Who will be exalted and who
   humbled,
   Who will be rich and who will be
   poor?
²¹And repentance, prayer, and charity
   Help the hardship of the decree
   pass.
²²For your glory is like your name,
   Slow to anger, quick to forgive.

²⁰מִי יִשָּׁלֵו וּמִי יִתְיַסָּר

מִי יָרוּם וּמִי יִשָּׁפֵל

מִי יַעֲשִׁיר וּמִי יַעֲנִי

²¹וּתְשׁוּבָה וּתְפִלָּה וּצְדָקָה

מַעֲבִירִין אֶת־רֹעַ הַגְּזֵרה

²²כִּי כְּשִׁמְךָ כֵּן תְּהִלָּתֶךָ

קָשֶׁה לִכְעוֹס וְנוֹחַ לִרְצוֹת

²¹*And:* Commonly, "but." We prefer "and" because it relates back to the "ands" that began the prayer.

²¹*Charity:* A poor English translation, but it's all we have.

²¹*Help the hardship of the decree pass:* This is the key to the poem. The line uses the same root *a.v.r.* ("pass") that we've seen throughout to explain the impact of three good actions ("repentance, prayer, and charity") upon God's decree, the mitigation of which is the essential goal of the High Holy Days. But the second half of the line is brilliantly ambiguous in a way that's hard to capture in English. The Hebrew may mean either (1) that the three good actions mitigate "the bad decree," as implied in the American Reform *Gates of Repentance*: "temper judgment's severe decree"— that is, they might make the decree less severe; or (2) that the three good actions might leave the decree unchanged but make its "badness" less. In other words, they might have nothing to do with what actually happens, but they might make it easier for us to deal with the inevitable consequences. We have chosen "hardship of the decree" because that phrase, like the Hebrew, is ambiguous. If "badness" were a common word, we might prefer "badness of the decree." "Misfortune" is another possibility.

²²*Name:* The Hebrew here, *shem*, entails "name" but it also includes the notion of "reputation," so the point is similar to "your reputation precedes you." The line here is taken from Psalm 48:11, in the context of justice filling God's right hand and of Zion and Judah rejoicing in God's judgments. The British Reform *Forms of Prayer* offers, "Your glory is Your nature."

²³ For You do not want the dead
  to die,
 But for them to turn from their path
  and live.

²⁴ You wait until the day they die,
 Accepting them immediately if they
  return.

²⁵ Truly You are their creator
 And You know their nature

²³כִּי לֹא תַחְפֹּץ בְּמוֹת הַמֵּת

כִּי אִם בְּשׁוּבוֹ מִדַּרְכּוֹ וְחָיָה

²⁴וְעַד יוֹם מוֹתוֹ תְּחַכֶּה־לּוֹ

אִם יָשׁוּב מִיַּד תְּקַבְּלוֹ

²⁵אֱמֶת כִּי אַתָּה הוּא יוֹצְרָם

וְיוֹדֵעַ יִצְרָם

²² *Slow:* Literally, "hard." In English, unlike in Hebrew, "hard" (and "easy"), in the sense the text intends here, must refer to the objects of verbs, not their subjects. For example, "He is hard to antagonize," but not "He is hard to frown." So we use "slow" (not "hard") and "quick" (not "easy"). The language is from *Pirkei Avot* 5:11, where there are four kinds of temperaments: quick to anger, quick to forgive (*Pirkei Avot* says their loss is cancelled out by their gain); slow to anger, slow to forgive (their gain is cancelled out by their loss); slow to anger and quick to forgive (the righteous); and quick to anger and slow to forgive (the wicked).

²³ *Want:* Or "take pleasure," a construction that would make the rest of the line awkward in English: "You do not take pleasure in the death of the dead." The line is adapted from Ezekiel 18:32, "It is not my desire that anyone shall die—declares the Lord God. Repent, therefore, and live," in the context of God's retribution on those who do repent.

²³ *Them:* Literally, "him." We use the plural here to avoid "him/her." The Hebrew is inclusive. The original line is based on Ezekiel 18:23, where the antecedent is "the wicked" ("Is it my desire that the wicked person shall die"). Here, the antecedent becomes "the dead."

²³ *Turn:* Or "return."

²⁴ *The day they die:* "Their dying day" is tempting, but that phrase is usually used idiomatically, and here the point is literal.

²⁵ *Truly You are:* The Hebrew phrasing mirrors "Truly You are judge" in line 3.

²⁵ *Their:* The Hebrew now switches to the plural ("they"). We have used the plural all along, so we can't mark this change in English.

26 For they are flesh and blood.

²⁶ כִּי הֵם בָּשָׂר וָדָם

27 Their origin is from dust
   And their end is to dust:

²⁷ אָדָם יְסוֹדוֹ מֵעָפָר

וְסוֹפוֹ לֶעָפָר

28 At their peril gathering food,
   They are like shattered pottery,

²⁸ בְּנַפְשׁוֹ יָבִיא לַחְמוֹ

מָשׁוּל כַּחֶרֶס הַנִּשְׁבָּר

²⁵ *Creator and You know their nature:* Our translation misses two important aspects of the Hebrew. First, the words for "creator" and "nature" in Hebrew—*yotzer* and *yetzer*—are nearly identical, creating an effect similar to "You made them and You know what they are made of." But though the second word means "nature," it also specifically means "inclination" in the sense that the Rabbis use it: each person has a good inclination (the inclination to do good) and a bad inclination (the opposite). Here we read that God created us, so God knows about both (and, in particular, since our sins are the issue, about the evil inclination).

²⁷ *Their:* The Hebrew gives us "man's," in the general sense of the word, but because "man" in many dialects refers only to men, we prefer "their." We cannot convey the fact that the Hebrew word here, *adam,* sounds like *dam,* the word for "blood" that ended the last line (line 26).

²⁷ *Origin is from dust and their end is to dust:* Commonly, "origin is dust … end is dust," but the Hebrew is more nuanced, as we indicate in the translation. The first part of the image is from Genesis 2:7. Both parts appear in Genesis 3:19. The Hebrew literally reads, "from dust … to the dust." We translate both as "dust," without the word "the" because we assume the point was to have two phrases that sound almost the same. For complicated grammatical reasons, the two Hebrew phrases "from dust" and "to the dust" actually sound closer than "from dust" and "to dust." The Reconstructionist *Kol Haneshamah*'s "all of humanity is founded on dust" plays on the dual meaning of the Hebrew word *y'sod,* here "origin," but also "foundation."

²⁸ *At their peril gathering food:* Based on Lamentations 5:9, where the line appears as part of a litany of suffering, the conclusion of which includes the recognition that our suffering is caused by our own sins (5:16) and then the famous plea that pervades the High Holy Day liturgy to "take us back to You that we might come back; renew our days as of old" (5:21) The British Liberal *Machzor Ruach Chadashah* offers, "Life is a struggle for daily bread."

²⁹ Like withered grass and like a faded
blossom,
Like a passing shadow and like a
vanishing cloud,

³⁰ And like blowing wind and like
sprouting dust
And like a dream that will fly away.

³¹ But You are king,
The living and everlasting God.

²⁹ כֶּחָצִיר יָבֵשׁ וּכְצִיץ נוֹבֵל

כְּצֵל עוֹבֵר וּכְעָנָן כָּלֶה

³⁰ וּכְרוּחַ נוֹשָׁבֶת וּכְאָבָק פּוֹרֵחַ

וְכַחֲלוֹם יָעוּף

³¹ וְאַתָּה הוּא מֶלֶךְ

אֵל חַי וְקַיָּם

²⁸ *They are like:* In Hebrew, we have a word that means "compared to" (*mashul*) followed by "like" (*k-*). We translate "they are like" because otherwise our English might mean "they gather food like …" rather than "they are like …" shattered pottery. The image is from *Genesis Rabbah* 14. The commentary there to Genesis 2:7 ("The Lord God formed man from the dust of the earth"), which was referenced in the previous line here (line 27, "Their origin is from dust and their end is to dust"), discusses two kinds of vessels—glass and pottery—and differing views about which of the vessels can be fixed and which are beyond repair.

²⁹ *Withered grass:* Based on Isaiah 40:7 ("Grass withers and the blossom fades, for the breath [or wind] of God blows upon it. The people are surely like the grass"), and perhaps also an allusion to Psalm 103:15–16, which similarly notes human transience: "People's days are like grass; they blossom like a blossom in the field" until wind blows and they are no more.

²⁹ *Passing shadow:* From Psalm 144:4.

²⁹ *Vanishing cloud:* Based on Job 7:9.

³⁰ *Blowing wind:* Still in keeping with Isaiah 40:7.

³⁰ *Sprouting dust:* The image is reminiscent of Isaiah 5:24: "their sprout rises like dust." In Isaiah, the image is "sprouts" (better, "flowers") drying up and floating on the wind like dust. The wording here probably means the same thing, though it completes the previous image. The sprouts have withered, and now the dust has sprouted.

³⁰ *A dream that will fly away:* From Job 20:8.

³¹ *Everlasting:* Literally, "lasting."

32 Your years are boundless
And the length of your days is
endless.

33 Your glorious chariots are priceless
And the eternity of your name is
limitless.

32 אֵין קִצְבָּה לִשְׁנוֹתֶיךָ

וְאֵין קֵץ לְאֹרֶךְ יָמֶיךָ

33 וְאֵין שִׁעוּר לְמַרְכְּבוֹת כְּבוֹדֶךָ

וְאֵין פֵּרוּשׁ לְעֵילוֹם שְׁמֶךָ

32 *Your years are boundless and the length of your days is endless:* The Hebrew for "boundless" and "endless" is "there is no *kitzbah*" and "there is no *keitz*," literally, "there is no bound" and "there is no end." Instead of "there is no," we have words that end with "-less" ("boundless ... endless"), both here and immediately below (line 33, "priceless ... limitless"). Unfortunately, in rendering *kitzbah* and *keitz*, we cannot also capture the replication of sounds (*k.tz.* in both).

In addition, the Hebrew reads, "the length of your days," a familiar translation that doesn't seem to make much sense here, but we include it because otherwise we would create more of a pattern in the English ("years ... days") than we find in the Hebrew ("years ... length of days").

33 *Your glorious chariots are priceless:* We find the same language in Isaiah 22:18, where the glorious chariots belong to a human and become a symbol of destruction. This line thus continues the contrast between humans and God.

33 *Limitless:* Literally, "beyond description." The "-less" ending in English, like the "there is no ..." construction in Hebrew, means different things in different contexts. "Valueless" means "having no value," but "priceless" means just the opposite, "too valuable to measure." What we really want here, to keep the "-less" pattern, is "descriptionless," but English offers no such word.

³⁴Your name suits You
And You suit your name.

³⁵You named us after You;
Act for the sake of your name.

³⁶And sanctify your name
Through those who declare the
sanctity of your name

³⁷For the glory of your name,
Honored and sanctified,

³⁸As the utterances of the assembly of
holy seraphim,
Who sanctify your name with "holy,"

³⁹Inhabitants above with inhabitants
below
Thrice call out the trio of holiness
with "holy."

³⁴שִׁמְךָ נָאֶה לְךָ
וְאַתָּה נָאֶה לִשְׁמֶךָ

³⁵וּשְׁמֵנוּ קָרָאתָ בִשְׁמֶךָ
עֲשֵׂה לְמַעַן שְׁמֶךָ

³⁶וְקַדֵּשׁ אֶת שִׁמְךָ
עַל מַקְדִּישֵׁי שְׁמֶךָ

³⁷בַּעֲבוּר כְּבוֹד שִׁמְךָ
הַנַּעֲרָץ וְהַנִּקְדָּשׁ

³⁸כְּסוֹד שִׂיחַ שַׂרְפֵי קֹדֶשׁ
הַמַּקְדִּישִׁים שִׁמְךָ בַּקֹּדֶשׁ

³⁹דָּרֵי מַעְלָה עִם דָּרֵי מַטָּה
קוֹרְאִים וּמְשַׁלְּשִׁים בְּשִׁלּוּשׁ
קְדֻשָּׁה בַּקֹּדֶשׁ

³⁴⁻³⁵ *Your name:* As in line 22, more than just "name," but we have no better English translation. This line begins the transition into the *K'dushah.* It parallels the more usual introduction, which is also built around combinations of the sounds *sh* and *m*, both in *SHeM* ("name") and elsewhere. See J. Hoffman in *My People's Prayer Book*, volume 2, *The Amidah*, p. 93.

³⁶ *Through:* Literally, "on."

³⁷ *Name, honored and sanctified:* We would normally prefer "honored and sanctified name." We reverse the word order here to preserve the structure of the original poem, which puts *name* on one line and the adjectives by themselves on the next.

³⁸ *As the utterances of the assembly of holy seraphim:* See J. Hoffman in *My People's Prayer Book*, volume 10, *Shabbat Morning—Shacharit and Musaf,* for a full treatment.

PART I

The Moral Challenge
of *Un'taneh Tokef*
Can the Prayer
Even Be Salvaged?

1

The Exodus and the Elephant

Rabbi Tony Bayfield, DD

One of my formative memories comes from a Yom Kippur when I was twelve or thirteen. In those days, British Reform positioned the Yom Kippur morning sermon at the end of the Torah service, which itself completed *Shacharit.*[1]

It must have been after 1:00 P.M. The rabbi—young, brilliant, and impassioned—stood impatiently waiting to deliver his sermon. The queue of people exiting Ilford Town Hall seemed endless.[2] As the improvised sanctuary emptied, the rabbi could stand it no more. Gesticulating toward the end of the queue, he thundered the importance of teaching Torah. The elderly German lady who had the misfortune to be the victim of the rabbi's pointing finger turned and said loudly, "Vy is he pointing at me? I'm only going for a vee vee."

The story kept me endlessly amused at the time. Much later, as a young and impassioned rabbi, I had learned from it as well. I positioned my sermon in the brief hiatus between the arrival of the last latecomers and the beginning of the exodus from the service. My Hebrew name is not Avraham ben Canute for nothing.[3]

I'd begun to fathom, at a superficial level, why so many people departed after a respectable couple of hours. Our liturgy was insanely boring and completely incomprehensible. It was an enormous relief when,

Rabbi Tony Bayfield, DD (Lambeth), is head of the Movement for Reform Judaism in the United Kingdom. He teaches personal theology at the Leo Baeck College in London.

twenty-five years ago, the British Reform Movement's liturgical geniuses Rabbis Jonathan Magonet and Lionel Blue produced a new *machzor* for the High Holy Days.[4] For me, the whole book was—still is—a revelation. The most revelatory section was the Yom Kippur *Musaf.*

What Magonet and Blue did was to place the *Avodah* in the context of tracing "holy history" from our beginnings through the Temple ritual to the martyrology, much expanded by a series of brilliantly chosen testimonies from nineteenth- and twentieth-century history. This climaxed with the Shoah and our defiant emergence, quoting the end of *The Star of Redemption*, "INTO LIFE."[5] Their innovation goes to the heart of the mystery behind the unceasing Jewish journey through time; it works wonderfully well. But it hasn't eradicated the post-*Shacharit* exodus.

Today, on the cusp of the journey from the confident theological proclamations of *Shacharit* to the probing questions of *Musaf* stands not a sermon but *Un'taneh Tokef,* in the hope that the people will at least postpone their leaving because they want to stay for it. They apparently don't. Why not?

Over the decade that I have been professional head of the British Reform Movement, we have developed an annual leadership day. It's a day that brings together the movement's board, the executive of the Assembly of Reform Rabbis, the leadership of the Leo Baeck College, and our senior professional staff. It was this group, more than any other, that transformed us from a trade association, an organization for synagogue lay leaders, into a movement—a movement with a philosophy of reaching out and engaging people in their individual Jewish journeys, thereby affirming the many ways of walking an authentic Jewish walk and deepening the quest for meaning and purpose in Jewish identity.

In 2007, my keynote address was unusually and explicitly theological, expressing anxiety over the movement's new *siddur,* then approaching finalization.[6] I talked about the "elephant in the sanctuary" that somehow never gets addressed: the liturgical language of a "great, mighty, and awesome God" who rescues and saves. I suggested that such a God strained the credulity of the overwhelming majority of our congregants, even those who come regularly to synagogue. I argued that the unwillingness to confront this traditional image and language was a failure of nerve and patently dishonest.

Which brings us to *Un'taneh Tokef.* I am sure that many other contributions to this book discuss the medieval origins and history of the prayer and its rich layers of poetic meaning. I would like to concentrate on the relationship between *Un'taneh Tokef* and the sensitivities of contemporary worshipers who encounter it on the High Holy Days.

Un'taneh Tokef portrays God as standing in judgment upon us. By Yom Kippur, God has decided who will live and who will die—and how they will die as well. I may be scheduled for terminal cancer next November, and you may be scheduled for a car crash two weeks later. Of course, until Yom Kippur the decree is only provisional: if, by then, we have changed our ways, prayed hard enough, and performed acts of righteousness, the decree will be averted. Do the right thing before the final gavel falls and neither the cancer nor the car crash will occur.

I find that promise loathsome. I have to be honest and not mince my words. I find it loathsome. All of my experience tells me that life doesn't work like that. But my expression of deep feeling comes from my unwillingness to abide a theology that is just plain blasphemous.

One might object that the mainstream of post-Shoah theology, as led by Emil Fackenheim and expressed by Dow Marmur, affirms the tradition of an infinitely distant and ineffable God who defies human reason and expectations. The Jewish way, we are told, is to wait for this geographical and logical distance to diminish while we get on with living authentically Jewish lives.[7]

Marmur is my mentor and friend, a very great rabbi. But I can't do it. I've tried. I've even pursued all of the well-known arguments for a naturalistic or post-theological God. Just when I think I've reached an intellectually satisfying, emotionally honest, twenty-first-century response, God finds a way to laugh at my smugness and evasion. But not at my objection to *Un'taneh Tokef.*

I am, you see, an unreconstructed theist, but not one who believes in an all-powerful Manipulator who has a level of control over our lives that defies credulity and morality.

Several times I've made statements similar to this one. I've been mystified at the lack of enthusiasm they encounter.

One of the most widespread responses has been to tell me that the words don't matter. The key to liturgy is music, and few people give a damn about the words. I can see that. In the more musically sophisticated Reform synagogues in Britain, *Un'taneh Tokef* is sung almost entirely in Hebrew. As we stand and listen, the dominant mood is of solemnity and of judgment—but judgment without specifying by whom or how.

Others say that the bane of liturgical effectiveness is excessive literalism. *Un'taneh Tokef* is a painting in words, open to creative understanding. It provides a constant wherever you are in the world and in whatever denomination you find yourself. As much as our individual understandings of the text will vary, the insistence on at least having the same text before us every High Holy Day season unifies us. I can see that as well.

Others maintain an embarrassed silence that I've come to understand as meaning that concepts of God are many in today's Jewish world and my particular God, who sounds both uncomfortably anthropomorphic and unhelpfully impotent, takes us into areas we would rather not go.

There are lots of reasons for not spelling out the nature of the elephant in the sanctuary.

So what is my conclusion after all this angst? It's that the main thrust of liturgy over the last thousand years has been in the direction of the prescriptive. In the last analysis, the editors of prayer books determine what should be prayed and what should not, what is in and what is out. I would argue that modern attitudes to authority and the patent preference for pluralism are such that universally prescriptive decisions may no longer be viable and choice must be offered. I would prefer doing away with the traditional *Un'taneh Tokef*, but I understand how others, apparently, feel differently. We will have to live with liturgical diversity.

The 1985 British Reform *machzor* reads, "On Rosh Hashanah, we consider how judgment is formed. On Yom Kippur we consider how judgment is sealed, for all who pass away and all who are born, for all who live and all who die...."[8] Some will argue that's a fudge, others that it's a dishonest translation of the Hebrew. For me, personally, it works fine.

But I'm not sure that when the British Reform Movement comes to revise its *machzor*, that approach will survive. It may well be that it will sit beside the traditional text with the traditional translation. Individuals and communities will have the choice. And I am content with that. Choice is good. It may just be the best we can do in these theologically troubled times.

Will it stem the post-*Shacharit* exodus? There, I have my doubts. A choice of fine words and fine music is no substitute for addressing the elephant in the sanctuary.

2

Awe-full Thoughts on Words a Melody Cannot Save

Rabbi Andrew Goldstein, PhD

Retiring after forty-three years in one congregation and not wishing to get in the way of my son, who had succeeded me, I sought another pulpit for the High Holy Days and was fortunate enough to be invited for Tishrei 5769 to Perth, Australia. You can't get much further away from London, and it was an interesting experience in many ways. Sukkot, our Jewish autumn festival, fell in the spring, and some of the symbolism of Rosh Hashanah and Yom Kippur I had grown up with didn't quite work. Think of Rabbi Jack Reimer's meditation "Now is the time for turning; the leaves turn ... to red and orange"—yet in Western Australia the trees were bursting with buds, the leaves newly green. But it was the official prayer books I had to use that challenged me the most.

I was raised in the Liberal Synagogue in Birmingham (England), and as a student rabbi, I began my long career at Northwood and Pinner Liberal Synagogue on the outskirts of London. I have prayed and conducted High Holy Day services from all three generations of British Liberal Jewish prayer books. Until 1973 it was the somber, black-covered *Liberal Jewish Prayerbook*, volume 2 of Rabbi Dr. Israel Mattuck, the first

---

Rabbi Andrew Goldstein, PhD, is chairman of the European Region of the World Union for Progressive Judaism and coeditor of *Machzor Ruach Chadashah* (London, 2003).

rabbi of the Liberal Movement (founded in 1902). Mattuck had been born in Lithuania but grew up in America and was ordained from the Hebrew Union College in Cincinnati. He brought to Britain the liturgy of the American *Union Prayer Book* and, despite notable differences, based his books on it.

Until writing this article I assumed that Mattuck did not include *Un'taneh Tokef* in his High Holy Day services, but Professor Eric Friedland pointed out to me a shortened and transformed version at the beginning of the Yom Kippur additional service in the original 1923 edition (pp. 198–200) and its 1937 revision (pp. 186–188). It commences with Ezekiel 18:30–32, which contains some of the phrases appearing in *Un'taneh Tokef,* and continues thereafter in Hebrew and English. Mattuck wrote an English meditation to precede the Ezekiel passage starting with "Deeply solemn and inspiring is this day," but the Hebrew words *Un'taneh tokef* do not appear. As Friedland puts it, "What Mattuck did was theologically and literally brilliant, but hardly any regular High Holy Day worshiper would realize it was the good old familiar *Un'taneh Tokef.*" I, too, had failed to notice its existence.

I was ordained in 1970 and soon got involved in the discussions taking place on the draft of *Gate of Repentance* being edited by Rabbis John Rayner and Chaim Stern (*zikhronam liv'rakhah*). As a junior member of the Rabbinic Conference, my only contribution to that book was to change "crocodile" to "armadillo" at the beginning of the Yom Kippur additional service (p. 265). I had done an undergraduate degree in zoology and was happy to see my three years of study vindicated.

Following the style of our *siddur, Service of the Heart* (1967), *Gate of Repentance* was designed to be far more traditional, with a stricter adherence to classical liturgical structure, than Dr. Mattuck's predecessor prayer books. I recall some discussion over the inclusion of *Un'taneh Tokef* but cannot remember who initiated its inclusion—was it the British Rayner or the American Stern? A few die-hard Liberals objected to it, but they had also resisted the change from "Thee" to "You" in the *siddur.* Most accepted it, especially when their choirs learned the music. However, the most disturbing paragraph had been omitted.

It appeared differently, depending on the occasion. On Rosh Hashanah, it was placed at the point where *Musaf* turns up in the traditional *machzor*—the time when the largest congregation of the year is present. It terminates there with the first punch line, "But repentance,

prayer and good deeds annul the severity of the judgement."[1] The version
at the beginning of the Yom Kippur additional service, however—when
the smallest congregation of the Yom Kippur services is present—continues
to the second climactic verse, "But You are the eternal King, the everlasting God" (pp. 255–56). It was preceded each time by an explanatory
meditation (in smaller font) by John Rayner, attempting to explain away
the theological problem that even the bowdlerized version presented. As
Rayner put it in a note at the end of the book (p. 459), "Much of it has a
strongly fatalistic ring, especially in portions omitted by us. Yet man's
ability to change his ways and therefore his destiny, is emphatically main-
tained, especially in the affirmation that 'repentance, prayer … etc.'"

It was the "portions omitted by us" that shocked me when I found
them included in Australia, but before dealing with those, let me bring
the British Liberal liturgical reformation up to date. Thirty years after the
publication of *Gates of Repentance*, I was privileged to coedit with Rabbi
Dr. Charles Middleburgh its successor, *Machzor Ruach Chadashah*
(2003). It was largely a modernized revision of its predecessor. As with the
new *Siddur Lev Chadash* that appeared in 1995, we too faced the die-
hards whose main objection was to our use of non-sexist English: "King"
becoming "Sovereign," and "Lord" becoming "Eternal One." I can't recall
any opposition to *Un'taneh Tokef*, although we included our "full" version
in the Rosh Hashanah as well as the Yom Kippur service.

Presumably people had got used to the poem, and why not? It contains wonderful imagery. What does it matter if we do not believe that
God actually sits as "Arbiter, Expert and Witness," remembering "deeds
long forgotten" and opening "the book of records" where "what is written
there proclaims itself for it bears the signature of every human being"?
Such a poetic vision can surely help us open our own book of records, to
try harder to recall the errors we made in the year past and seek to make
restitution. And the closing poetry of our version can surely inspire us to
take seriously the passage of time and encourage us to use our years more
wisely: "We are like a fragile jar, like a shadow moving on, a cloud passing
by, a particle of dust floating on the wind, a dream soon forgotten." Surely
this is meaningful even for the agnostic who might have trouble with the
ending that follows: "But You are the Eternal Ruler, the everlasting God."

For me the *Un'taneh Tokef* is one of the high points of the High
Holy Day liturgy. The music is beautiful and the Hebrew majestic.
Reading out the English never fails to give me a thrill.

All this changed in Perth. Although part of the British Commonwealth, Australian Jews use the American Reform prayer books, which confronted me with the full *Un'taneh Tokef.* I pondered before the service whether I could bring myself to read that much-debated passage, "How many shall pass on and how many will be created, who will live and who will die ...," with its long list of ways we might perish in the ensuing year: fire, water, sword, plague ... it goes on and on. Only a sadist could take pleasure in this catalogue of violent ends. I just had to skip the passage and, to my relief, was not summarily expelled from Australia; previous rabbis in Perth had also omitted the offending paragraph, and the congregants I spoke to agreed with my decision.

I had forgotten that when he got back to America, Chaim Stern (who edited the American liturgy after coediting our own) had included this passage. I recall asking him, while working on our new *machzor*, why he had included it. He said, "Because it has a nice tune and people like to hear it sung."

I got similar reasons for the inclusion in the American Reform liturgy of other phrases and passages excised by most other Progressive liturgies: a Davidic messiah (in the *haftarah* blessing) and Satan (in the *Hashkivenu*) for example. The devil might have the best tunes, but is this justification for including in our Progressive worship passages and words that are intellectually unacceptable, especially where the accompanying English is not a true translation, but a paraphrase hiding the true meaning of the Hebrew? I am relieved to find that *Mishkan T'filah* does not follow this practice.

Reform and Liberal Judaism have changed a lot since the days of our founders, and, I believe, mostly for the better. I am comfortable with calling the festivals Sukkot and Shavuot rather than the Tabernacles and Pentecost of my youth. I feel proud and satisfied to have been involved in the editing of new generations of prayer books that follow a more traditional pattern than their predecessors. I rejoice that we have reintroduced *Havdalah* and *S'lichot* and *Tikkun Leil Shavuot,* literally "an act of repair on the night of Shavuot," which manifests as a gathering for study on *Erev Shavuot* that often continues until dawn. I am inspired by many of the ancient prayers we have reintroduced to our liturgy. But I am disturbed by the prayers or phrases that have been reinstated just because they have a nice tune, or for chauvinistic reasons, or because "they are traditional." We have our own

Reform and Liberal traditions. I just cannot believe in a God who decides who will live and who will die, and I do not find it acceptable to ask the congregation to make such assertions at the most sacred services of the Jewish year.

3

Is *Un'taneh Tokef* Palatable?

Rabbi Delphine Horvilleur

Our minds freely associate, producing thoughts and conclusions ranging from the profound to the mundane. As I prepare for the High Holy Days, I find that the quantity of ruminations increases. A case in point: each time I hear the word *tokef,* I think about a modern Hebrew expression that consumers encounter daily in Israel's grocery stores—*pag tokef.*

This phrase is found on almost every product: on yogurts and cereals, on packaged food and gallons of milk. *Pag tokef* followed by a date is accurately translated as "best used before ..." or even "expiration date is...." More literally, the phrase means "beyond relevance." Food is perishable. It can be preserved for a while, under certain conditions, but eventually, it becomes inedible and *pag tokef.* Beyond that date, do not use and beware! Those products are indeed "beyond relevance."

As I read *Un'taneh Tokef* and its dreadful threats to life ("who will live and who will die ..."), and as I listen to its deterministic theology (on this day our fate is sealed), I can't help but wonder: Isn't this entire liturgical piece *pag tokef*? Are these words still germane to twenty-first-century worshipers, or is this theology "beyond relevance" for us? Are we

---

Rabbi Delphine Horvilleur is the rabbi of congregation MJLF (Mouvement Juif Libéral de France in Paris). She was ordained at Hebrew Union College–Jewish Institute of Religion in New York in 2008 and became the third woman rabbi in France. She is the creative director of Le Café Biblique, a pluralistic group of Jewish study, and the chief editor of *Tenou'a,* a French magazine of Jewish thought.

serving outdated ingredients to our worshipers on the Days of Awe? Are we feeding them inedible matter on their day of fast?

Un'taneh Tokef is undoubtedly one of the most challenging pieces of Jewish liturgy. The problem is that it is also one of the most famous, as it seems to embody the traditional liturgical messages of the season: on this day, your fate is sealed, your future determined.

For many, this liturgical piece at the core of the holiest days of the year elicits discomfort. "How can modern Jews accept the fatalistic theology of *Un'taneh Tokef*?"

As a rabbi in a Reform congregation, I teach, all year long, the most precious ideas of our theology. Being a Jew is about being empowered to act as God's partner. I teach a nonfatalistic attitude to life, an approach that addresses our ability—indeed, our responsibility—to change the world at large and our personal world within it. In modern Jewish thought and teaching, I find comfort. In my Judaism of responsibility and covenant, humanity is engaged in a face-to-face dialogue with the divine.

But here come the High Holy Days, the one time a year that so many of my congregants show their faces. Here they are, opening their book as God opens his, instructed to kneel at the Great *Alenu* and to listen to the *Un'taneh Tokef,* both of which implacably convey, and even seal, a totally different relationship between humanity and the divine.

Un'taneh Tokef assumes a vertical relationship between God, the king, and human beings, his servants. He has the power, and we are his slaves, simply and passively dependent upon his goodwill or his bad plans for our future. Most of Tishrei's liturgical pieces position the worshiper in this passive role of someone who is inevitably acted upon. The prayer texts in general, and *Un'taneh Tokef* in particular, seem to say, "There is nothing you can do but accept the decree."

It seems to me that the liturgy of Yom Kippur is the best Jewish adaptation of a Greek tragedy. The entire drama takes place in twenty-four hours. The heroes (us) are in the hands of the gods, turning from subjects to objects of a determined fate, left to experience what has been sealed for them. This theology is quite infantilizing. Things are decided for us, decreed from above, and delivered like manna in the desert. Except this time, the manna doesn't sustain us; it threatens us with destruction "by fire and ... by water ... by earthquake and ... by plague."

Of course, one can always impose relevance on a text by engaging in the ancient Jewish activity that Moshe Halbertal calls "charitable reading."

My title "rabbi" makes me part of a chain of "charitable readers," interpreters of our ancient texts, committed to look for relevance. And I have to admit (thank God!) that *Un'taneh Tokef* does tolerate "charitable reading" for an inspired reader.

The climactic line *Ut'shuvah, ut'fillah utz'dakah ma'avirin et ro'a hag'zerah* is usually taken as a claim that "repentance, prayer, and charity" can nullify a decree from on high (line 21). Surprisingly, these words come at the end of a text that just claimed the opposite: that our fate was already irrevocably determined. Paradoxical! It seems, actually, that *Un'taneh Tokef* is a masterpiece of theological contradiction, as if to say, "Beware! Everything is written … but everything can be changed. And remember that your thoughts (*t'shuvah*), your words (*t'fillah*), and your deeds (*tz'dakah*) can save you."

Tolerating contradiction is the charitable reading I am willing to provide for my congregants. Our liturgy is ambivalent, and as such, it reflects who we are: paradoxical beings, ambivalent believers.

Yes, *Un'taneh Tokef* is, in many aspects, a *pag tokef* liturgy. I admit it, I accept it, but I am still rabbi and a worshiper, left to ask myself the central question of modern Jewish thought: do I throw away my text when it seems to "smell bad"?

From the (very) profane to the sacred—I am aware that what *Un'taneh Tokef* does for me it may not do for others. For some, it offers comfort as it is, or precious memories, perhaps—simply because it sings a melody from the past. And others may still find it unsalvageable.

As a rabbi I am committed to never allowing words of our tradition to remain uninterpreted, never letting their literal meaning be read unambivalently. I keep reading my *pag tokef* prayer *because I am committed to refreshing and refining its relevance from generation to generation.*

We are told that a portion of manna was to be kept in the ark. I am convinced that it wasn't meant to be eaten again. It was to serve as a memory, to enable future generations to look back at the journey and all the learning that came with it in their (and our) ancient history.

Acknowledging where we were five thousand years ago and all the time we have walked a long road to where we are now will never be *pag tokef.*

4

From Text to Life to Text
The *Un'taneh Tokef*
Feedback Loop

Rabbi Noa Kushner

Un'taneh Tokef is only the liturgical, poetic piece of a larger whole—the existential whole, the way we live our lives. I think of the relationship between the liturgy and our lives as a feedback loop that goes in both directions. One piece without the other is incomplete. Liturgy requires life as life requires liturgy.

Un'taneh Tokef (the liturgical piece) is a text, just a text, that reflects how we might live and how we will die. If we only considered the liturgy abstractly, removed from life, removed from the reality of experience, it would feel less of a personal challenge. Only when we understand it as a liturgical comment on our existence do our problems with it begin; only then does it feel too authoritative on subjects that resist authority. It feels like it is overreaching, trying to prescribe generalities about life and death when we know that there are always exceptions to these rules.

However, if we consider *Un'taneh Tokef* as a vantage point from which to look out at life, we begin to see an exchange taking place. The ongoing story of our lives informs the prayer, filling in where the liturgy can only gesture. Without us, the people who say the words, the liturgical text would have no point. Without the work of our lives, the prayer would

Noa Kushner is the rabbi for Nita (www.nitamarin.org), an independent project of Congregation Rodef Sholom in Marin, California.

be incomplete, shallow to the point of being flat, words stuck to the page. So, we truly pray only when we bring our lives to the act of prayer.

But the idea of bringing life's experience to prayer is not as easy as it sounds. What do we do when we see contradictions between our lives and the prayer? That is our problem with *Un'taneh Tokef. T'shuvah* (self-reflection and change), for example, is said to "help the hardship of the decree pass" (line 21). Regardless of whether we read this as the act of *t'shuvah* allowing us to change the end result of a life situation or the act of *t'shuvah* helping us to weather an existing life situation, there may be times in our lives when all the honest *t'shuvah* in the world seems to do neither. It neither mitigates our circumstances nor improves our outlook. Perhaps, we hope, over time, *t'shuvah* will work quiet miracles for us, but at this moment, our "decree" has not changed and our feelings about our situation have not altered. Now we have a real contradiction. And at this moment, it might be easy to give up on this prayer altogether.

Our problem exists, however, because we treat the text as so sacrosanct that it is supposed to *only* compel us to change *our* view on life. That does happen—the relationship between text and life is mutual, after all. But feminist writers have taught us how contradictions between life and text should also force reinterpretations of the text. We need nullify neither our lives nor the text. We need only abandon the idea that the text (in this case, a prayer) is supposed to be able to fully describe our lives (and even our deaths) on its own, without us. Of all the texts we read, prayers, especially, illustrate this reality, since they do not become prayers until someone prays them. The prayers and the pray-ers need each other. Life is informed by text, but the meaning of the text must also change with what it inherits from life.

Moreover, we pray as a community. Imagine if we asked people who had suffered tragedy or who found that *t'shuvah* did not lighten their difficult situations to leave the room during *Un'taneh Tokef.* The prayer would immediately be stripped of its power. To the contrary, precisely because those who have suffered stay in the room do we experience the weight of what the prayer is trying to express. Now we are forced to interact with its message. We live through the prayer together, actually completing it by bringing our complicated lives to it. Together, with all of our contradictions in the room, we work our way to a reading that expresses more than what is on the page. It is not an affirmation that some of us deserve to suffer(!) but a realization that, for some of us, suffering exists.

At that point, if we are willing, *Un'taneh Tokef* can become an instigator. It can provoke us to a new awareness of God. We may see that not all connections to God are straightforward; God does not work "by the book," even "by the prayer book." Some connections to God are messy. They still require the prayers in our books (it is Judaism, after all), but they also require honesty in our reading of the prayers, and in our consideration of our lives. A room full of people who know each other's lives and the moment of praying *Un'taneh Tokef* together can then combine to become a way of connecting our experience, no matter how challenging, back to God.

Remember the feedback loop? It goes in both directions. Just as the reading of *Un'taneh Tokef* needs us, we need *Un'taneh Tokef.* When we allow its contents, especially over time, to seep into our collective consciousness, we see that some of the prayer's poetry has a strong impact; there are indeed patterns that overlay the chaotic experience of being alive. The sweeping categories offered here ("who will live and who will die," for instance) have a way of helping us to leave the unimportant stuff behind, even after the High Holy Days are over.

Un'taneh Tokef also provides a safe passage to a landing from which we can examine our lives and even the reality of our deaths—in ways we would not dare face on our own. Take, for example, that sober list of the ways people die. We know these things happen—to someone, even if not to us, every day. We watch the news, hear stories. We ourselves grieve for someone who died too early, too young. The very idea of it is enough to shake us, to set our teeth on edge. We would rather not think about it, so we put it out of our minds.

However, when we read that list in *Un'taneh Tokef,* we are brought back again to these sober realities. The list is a specific, unyielding look at what we know but regularly try to forget—namely, that we will die. Everyone in or out of the room, everyone reciting and everyone not reciting this prayer, you and I, we all will die. There is no getting around it. Too many whom we know, too many whom we love, will die too young, in ways we can't even talk about.

Un'taneh Tokef calls all this to mind. It says, "You will remember everything that has been forgotten, and You will open the book of memories" (line 5). We presumably say this line to God, but here is another example where our interpretation and our lives add meaning to the text. We cannot read these words without addressing ourselves as well, because it is precisely in saying this very prayer that we ourselves are forced to remember everything we would rather forget.

Usually, when we are most near to death, we are, very simply, mourners. When someone we love has just died, we don't think in abstract terms—we don't think at all. We feel a heavy absence, and we miss the ones who are gone. *Un'taneh Tokef* makes for poor consolation. We would never read it at a funeral. It gives us no comfort.

But on the High Holy Days, the days of fear and wonder, we are not typically in mourning. We can feel *and* we can think. *Un'taneh Tokef* takes advantage of this unusual moment when we might stretch ourselves to look over the precipice, knowing that we are not falling. At this moment, finally, it is safe to pry open difficult memories and expectations. We can allow ourselves to wonder if there is anything to be learned from the fact of our death. We might even have the presence of mind to ask, "Given that I am going to die, given that my death is a fact, what will I make of my life?"

And it is this question, "What will I make of my life?" that is at the very heart of the prayer. This question is the reason we go through that painful list; it is the reason we contemplate our own deaths and the deaths of those we love; it is the reason we force ourselves to remember that we have power in shaping our lives even in the face of real suffering. All of this works together to create a space where we can humbly ask ourselves, "What will I make of my life?" And then, our answers, the next cycle of the feedback loop, the rest of the year, begin again—at this moment, on the day the world was created, we re-create ourselves.

5

A Rationalist's View

Rabbi Charles H. Middleburgh, PhD

It is beyond question that *Un'taneh Tokef* is one of the most beloved and prominent pieces in the Ashkenazi High Holy Day liturgy, an almost perfect combination of words and music set against the background of a heavenly court in session to consider judgment against sinners. The deity itself is ensconced to fill every role necessary—"judge and prosecutor and litigant and witness" (lines 3–4)—doesn't sound like the sort of multitasking I'd be happy to see in a courtroom, but then, this isn't just any old courtroom! The impact of *Un'taneh Tokef* as a whole cannot be doubted. Herman Kieval looks at the careful way its music alone is orchestrated:

> The musical rendition of *Un'taneh Tokef* marks the high point of the cantorial repertoire for Rosh Hashanah. It features a wide range of modes and motifs, major and minor. In it, we hear the majestic music of the Heavenly Court, the peal of the Shofar at which even the angelic hosts tremble, the soothing pastoral of the shepherd mustering his flock. Then the mood changes again into the tearful supplication of "who will live and who will die" and the humble sigh of "their origin is from dust and their end is to dust." Finally the music soars into the promise of "You are King, the living and everlasting God."[1]

Rabbi Charles H. Middleburgh, PhD, is rabbi to the Reform Jewish Celts of Ireland and Wales; honorary director of studies at Leo Baeck College, London, where he has taught since 1984; and coeditor with Rabbi Andrew Goldstein, PhD, of the Liberal Judaism *Machzor Ruach Chadashah*.

However, it is not the piece overall that has caused me grief every time I have had to endure it in my Reform synagogue over the last six years, nor the music to which it is always beautifully sung by my *chazzanit* Professor Fiona Karet, but one paragraph, the one that begins, "On Rosh Hashanah they will be written down ..." (*b'rosh hashanah yikatevun ...* [line 14]), with which, says Kieval, *Un'taneh Tokef* "reaches a peak of dramatic urgency."

To do the specific paragraph in the prayer to which I so strongly object justice, let me give you the translation of the strictly Orthodox ArtScroll Ashkenazi *machzor*, which provides a stark view of what the prayer is traditionally intended to portray:

> On Rosh Hashanah will be inscribed and on Yom Kippur will be sealed how many will pass from the earth and how many will be created; who will live and who will die; who will die at his predestined time and who before his time; who by fire and who by water, who by sword, who by beast, who by famine, who by thirst, who by storm, who by plague, who by strangulation, and who by stoning. Who will rest and who will wander, who will live in harmony and who will be harried, who will enjoy tranquillity and who will suffer, who will be impoverished and who will be enriched, who will be degraded and who will be exalted.

Now call me an old-fashioned left-wing Liberal Jew—in fact, *please* call me an old-fashioned left-wing Liberal Jew—but in my view, there is no place for that sort of primitive material in a *machzor* used by nontraditional Jews in the twentieth century, let alone the twenty-first. And to our credit, Reform Jews faced this reality very early on, albeit without the wholehearted consistency that would have made the lives of subsequent liturgists much more straightforward! My dear friend and liturgical mentor Professor Eric Friedland describes the version of *Un'taneh Tokef* found in Rabbi David Einhorn's seminal *Olath Tamid* from 1858:

> Einhorn's *Un'taneh Tokef* is also divergent, rejecting anything savouring of the supernatural or the mythological. No longer do we behold angels trembling at the call of judgement, or God enthroned in lofty splendour conduct-

ing His heavenly assize. Instead we envisage humankind passing through the Shepherd's tally before its fate is decreed. The old court of appeal, based on repentance, prayer and *caritas* ["charity"], gives way to the less Damoclean notion of Psalms 8:5–6, which casts human beings as both lowly and *engelgleich* ["like angels"]. That biblical paradox is a recurrent theme in *Olath Tamid*, which often juxtaposes the child-of-earth image with the loftier child-of-God one.

What Einhorn seems to be suggesting is that as prone as man is to sin, he does have the capacity to transcend his sensual bounds and attain a worthy spiritual state. Although this bifurcated view in *Olath Tamid* may seem to be more Christian than Jewish, the Pauline-Augustinian contempt of the things of earth is nowhere evident in *Olath Tamid*. Einhorn's strong Jewish sensibilities did not allow for a Manichean scorn of the material and the physical which, after all, "God saw was good." Indeed, it is somewhat surprising that Einhorn, known for his rigorous consistency, even bothered to include this *piyyut*, with its sense of foreboding, so out of tune with *Olath Tamid*'s overall optimistic tendency.

The popularity of the prayer, particularly of its "Who will live and who will die" sequence, doubtless accounts for its longevity even in uniformly "rationalist" Reform liturgy.[2]

As Friedland makes clear, even Einhorn retains the powerful and, in my view, pernicious paragraph, but, mercifully, without the "strangling and … stoning" (line 18). He was not thoroughgoing in his rejection of this prayer's difficult theology, but at least he made a courageous start.

In Britain, we Liberal Jews looked at all this. Our new *machzor* came out in 2003. Its two predecessor volumes were the 1973 *Gate of Repentance* (*GOR*) and, before that, the 1937 *Liberal Jewish Prayer Book* (*LJPB*). The 1973 *GOR* included *Un'taneh Tokef*, but without those portions that its coeditor John Rayner (*zekher tzaddik liv'rakhah*) described as possessing a "strongly fatalistic ring." But its predecessor, the 1937 *LJPB*, edited by Rabbi Israel Mattuck (*zekher tzaddik liv'rakhah*), omitted it altogether. Mattuck provided instead an ingenious, if unconventional, paraphrase, of which the following is a brief excerpt:

> Deeply solemn and awe-inspiring is this day. It has been ordained because man feels heavily the inevitable judgement upon his sins, and the sadness of separation from God. For no man is free from impure feelings, and all are assailed by temptations. When we become aware of our sinfulness, our souls within us feel as if the sting of death has touched them. Yet if we turn to God, he will revive our hearts in purity and strengthen in us the power of goodness. God is the true Judge, whose throne is established in mercy. We hope for his forgiveness, the assurance of a new life which shall be stronger in righteousness, richer in love, and, above all, more deeply and fully imbued with that which includes all excellence and impels to highest endeavour—the love of God.[3]

The story of English Reform liturgy is equally interesting. In the 1931 liturgy (*Forms of Prayer*), *Un'taneh Tokef* appears for Yom Kippur, but not for Rosh Hashanah, probably due to the continuing strong influence of the Sephardi tradition, which has no similar prominent usage of *Un'taneh Tokef* on either holiday. This radical excision must have met resistance, however, because the 1961 reprint inserts a little six-page section called "Additional Prayers," which provides a severely abbreviated *Un'taneh Tokef*, omitting most of the first and all of the second paragraphs. Exactly the same thing happens on Yom Kippur. Professor Friedland is of the view that this addition may have been due to the influence of liberal German Jews who emigrated to the United Kingdom, joined Reform synagogues, and missed the prayer they were used to back home.

But, amazingly, the 1985 Reform liturgy restores *Un'taneh Tokef* in all its awesome, or awful, completeness! And there is no reason to assume that attitudes will change any time soon. As a counterbalance to my perhaps overrigid rationalist approach, Professor Friedland has suggested that the experience of the Shoah had "brought home the stark unpredictability and unappeasable fragility of life," as a result of which "the antiquated language of the poem" took on "a reality of its own and began to resonate even for the most steadfast rationalist." That would explain why both the Liberal and the Reform Movements in Great Britain returned to the prayer in 1973 and 1985, respectively, even though their predecessors were much more daring in omitting it as much as possible.

I talked some months ago to Dr. Annette Boeckler, librarian at Leo Baeck College and liturgical scholar, about this subject and told her how puzzling I found it that in modern prayer books a formerly omitted piece of text of such dubious theology should have made a triumphant reappearance, and her view was that the power of the *tune* clinched it. I countered with the question, "Can a *melody* be more powerful than a series of theological statements that no truly Progressive Jew could still possibly believe in?" and then answered it myself, "Of course. Why would the average Jew in the pew set the demands of rational theology over a good tune!"

The *machzor* that Andrew Goldstein and I edited for the Liberal Movement (2003) retains the version of *Un'taneh Tokef* that appeared in its predecessor, and having grown up hearing it sung without the "offensive" paragraph, I can say that I never felt the version I knew as a child, and still prefer as an adult, to be in any way deficient. Eric Friedland has reminded me, however, that beautiful and touching as the abridged version is, the language is no less mythological and, at root, no more palatable to the aforesaid confirmed rationalist! All of that notwithstanding, I would be both shocked and dismayed were our liturgy to march backwards intellectually and spiritually by including the complete prayer in a future edition. Hopefully I will be dead before that occurs!

We are all aware that our response to specific texts in the liturgy is hugely influenced by what is familiar, and it is often hard to maintain a forensic approach to texts that have been in our hearts and minds, and on our tongues, since childhood.

Anyone who has been involved with the writing and editing of liturgies is also aware that one tampers with cherished texts at one's peril and, further, that the strictly rational approach is almost immediately undermined by this unspoken thought (with which I disagree): If you start off on that tack, you'll end up with next to nothing in this postmodern, secular age! Nevertheless, I nail my colors, of choice, to the radical and rational mast, and although I have to acknowledge my practical and intellectual inconsistency, as Martin Luther remarked in another context, "I can do nothing else" (*Ich kann nicht anders*)!

6

Universalism versus Martyrdom

UN'TANEH TOKEF AND ITS FRAME NARRATIVE

Rabbi Marc Saperstein, PhD

In the summer of 1981, near the beginning of my rabbinic and academic career, I published an article that was triggered by an experience leading a Rosh Hashanah worship service the previous year.[1] Looking out at the congregation, I saw in one of the first few rows an eleven-year-old girl whose thirty-nine-year-old mother was dying of metastasized breast cancer. As this girl was reading with the rest of us the climactic proclamation *Ut'shuvah ut'fillah utz'dakah ma'avirin et ro'a hag'zerah*, translated as "Penitence, prayer and charity avert the stern decree" (cf. line 21), I remember thinking, "What conclusion will she draw when her mother dies?" as indeed she did a week later? That her prayer was not sincere enough, that she was not good enough, to avert the decree? Is that what the sentence meant?

Rabbi Marc Saperstein, PhD, relocated to London in June 2006 to become principal of Leo Baeck College. Previously he had taught and headed Jewish studies programs for twenty-nine years at Harvard University, Washington University in St. Louis, and George Washington University in Washington, D.C., and was vice president of the American Academy for Jewish Research.

My investigation led to many insights new to me. Perhaps most important was that the midrashic source of this statement is "Three things annul the decree [*m'vatlin et hag'zerah*]: they are penitence, prayer, and charity" (*Genesis Rabbah* 44:5). The changes introduced into the liturgical poem are significant: *ma'avirin et ro'a hag'zerah* (literally, "cause the evil of the decree to pass") is fundamentally different from *m'vatlin et hag'zerah* ("annul the decree"). My conclusion was that the affirmation is not that "it is within man's power to annul an evil decree," as a leading commentary on the High Holy Day liturgy explains it;[2] it is, rather, a statement about human response to the arbitrary misfortunes and catastrophes that occur all around us.

Since that initial article I have remained fascinated by the power and beauty of the language in this passage, though continually challenged by its meaning. Among the many other dimensions of the text are its significance for the history of Jewish-Christian dialogue.

Scholarship has determined that the literary form of the passage reflects currents that were common to both Jewish and Christian (Byzantine) liturgy: biblical references to trembling on high, the opening of the books, the sounding of the trumpet, the image of a shepherd counting the sheep of his flock.[3] The first such claim came from the father of Jewish musicology, Professor Eric Werner, who tied it also to themes from Christian liturgy that are found in a well-known prayer, *Dies Irae*. What Werner did not emphasize, however, is the critical difference in the context of the awe-inspiring event. In the Christian liturgy, it is eschatological: the prelude to the resurrection of the dead and the Last Judgment. In Jewish liturgy it is an event that occurs each year, when human initiative may still be efficacious.[4]

I have also been struck by the universalistic character of the liturgical discourse. Shlomo Eidelberg, the noted scholar of Ashkenazi Jewry, wrote a Hebrew article, "The Historical Background of the Story of R. Amnon and the Prayer *Un'taneh Tokef*," in which he asserted that "in this liturgical poem, the judgment of the Jew [*ha'adam hay'hudi*] on the Days of Awe is described."[5] But, despite the reference to the Days of Awe in the Jewish calendar, there is nothing distinctively Jewish about the people described in the text. To the contrary, the universalistic formulations recur as a leitmotif, for example, in the introductory section, "the signature of every human being is in it" (line 6), "all who enter the world will pass before You" (line 10), "You record and recount and review all living beings" (line 12), and "You decide the end of all creatures" (line 13).

Toward the close, we find a similarly universalistic passage of stunning power, a collection of striking biblical similes for the precarious nature of human life and the ultimate futility of our endeavors and aspirations: "[Human beings'] origin is from dust and their end is to dust: ... they are like shattered pottery, like withered grass and like a faded blossom, like a passing shadow and like a vanishing cloud and like blowing wind and like sprouting dust and like a dream that will fly away" (lines 27–30). How can one fail to appreciate that this is not about "the judgment of the Jew" or about the destiny of the Jewish people, but about the human condition, what we share with every human being?

This powerful universalistic message is in irresolvable tension with the story of Rabbi Amnon that provides the setting for *Un'taneh Tokef* in Ashkenazi communal memory and (in a highly apocopated and moderated version) in the latest American Reform *machzor* (*Gates of Repentance*). It appears first in a thirteenth-century Ashkenazi law code and is attributed to the twelfth-century historical writer Ephraim of Bonn.[6]

Given in detail elsewhere in chapter 3, its outline is relatively simple. Amnon, pressured by the local bishop to convert to Christianity, decides to stall for time by asking for three days to think it over. On the third day, he is brought before the bishop, who orders that Amnon's fingers and toes be chopped off, one by one. He repeats the option to convert after each amputation, but Amnon steadfastly refuses. Finally, allowed to attend the synagogue on Rosh Hashanah, he is placed next to the *sh'liach tzibbur*. During the *K'dushah*, he recites *Un'taneh Tokef*. He dies a martyr as the liturgical poem is completed.

The narrative about the bishop's behavior is deeply problematic. Eidelberg writes, "The [Crusade] chronicles tell of the cruel deeds performed by the Crusaders, about cutting off of hands and feet and mutilating limbs of the martyrs who refused to renounce their faith in order to save their lives." This suggests that the story has a clear historical basis. But the only reference to mutilation in the chronicles of the First Crusade applies to Christian victims, not Jews: at the first outbreak of violence, Bishop John of Speyer seized burghers who participated in the murder of Jews and "cut off their hands."[7]

The general pattern is that the Christian warriors gave the Jews a choice and killed them when they refused to convert.[8] There are also references in the chronicles to Christians torturing Jews in order to induce them to convert.[9] Occasionally, we read of forcible conversions without consent.[10] But there is no description in these texts of the behavior that is alleged in the Amnon narrative. That narrative does not even make reference to the Crusade.

The Hebrew accounts of the Crusade, supported by contemporary Christian chronicles, describe Christian warriors running amok and acting against the accepted doctrines of their faith, in conflict with the local bishops. The Amnon story, however, attributes the mutilation to a bishop, who makes a calculated decision to order the fingers and toes of a Jew to be amputated in order to get assent to conversion. Not only is this in blatant violation of accepted Church doctrine prohibiting conversion under duress, it is also inconsistent with the record of the contemporary Rhineland bishops, including Rudiger of Speyer, who welcomed Jews to his community in 1084 with a generous charter of privileges. The local bishops during the First Crusade are actually described in the contemporary Jewish accounts as having made a good-faith effort to protect the Jews. The behavior attributed to the bishop in this narrative appears to be a calumny, a libel, without any basis in fact.

The Amnon story totally transforms the meaning of the magnificent poem. A passage that repeatedly insists on the common experience of all human beings and shares central literary motifs with contemporary Christian liturgy is transformed into an expression of martyrdom, the exemplification of an unbridgeable gap between the two religions.

Apparently the connection between the frame narrative and the poem is the judgment imagery with which the poem begins: an affirmation of God's justice under excruciating circumstances. The implication seems to be that Amnon's hesitation about conversion was an offense of such magnitude that he accepts the torture as the verdict of a just Judge. That is of course deeply problematic in itself. But making this liturgy a clarion call to martyrdom? One can imagine martyrs, as they face death, proclaiming the first paragraph of the *Sh'ma*, commanding love of God (in the interpretation of Rabbi Akiva) even at the cost of one's life (Talmud, Berakhot 61b). One can imagine them singing *Alenu*, the first part of which asserts the unique destiny of the Jew in contrast with the other nations of the earth.[11] But the universalistic *Un'taneh Tokef* and martyrology are extremely difficult to reconcile.

Yet the current American Reform *machzor* introduces the passage with a meditation about its traditional context: "It is said[12] that the words we are about to utter were born of the martyrdom of Rabbi Amnon of Mayence. He chose to die that his faith might live."[13]

Even with the proper translation and understanding of the climactic affirmation about the efficacy of penitence, prayer, and charity, the text of the *piyyut* is not free of theological challenges.[14] To present it as a text celebrating Jewish martyrdom, evoking a historical setting of the First Crusade, which produced appalling behavior on the part of Christian warriors, chilling responses on the part of many Jewish victims (who slaughtered their own wives and children and killed themselves in order to avoid forced conversion), and some of the most intolerant discourse about Christianity ever written in Hebrew texts, is to violate the universalistic vision of the poem. Penitence, prayer, and charity can serve to create bonds across religious lines; reference to a problematic story about a Christian bishop mutilating a faithful Jewish martyr feeds the worst stereotypes in our collective memory. *Un'taneh Tokef* deserves a place in a contemporary Progressive High Holy Day *machzor*. The frame narrative about Amnon of Mainz does not.

7

Somehow Linked to God

Rabbi Daniel G. Zemel

Each year, as Rosh Hashanah approaches, I am overwhelmed by the mysterious power of the High Holy Days. Why do Jews who do not set foot in the synagogue on any other day of the year feel they must at least drop by during Rosh Hashanah and Yom Kippur—even (in some places) at the cost of special tickets that give them seats in an overflow room where the best they get is closed-circuit TV? The words of *Un'taneh Tokef* echo reality: "All who enter the world will pass before You" (line 10). Looking out at a sanctuary filled with people, I think, for a moment, that they really will—that they really are—precisely here, precisely now.

Although leading very secular lives, we American Jews are not ready to abandon the traditions of our parents and grandparents completely. We have faith that somewhere in this tradition we can find wisdom and strength of spirit. Holding on, even for two or three days a year, reconnects us to a past that we are simply unwilling to forget.

But there is more. There are the words of *Un'taneh Tokef,* which haunt us with the sobering reminder that even "forgotten" things are being inscribed and recorded.

Un'taneh Tokef assures us that there is something beyond, that we are in touch with it, and that this day is indeed holy.

By connecting us to memories of the past and to holiness beyond ourselves, *Un'taneh Tokef* gives us the roots we sorely need when every other area of our lives is rootless. We live in cities where we did not grow up. Parents and children are scattered elsewhere. We regularly work new

---

Rabbi Daniel G. Zemel is the senior rabbi of Temple Micah in Washington, D.C.

jobs, inhabit new neighborhoods, and visit new vacation spots. For lives that are whirlwinds of change, these holy days provide a constant, a reference point from which to take stock. When everything is change, nothing can be measured. Only in a moment of pause can we measure what we are doing, where we are going, how we are living. We remain, in some important measure, who and what we come from. *Un'taneh Tokef* keeps aglow the flame of our past.

We would not come so faithfully if the message of the day were not the certainty of connectedness, holiness, rootedness, and constancy. But there is a price. The voice of these Days of Awe is the *machzor*, and the *machzor* makes demands of us. It asks that we consider our lives as a gift, that we take not one life-moment for granted, that we give thought to the direction our lives are taking. We leave fingerprints wherever we go; the book of our life bears our own signature. This prayer asks us to confront the fundamental seriousness of being. Our lives are not jokes; we are created in God's image.

The prayer book provides an interesting dialectic. On the one hand, we are invited to delve deeply into our individual souls. Who are we? What have we become? What vows have we made? What loyalties will we stand by? Nothing could be more personal. On the other hand, so much of the prayer book is couched in the plural, "we." We are alone, but we are not alone. We are part of a community. Each of us is responsible for the other. The sin of one affects all. We can influence each other for good or for ill. We are judged—not just for our individual deeds, but for the kind of community we inhabit.

Who we are, personally and communally, prompts the climactic questions, "Who will live and who will die ... who by fire, who by water ..." (line 16). But is it really possible that while we're down here simply trying to hold on, God is up there with a scorecard? I frequently wonder if some personal tragedy led the author of this poem to such a harrowing conclusion. Is this his effort to make sense of some loss that he suffered or witnessed? Did he himself really believe his own words when he wrote the following:

> [On Rosh Hashanah] All who enter the world will pass before You like sheep. As a shepherd searches for his flock and has his sheep pass under his staff so too will You record and recount and review all living beings; and You as You

> have them pass by will decide the end of all creatures and
> write down their sentence. (lines 10–13)

Can we not ask: In what way, God, do you think about the souls of those
who are taken young, before what You yourself call "their end?" What are
your calculations in these cases? How are you counting?

The great poet who wrote *Un'taneh Tokef* knows that some are called "not
at their end" (line 16). He is asking our deepest question: Why? What can
faith mean when the young are taken before their time, when senseless
tragedy abounds? Why do some reach old age and some but a few moments?
On one side of the scale is justice, on the other that searing "Why?" How
can we be persons of faith when consumed by this mystery of life and
death, fairness and injustice? These mysteries can be too enormous for us to
bear. We fall back on ourselves and are nearly broken by our own weakness,
our limitations—physical, emotional, spiritual, conceptual.

Our poet too, I believe, was confounded. "Their origin is from dust
and their end is to dust" (line 27), and between dust and dust lie lives of
impossible struggle. Unable to bear the enormous cost that life extracts
from deep within us, the poet sums up the burden very simply, in just a
few words: "At their peril gathering food" (line 28). I read this line more
poetically: *B'nafsho yavi lachmo*, "At the risk of our souls, we earn our
keep." Death comes without explanation, but life is an inordinate effort.
This prayer leaves no stone unturned, no question unasked.

Our poet, like us, cannot face life as an unremitting black hole. He has
suffered a loss too great to bear. He wants to go on living, to play again
and laugh again and feel joy again. He yearns for something to hold on
to, something that will keep his own spirit afloat. In desperation, perhaps,
he finds them in those famous words, "Repentance, prayer, and charity
help the hardship of the decree pass" (line 21).

That is not how we have traditionally read them. We have more
usually understood them to say that these three actions "avert the severe
decree"—as if to say, "There is a cure!" Each year as I say those words, I
pray that they were written with regret, that our author was grasping at
straws, for that too is part of our life: clutching for something that is not

really there. There is no cure. But what a false hope to offer, blaming the victim for the crime, as if to say that those who suffer do not sufficiently repent, lack a vital enough prayer life, or are somehow lacking in generosity. Despite the many attempts to explain them away, these words disturb me deeply.

I choose to think that our poet also knew them to be untrue, for he could have chosen to end his poem with this reassuring curative. Instead he struggles on, searching for a truer end.

He finds it with a final burst of hope, calling out to whomever in the universe might listen: "Your years are boundless and the length of your days is endless. Your glorious chariots are priceless and the eternity of your name is limitless. Your name suits You and You suit your name. You named us after You" (lines 32–34).

This is true faith: the proclamation, despite it all, of God's greatness, and the assertion that God's name is included in ours. We are somehow linked to God; being so linked is our definition. God shares God's holiness with us. We are God's image, God's partner. We are God's helpmate from the dawn of creation. And the poet says it is through our names. When we cry out God's name, we voice our own as well.

"What's in a name?" Juliet asks Romeo. Our poet might say, "Everything." He calls on us to live our lives by linking our names to holiness and nobility.

Un'taneh Tokef is God taking attendance: we are called to remember the names of those who said *Hineni*, "Here!" to God's call to the service of justice and good deeds. We also yearn to link our names to God.

The High Holy Days compress our lives into the most basic and essential terms, restoring our souls in a manner so critical as to be beyond our ability to articulate. Is that not what poetry and prayer are about—expressing the inexpressible? We sing prayers to melodies that remind us of our childhood, that feel as though they reach into antiquity and root us in a past. We reach for something bigger in our lives, for holiness itself. We consider the dialectic of the prayer book: we are alone but connected to others. We, like God, take attendance, recount the names of those we love and those we see, those we know and those we just know of, those with us and those around the globe. We more slowly recount the names of those we miss but whom we continue to love. We pray that by *Un'taneh Tokef*'s glorious end, we will have linked ourselves to all of them—and to God.

PART II

Reinterpreting *Un'taneh Tokef* for Our Time

8

A Biblical Perspective

Dr. Marc Brettler

I find *Un'taneh Tokef* deeply moving. Its words scare me, especially "who will live and who will die" (line 15). Its tunes, too, are haunting—both the traditional melody and the newer one introduced in 1990 by Yair Rosenblum to commemorate those killed in the Yom Kippur War from Kibbutz Beit Hashita. I appreciate why it has developed into such an important prayer and why a myth developed to suggest its divine origin. But especially after writing commentaries for *My People's Prayer Book* and *My People's Passover Haggadah* on the relation between the liturgy and the Bible, I cannot recite any prayer without thinking: How biblically inspired is it in phraseology and content? What post-biblical ideas does it contain? Which of the wide variety of biblical theological notions and texts does this text further? Which does it ignore?

On one level, *Un'taneh Tokef* is very biblical—more than 90 percent of its phrases are from the Bible. Take, for instance, the three couplets from "Their origin is from dust" through "like a vanishing cloud" (lines 27–29). The idea of people as created from dust is from the second creation story

---

Dr. Marc Brettler is the Dora Golding Professor of Biblical Studies at Brandeis University and has published and lectured widely on metaphor and the Bible, the nature of biblical historical texts, and gender issues and the Bible. He contributed to all volumes of the *My People's Prayer Book: Traditional Prayers, Modern Commentaries* series, winner of the National Jewish Book Award, and to *My People's Passover Haggadah: Traditional Texts, Modern Commentaries* (both Jewish Lights). He is coeditor of *The Jewish Study Bible*, which won the National Jewish Book Award; and author of *How to Read the Jewish Bible*, among other books and articles. He has also been interviewed on NPR's *Fresh Air* by Terry Gross.

(Genesis 2:7); "their end is to the dust" comes from Job 10:9; "at their peril gathering food" paraphrases Lamentations 5:9; the image of "shattered pottery" is found in Jeremiah 19; "like withered grass" and "like a faded blossom" cite Isaiah 40:7; "a passing shadow" is based on Psalm 144:4; and "a vanishing cloud" is from Job 7:9. The poem's author knew even the most obscure biblical books (like Habakkuk and Daniel).

Like other liturgical poets, this one has woven the compilation of biblical phrases into a meaningful new creation, using biblical expressions in highly innovative ways—like "a thin whisper of sound" (line 7) from 1 Kings 19:12 and "shaking and trembling" (line 8) from Psalm 48:7. He also creates new wordplays, such as *yanu'ach* ("rest") and *yanu'a* ("wander"; line 19), employs biblical parallelism creatively, and uses several key terms such as "the day of judgment" (line 9) that are distinctly Rabbinic and post-biblical.

Un'taneh Tokef is also highly innovative with respect to the Bible in its theological vision. We know very little about Rosh Hashanah and Yom Kippur in the biblical period. They are absent in the festival calendars in Exodus 23 and 34 and Deuteronomy 16 and are found only in the (later, Priestly) calendar of Leviticus 23 and Numbers 29. Clearly, they were not always the major Jewish festivals that they have become.

In the Bible, Rosh Hashanah never even has that name—it cannot be the new year, since it is "the seventh month, on the first day of the month" (Leviticus 23:24). It is a day of "complete rest, a sacred occasion commemorated with loud blasts" (ibid.) when work was prohibited and sacrifices were offered (v. 25), and no more.

A bit more is said about Yom Kippur, which should be translated as "the Day of Purgation," in which the Tabernacle, the prototype for the Jerusalem Temple, was cleansed ("purged") of ritual impurity. The high Priest used the blood of a goat (Leviticus 16) for this purpose to assure that God would stay and protect Israel; a scapegoat ritual was also enacted. These rituals seem to function automatically—no repentance is needed. Only once is Yom Kippur connected to cleansing people rather than the Sanctuary (Leviticus 16:33). But there is no public prayer for Yom Kippur, which is not connected to Rosh Hashanah as the climax of the Ten Days of Repentance—a term and idea that is post-biblical. Indeed, the very notions behind *Un'taneh Tokef*—the period between Rosh Hashanah and Yom Kippur as a time for intense personal introspection culminating in final judgment by God—are totally foreign to the Bible.

The biblical Israelites would not even have recognized the central climactic phrase, "Repentance, prayer, and charity help the hardship of the decree pass" (line 21). They would have asked: what does "the hardship of the decree" mean? Why the triad "repentance, prayer, and charity"? And what is repentance (*t'shuvah*) anyway? The related verb *shuv*, "to (re)turn," appears in the Bible, sometimes in the sense of "returning to God," but the noun *t'shuvah* never means "repentance" there. Thus, the main theology, and even some of the crucial terminology of this prayer, would have been foreign to our ancestors. The very Rabbinic notion of the "High Holy Days" or "Days of Awe" reflects a transformation of biblical theology.

The most significant change is the turning of the biblical judgment *period* into the annual judgment *day*. This is accomplished through three images from Ezekiel: God caring for the flock (Israel), God judging each person individually; and God punishing Israel. All three are connected in our prayer. The image of a "book of memories" (line 5) is also borrowed from biblical, and even ancient Near Eastern, roots.

Ezekiel the prophet offered comfort to the Judeans exiled to Babylon. We can imagine the despair of these exiles, who felt punished for the community's sins and for the cumulative sins of several generations. In response, Ezekiel insists on two theological realities: (1) God does not punish intergenerationally—"The person who sins, he alone shall die" (18:20); and (2) everyone has the right to repent, even from serious sins—"If the wicked one repents of all the sins that he committed and keeps all my laws and does what is just and right, he shall live; he shall not die. None of the transgressions he committed shall be remembered against him; because of the righteousness he has practiced, he shall live") (vv. 21–22). The prophet adds, "You do not want the dead to die" (v. 32) but only to "return from their path" (v. 23). This rationale is cited in the *Un'taneh Tokef*, whose author was certainly thinking of Ezekiel 18 and its guarantee that during times of disaster, both personal and national, people must look inward and repent. This is a remarkable response to powerlessness caused by the exile, and to us as well.

But when and how does repentance happen? How patient is God? Ezekiel does not answer these questions, but the Rabbis do, by creating an annual time of reckoning.

Un'taneh Tokef (lines 11–12) describes this reckoning with another image from Ezekiel: "As a shepherd seeks out his flock when some [animals] in his flock have gotten separated, so I will seek out my flock" (34:12). In contrast to Psalm 23, "Adonai is my shepherd; I lack nothing" (v. 1), this "seeking out" is not necessarily beneficial: "I will look for the lost, and I will bring back the strayed; I will bandage the injured, and I will sustain the weak; and the fat and healthy ones I will destroy. I will tend them rightly [*b'mishpat*]" (v. 16). In other words, selection will occur using the shepherd's crook; some sheep will be rewarded and others punished—this image is the model for the *Un'taneh Tokef.*

The long inventory of punishments in lines 15–20 of *Un'taneh Tokef* includes some that are called for by the Talmud, such as strangling. But the core is an expansion of Ezekiel 14:21, which lists "the sword, famine, wild beasts, and pestilence." We also find "fire and water" from Psalm 66:12, and Psalm 75:8 proclaims, "For God it is who gives judgment; He brings down one man, He lifts up another." This expansive collating of biblical punishments highlights God's great power. Yet people are not powerless before this mighty God; they can control their destiny by repenting.

Before imposing punishment, God must record transgression—the biblical image of heavenly books serves this purpose. It is found about a dozen times in the Bible, for example, in Exodus 32:32, where Moses says to God, "Now, if You will forgive their sin [well and good]; but if not, erase me from the record which You have written!" The form of this book is never detailed and we do not find an individual's signature in it. The book, or more accurately, scroll, likely originates in accounts of pre-Israelite, Mesopotamian "tablets of destiny" that the gods had, and it further developed as a scroll or book in Psalm 69:29 and in the New Testament, too (e.g., Luke 10:20; Philippians 4:3; Revelation 13:8).

If the "book of life" is used to reckon punishment, when is this book "closed" in the accounting sense? The Bible offers no hint, but it often speaks of an accounting day, "the *Day* of Adonai," a day or an era when God will reappear on earth, punishing the wicked and ushering in an ideal age. *Un'taneh Tokef* depicts each High Holy Day season as a miniature Day of Adonai by citing biblical texts that deal with the *eschaton*, or end of days:

- Isaiah 16:5: And a throne shall be established in goodness / In the tent of David, / And on it shall sit in faithfulness / A ruler devoted to justice / And zealous for equity.
- Isaiah 27:13: And in that day, a great ram's horn shall be sounded; and the strayed who are in the land of Assyria and the expelled who

are in the land of Egypt shall come and worship Adonai on the holy mount, in Jerusalem.
- Isaiah 24:21: In that day, Adonai will punish / The host of heaven in heaven / And the kings of the earth on earth.

In our prayer, these judgment scenes, which were originally associated with the end of time, become an annual event.

Every Rosh Hashanah and Yom Kippur, I am moved by *Un'taneh Tokef*'s strong and evocative biblical language, which helps me stand, requesting mercy, before "the living and everlasting God." I stand in awe of something else as well—the Jewish tradition, which in so many places remains nourished by the Bible, yet has flourished precisely because of the way it has reworked biblical ideas in such an inventive fashion. I am awestruck by the vitality and flexibility of the Jewish tradition, which has captured such a creative balance of the old and the new: old words appear in new meanings and new contexts, and old tunes are revitalized to fit new times and events.

9

God as the Ultimate Writer

Dr. Erica Brown

One of the most striking and prominent images of the High Holy Days is that of the book of life (*sefer hachayim*), a magical document where past deeds are recorded and futures written. I remember as a child, having a vivid picture in my mind of an old bearded man opening up a book even longer than the *Encyclopedia Britannica* and checking off name after name. And my name would be there, too. Oy!

In *Un'taneh Tokef* we read words that validate this image: "Truly You are judge and prosecutor and litigant and witness and author and sealer, and record and recounter. And you will remember everything that has been forgotten, and you will open the book of memories and it will be read from: everyone's signature is in it (lines 3–6)."

God is a writer, the ultimate writer. And once our fates are written, there is something about the ink that terrifies us: what if it is really permanent? The High Holy Day liturgy confirms this fear. For most of the services, our *Amidah* prays that "we be remembered and written in the book of life for blessing, peace, and ample sustenance: (*b'sefer chayim,*

Dr. Erica Brown, director for adult education at the Partnership for Jewish Life and Learning, is an Avi Chai Fellow and the recipient of the 2009 Covenant Award. She is the author of *Inspired Jewish Leadership: Practical Approaches to Building Strong Communities,* a National Jewish Book Award finalist, and *Spiritual Boredom: Rediscovering the Wonder of Judaism;* and coauthor of *The Case for Jewish Peoplehood: Can We Be One?* (all Jewish Lights). She writes a weekly Internet essay, "Weekly Jewish Wisdom," for the *Newsweek/Washington Post* site "On Faith."

b'rakhah v'shalom, ufarnasah tovah, nizakher v'nikatev). And then comes *N'ilah,* where we change the verb. No longer are we being written. The writing is complete. This year's book of life is finished. We are "sealed" (*v'nekhtam*).

Un'taneh Tokef introduces the idea of God as writer, but the image of God as a writer and man's fate as written and recorded is not only reserved for our *machzorim,* our High Holy Day prayer books. It is present in any number of biblical verses:

- Exodus 32:32: "Forgive their sin, but if not, erase me from the record which you have written." But Adonai said to Moses, "He who has sinned against Me, him only will I erase from my record."
- Psalm 69:29: "Let them be blotted out of the book of the living; let them not be enrolled among the righteous."
- Isaiah 4:3 contains a list of those written for life in Jerusalem. If your name was erased from such a list, it signified death.
- Malachi 3:16: "Those who revere Adonai have talked to one another. Adonai has heard it and noted it, and a scroll of remembrance has been written at His behest...."

The image of God as a writer is very, very old indeed and was shared by others in the ancient Near Eastern world. In Mesopotamia, the gods were said to possess tablets inscribed with the deeds and destinies of human beings. God appears as writer in Rabbinic sources too. In *Pirkei Avot* 3:17, Rabbi Akiva mentions a heavenly ledger, an image found also in the Talmudic text upon which *Un'taneh Tokef* is based: "The righteous are written in the book of life, the wicked in the book of death, and those in the middle ground are held in abeyance" (Rosh Hashanah 16b).

One Yom Kippur I amused myself with this idea: if God writes a book of our deeds, what kind of book is that? Is God a technical writer or a fiction writer, for example, and if a technical writer, does God write only numbers or checks after certain information and in certain standard boxes, requiring the proverbial number-two pencil? Is Rabbi Akiva's ledger graph paper where God adds up columns like an accountant? Let's pray God is a novelist, a magical realist! Or maybe a journalist, striving for objectivity but naturally failing because of the balance of justice and mercy? Or even a researcher, using a system of controls and variables to test our judgments and behaviors. And how would we shelve God's writing in a bookstore: Psychology? Self-help? Religion? Fiction? History? Humor?

If God is going to be a fiction writer—and how, honestly, can God be anything other?—I wonder if God is a poet, a mystery writer, graphic novelist, or playwright. Well, perhaps that depends on the life we lead. After all, if we are the "copy" that makes it into God's journal, then we ourselves determine what kind of material we are. And then, of course, when we fail to understand ourselves, there are always the Cliffsnotes.

For all of the whimsical questions about God as a writer in *Un'taneh Tokef*, something more serious underlies the prayer: the sacredness of the writing process itself. *Pirkei Avot* 5:6 tells us that ten things were created right before Shabbat; one of them is *hak'tav v'hamikhtav*, "writing and a writing instrument." Writing precedes creation and is, arguably, the most transcendent way that God communicates with us. God gave us the Ten Commandments in written form; our life text is written; Kabbalah is predicated on the study of divine names and letters.

Our Jewish lives are shaped every day by sacred writing. This kind of writing is at once permanent and changeable. Torah scrolls must be written with permanent ink and on hides that preserve the ink in the most permanent way. The kind of writing on Shabbat that is prohibited is permanent writing that cannot be blown away or simply vanish. There is permanent writing, the kind that is chiseled on tablets, and it records the things that are most constant about our lives and our values.

But Jewish law discusses nonpermanent writing too. The trial of a suspected adulteress requires writing with nonpermanent ink, so that God's own name can be erased for the sake of *shalom bayit*, domestic tranquility. There is a lengthy discussion in Mishnah Shabbat (11:8) on what vegetables and materials produce nonpermanent ink. Not everything that is recorded need be saved.

Because of expense in the ancient world, paper was used more than once. Writing was rubbed out with stones, and then new writing was superimposed upon it. In *Pirkei Avot* 4:20, the scholar and heretic Elisha ben Abuya compares the learning of a child, which is "ink on clean paper," with learning in old age, "ink on erased paper." In other words, the fact that God writes down our *zikhronot* and *atidot*, our past deeds and our future, does not mean that our account cannot be erased or altered. Even in the ancient world, where it was much harder to correct errors in writing, mistakes were corrected.

As I grew older, my image of the *sefer hachayim* came to reflect other aspects of my emerging adolescence. My father is a writer, and one of my enduring childhood memories is going to sleep with the sound of the Smith Corona typewriter in his study on the third floor reaching the end of the roll, and then dinging and being brought back to the other side. So, in my vision of the heavenly scorecard, God no longer wrote with a quill pen. God used a Smith Corona.

As I progressed through high school and college, the process of writing advanced beyond recognition. How easy it became to correct mistakes. Nowadays, we simply spell-check and cut and paste or erase with ease. There is no excuse today for not handing in corrected writing. What a metaphor! We are the writers, but God is our editor, handing back what we have written and challenging us to correct our mistakes.

Writing is the perfect metaphor for *t'shuvah*. Thomas Mann once said, "A writer is somebody for whom writing is more difficult than it is for other people." So *t'shuvah*, like writing, is most difficult for people who do it best. F. Scott Fitzgerald once said, "Writers aren't exactly people … they're a whole lot of people trying to be one person." *T'shuvah*, too, requires an understanding of the multiple and contradictory forces that beset us as humans. Those who are most reflective about their behavior have the hardest time because they understand the emotional enormity involved.

In *Un'taneh Tokef*, we ask God to record us in the book of life, and on Yom Kippur we note when that writing is sealed and permanent. Until that moment, that very moment indicated by a shift of language, the gates of prayer are closing. Yet we know that the writing process is still going on. God is a writer in process.

Words build worlds. God built the world with words of creation and our Jewish world with words of Torah—then made us coauthors and editors in them both. We do more than walk beneath God's quill awaiting evaluation; we write our own destinies, knowing that God will do the fact-checking.

So this year, as we stand and say *Un'taneh Tokef* with our eyes closed and our hearts open, let us think not only about God as a writer but about ourselves, too, as authors of a future. Write well. Write thoughtfully and elegantly. Select words with extreme care, because words not only build but can also destroy worlds. Be open to the red pen of improvement. View relationships as an opportunity for self-editing. Embrace the difficulty of it. And then perhaps we can echo poet Yehuda Amichai's aspiration: "I want once more to be written in the Book of Life, to be written anew every day until the writing hand hurts."

10

"How Was Your Flight?"

Dr. Joel M. Hoffman

I have a love-hate relationship with worship.

When people ask me, "How were services?" I hear a question not unlike, "How was your flight?" The options for an answer start with "fine" at the positive extreme of the spectrum and seem to have no clear terminus at the other: flights are delayed, canceled, misrouted, turbulent, uncomfortable, inconveniently scheduled, overbooked, and worse, to say nothing of what some people think counts as dinner or what they do with my luggage.

Services, too, are too long for me and frequently boring. And that's on a good day, only going downhill when the seating is uncomfortable, the climate control not set to my preference, the music not to my liking, the poetry unsuited to my mood, the sermon a repetition of something I've heard, or a great number of other things that people around me seem to like much more than I.

Dr. Joel M. Hoffman lectures around the globe on popular and scholarly topics spanning history, Hebrew, prayer, and Jewish continuity. He has served on the faculties of Brandeis University, the Academy for Jewish Religion, and Hebrew Union College–Jewish Institute of Religion in New York. Hoffman writes about Hebrew for the international *Jerusalem Post,* and is the author of *In the Beginning: A Short History of the Hebrew Language* and *And God Said: How Translations Conceal the Bible's Original Meaning.* He contributed to all volumes of the *My People's Prayer Book: Traditional Prayers, Modern Commentaries* series, winner of the National Jewish Book Award, and to *My People's Passover Haggadah: Traditional Texts, Modern Commentaries* (both Jewish Lights). He lives in Westchester, New York.

And yet I keep going, almost every Shabbat and certainly every Rosh Hashanah and Yom Kippur. For me, not being in shul for the High Holy Days is unthinkable.

I am lucky. I understand Hebrew, so the accumulated poetry of over a hundred generations so compactly assembled and conveniently laid out in the prayer book is mine for the taking, if I so choose. And frequently I do. My thoughts and eyes wander, reading this prayer or that, sometimes taking in an especially beautiful image: the trees themselves clapping in joy, the glorious Jerusalem offering refuge to the poor, peace cascading down from above. Or I contemplate a particular turn of phrase or a grammatical construction that (at least to me) seems interesting.

Other times I wonder about the broader messages of the liturgy. Is God our ruler? If so, is God our king or our queen, and what would be the difference? Who are the people who sleep in the dust? Does God watch over me? Would it help if, as *Adon Olam* declares, I put my soul and body in God's hand? Does God have hands?

And sometimes I just marvel at the whole thing. I look around and I can't believe what I'm doing. Why am I wearing a *tallit*, singing texts I know are not true, reading words I've memorized from a pigment-inscribed scroll of parchment, or listening to a cascade of sounds produced from an unsophisticated animal's horn? Who would do such things?

It is against this backdrop that I encounter *Un'taneh Tokef* every Rosh Hashanah. Then again the prayer greets me on Yom Kippur, like a rerun of a movie on a very long flight (during which no food at all will be served), a reminder that I'm just beginning my yearly trudge through a day of fasting.

The prayer's poetry is lofty, brilliant even, and its imagery is vivid: the courtroom prosecutor doubles as judge and witness, stacking the cards against the defendant (me!) when the stakes are no less than life and death. The detail—will it be death by starvation or by dehydration?—drives home the point.

For all of the prayer's sophistication and elegance, though, its message at first glance seems to be straightforward, simple, and clear: good people live and bad people die. The only path to long life is repentance, and even though God waits until the very last minute, hoping for our return from sinful ways, the people who die deserve their death, and those who live merit their continued existence.

There are nuances—Does God mete out the punishment directly? Is a painful death the punishment for particularly egregious behavior?—but the point is not complicated, and it's a message that intuitively resonates deeply with most people.

That is because as children we are taught that our actions have consequences. It doesn't take us long to understand the model, and by the middle of our first decade of life we are fully aware that we will be punished when we do something wrong and rewarded when we do something right.

Our next step as children is to demand what we think of as equity. The child's complaint that "it's not fair" is always a damning accusation, because as children we are vexed when we do not get the reward we think we deserve, but, perhaps oddly, we are equally upset when the undeserving garner prizes. We learn to tolerate punishment when we deserve it, but we are outraged at the possibility that someone who behaved just as badly as we did might not suffer with the same severity.

By the time we are adults, we have so firmly internalized this doctrine of reward and punishment that, sometimes subconsciously, it pervades our life. We ask of some minor misfortune—a cold, say, or a flooded basement or a crashed computer or a delayed flight—"What did I do to deserve this?" Then we answer the silly question, in our minds searching for some error we must have made for which this is punishment. "If only I'd been kinder to my parents" or "I should have given more money to charity."

Intellectually we know that the question makes no sense. Colds are caused by germs, and the germs don't target us in retribution. The rain water doesn't seep through the basement because of our moral failings. The computer crashes purely of its own accord. And so forth. But the child in us never gives up, and we find ourselves plagued by bad answers to a worse question.

Oddly, this outlook attacks even adults who don't believe in God and don't go to services. When tragedy strikes, they too try to appease the God they don't believe in, in a manner they don't think is effective.

We react especially strongly regarding those we love. A parent who sees a child suffering might plead with no one in particular, "Let me suffer instead." We know that the world doesn't work that way—and belief in a God with whom to make such a bargain almost entails a rejection of the premise in the first place—but petitions like these cross our minds and even our lips, as prayers we almost cannot help but utter. Thoughts about equity, reward, and punishment keep us awake at night and haunt our days.

Deuteronomy promises that crop-nourishing rain will only fall if we follow God's commandments, and we Jews have always considered that passage important enough to include in our *m'zuzot, t'fillin*, and prayer books as part of the *Sh'ma*. God destroys Sodom and Gomorrah in response to the behavior of their inhabitants, and the prophets equate exile with our moral failings. The Bible is unrelenting in its classical doctrine of reward and punishment.

In this regard, *Un'taneh Tokef* seems like simply a poetic repetition of what we already know: we will thrive only if we behave well. But the compilers of the Bible knew something important about classical reward and punishment. They knew it wasn't true!

The book of Job—the Bible's only full-length treatise on human suffering—is a nearly total rejection of the idea that we are punished only in response to sin. Deuteronomy is wrong, says Job, as are the prophets in this regard. The righteous suffer just like everyone else, because misery is not a punishment, and it's not deserved. The book of Job explains to the reader—though not to Job himself—why Job is suffering. It's because God has been challenged to run an experiment. Will the super-righteous man Job blaspheme God if God ruins his life?

But the end of the book rejects any possibility of our understanding why bad things happen. "Were you around when I made the sea?" God chastises Job in response to his attempt to understand his suffering. "If you can't understand how I spoke the world into existence," God seems to be saying, "what makes you think you could ever understand the nature of human pain?"

In fact, the book of Job is more nuanced. For while it forces us to reject the doctrine of reward and punishment, it also acknowledges our natural tendency to rely upon it. We should be careful not to think that our suffering is our fault, says the book of Job, but equally we should always be cognizant that that outlook will be our default way of understanding misfortune. Job is rebuked for his question, not for being the kind of person who would ask it.

In that sense, we are all Job. We demand to know why we are suffering, and we are practically unable to accept our inability to understand the answer.

This is the real power of *Un'taneh Tokef.* While at first glance it seems to support reward and punishment, it quotes the book of Job more than any other source! Its biblical quotations remind us not to take the tempting doctrine of Deuteronomy too seriously.

The High Holy Days may be when it is decided who shall live and who shall die, and each year is marked by uncertainty about the future and, often, regret about the past. Some of us didn't make it through the year gone by. Others will likely not make it to the end of the next. Faced with this combination of terror and horror, we naturally ask what those who died did to deserve their fate, what we did to merit the unbearable longing for those we miss, and what we might already have done that will spell the end of our own lives.

But *Un'taneh Tokef* demands that we look more closely at our first instinctual reaction. Job is woven throughout the prayer and, by extension, throughout our lives. We have to overcome our natural inclination to look for a cause for every negative effect.

In this sense, too, *Un'taneh Tokef* is like a long flight, whose value lies not in the experience but in where it takes me. Over the course of the year I fret about suffering, worry about why things happen, and make unreasonable demands of God. *Un'taneh Tokef* brings me back to where I need to be.

11

Passing before God
THE LITERARY THEME OF
UN'TANEH TOKEF

Rabbi Elie Kaunfer

W hat does it mean to read *Un'taneh Tokef* as a poem? Modern Jews are quite comfortable creatively interpreting biblical and Rabbinic texts, but not liturgy. Prayers, therefore, remain simple statements with nothing but surface meanings inviting inspiration or—too often—rejection. But prayers also are works of literary art; they too demand interpretation, even though (or precisely because) such an approach complicates a seemingly straightforward picture of the divine-human relationship. This is especially true of *Un'taneh Tokef.*

Understanding *Un'taneh Tokef* in all its fullness requires a poetic reading that focuses on the literary key to the prayer—the multiple use of the Hebrew verb *avar.* The prayer is easily divisible into distinct sections, each with its own discrete theme, and each containing a different form of *ayin vet resh*, the root letters for the word *avar*, which unites them. All in all, *avar* appears a total of seven times in *Un'taneh Tokef,* a significant number in any Jewish text. Rich in meaning, *avar* unlocks a wealth of interpretations through allusions to the Bible and Rabbinic literature.

Rabbi Elie Kaunfer is cofounder and executive director of Mechon Hadar (www.mechonhadar.org). He is an Avi Chai Fellow and the author of *Empowered Judaism: What Independent Minyanim Can Teach Us about Building Vibrant Jewish Communities* (Jewish Lights). In 2009, *Newsweek* named him one of fifty top rabbis in America.

WIN A $100 GIFT CERTIFICATE!

Fill in this card and
mail it to us—
or fill it in online at

**jewishlights.com/
feedback.html**

—to be eligible for a
$100 gift certificate for
Jewish Lights books.

JEWISH LIGHTS PUBLISHING
SUNSET FARM OFFICES RTE 4
PO BOX 237
WOODSTOCK VT 05091-0237

Place
Stamp
Here

Fill in this card and return it to us to be eligible for our quarterly drawing for a $100 gift certificate for Jewish Lights books.

We hope that you will enjoy this book and find it useful in enriching your life.

Book title: _____

Your comments: _____

How you learned of this book: _____

If purchased: Bookseller _____ City _____ State _____

Please send me a free JEWISH LIGHTS Publishing catalog. I am interested in: (check all that apply)

1. ☐ Spirituality
2. ☐ Mysticism/Kabbalah
3. ☐ Philosophy/Theology
4. ☐ History/Politics

5. ☐ Women's Interest
6. ☐ Environmental Interest
7. ☐ Healing/Recovery
8. ☐ Children's Books

9. ☐ Caregiving/Grieving
10. ☐ Ideas for Book Groups
11. ☐ Religious Education Resources
12. ☐ Interfaith Resources

Name (PRINT) _____

Street _____

City _____ State _____ Zip _____

E-MAIL (FOR SPECIAL OFFERS ONLY) _____

Please send a JEWISH LIGHTS Publishing catalog to my friend:

Name (PRINT) _____

Street _____

City _____ State _____ Zip _____

JEWISH LIGHTS PUBLISHING

Tel: (802) 457-4000 • Fax: (802) 457-4004

Available at better booksellers. Visit us online at www.jewishlights.com

The derivative forms of *avar* are many and multivalent. Some (like "pass," "remove," and "cross") are value neutral. Others (like "sin" and "anger") have negative meaning. Others still (like "conceive" and "appease") are positive. The root is also possibly related to the original meaning of "Hebrew" (*ivri*).

In the beginning of the poem, the poet plays out some of these different valences in reference to the act of passing. First, referencing Mishnah Rosh Hashanah 1:2, the poem notes how the entire world passes (*ya'avrun*) before God as sheep (line 10). This passing denotes an unfeeling and objective judgment process, since the broader context of the Mishnah describes the four times of year that God judges the world. This is the classic Rosh Hashanah theology associated with *Un'taneh Tokef*—Rosh Hashanah is the time we pass before God to be judged for our deeds.

But the next line of the poem offers a very different view of passing before God. The line reads, "As a shepherd searches for his flock and has his sheep pass under his staff ..." (line 11). The beginning of this line ("As a shepherd searches for his flock") recalls the intimate image of the relationship between God and Israel presented in Ezekiel 34:12. There God acts as shepherd to stray sheep, which are explicitly compared to the most vulnerable of society: the sick, injured, and lost. God castigates Israel for not tending this flock and steps in as the ultimate shepherd to seek out the lost and neglected. It is at once an image of intimacy with the downtrodden and a critique of the powerful. This is not an impartial, unfeeling judge, but a justice-demanding shepherd.

The second half of that line ("has his sheep pass under his staff") also cuts against the first use of *avar* as "passing in judgment." People are usually judged on their merits. Here, however, a reference to Leviticus raises a different approach. Leviticus 27:32 describes sheep passing under the Israelite shepherd's staff, with the tenth one selected as a sacred tithe. The following verse (27:33) challenges the notion of being judged only on our merits, for in the tithe, the shepherd "must not be on the lookout [*y'vaker*, which recalls *k'vakarat* in our poem] for good as opposed to bad." No matter which sheep passes under the staff as number ten, it is reserved for sanctification. This image recognizes the role that randomness plays in fate and the ways in which good and bad deeds don't always correlate to good and bad judgments.

The next line of *Un'taneh Tokef* employs *avar* in yet a third manner: "So too will You record and recount and review all living beings as You have them pass by [*ta'avir*] ... and write down their sentence" (lines 12–13). While the surface reading may imply judgment, these lines recall the glorious return to Zion described in Jeremiah 33:10–13, in which sheep pass under God's staff for counting all across the Holy Land: "Thus says Adonai of hosts: In this ruined place, without man or beast ... there shall again be a pasture for shepherds, where they can rest their flocks.... Sheep shall pass [*ta'avornah*] again under the hand of one who counts" (Jeremiah 33:12–13). Here in Jeremiah, sheep passing by is a sign of life in a previously desolate land. This reference implies a redemptive end to judgment day rather than a sentence that is purely objective (the first reference in the poem) or random (the reference to sheep in Leviticus). It is also a collective judgment rather than an individual sentence.

Taking all three perspectives together, we see how, in just three consecutive lines, the poet elides disparate biblical images, complicating the definition of relationship to God on judgment day. It is objective; it favors the downtrodden; it can be randomly determined; it is collective and redemptive—all these meanings are united with the common root *avar*.

Un'taneh Tokef then applies *avar* to a list of "who will live and who will die": "How many will pass on [*ya'avrun*]" (line 15). Here, too, there are a number of interpretations. Perhaps, instead of "passing away" as in death, this word is connected to passing into life through the miracle of conception—how many will be conceived, that is, prior to the next stage of life mentioned immediately afterward, "how many will be created [*yibarei'un*]." The ambiguity between dying (passing away) and being born (conceived) speaks to the nuance the poet sees in the judgment process in general. This is not a simple world in which good people live and bad people die. The lines between life and death are foggy, blurred linguistically in the poem by the root *avar*.

By the time we arrive at the core line "And repentance, prayer, and charity help the hardship of the decree pass [*ma'avirin*]" (line 21), we know enough about the poet's usage to suspect that we cannot take this line on its surface level only (i.e., do good, and good will happen to you). The deliberate use of the verb *ma'avirin* complicates the simplistic conclusion that we need only act piously to effect a better future. Perhaps those acts will objectively lead to justice, as in the initial judging scene of the poem; perhaps randomness will prevail, as with the tithed sheep in

Leviticus. Perhaps, also, we will turn our hearts to Ezekiel's downtrodden sheep whom we have neglected.

The final two instances of *avar* expand the range of poetic connotations. First, humankind's transience is likened to a "passing [*oveir*] shadow" (line 29), the ultimate in human insignificance, in contrast to the "king, the living and everlasting God" (line 31). One is tempted toward self-loathing—we have no worth; only God has value. But this phrase is taken from Psalm 144, where David prays for a relationship with God. Despite the absurdity of the Infinite rescuing a mere mortal, whose days are like a "passing shadow" (v. 4), David pleads with God to "reach your hand down from on high; rescue me, save me from the mighty waters" (v. 7). Even while noting that humans are insignificant compared to God, the psalmist—and, in turn, our poet—claims that we deserve a relationship with God and a world where God does not abandon humankind despite its frailty. What on the surface looks like a self-deprecating description of humankind can be read as a subtle plea for connection with God.

At the poem's end, the literary theme shifts to the word "name" (*shem*), which appears ten times in the final eight lines alone. *Avar* makes one last appearance there, through the preposition *ba'avur*: "for (*ba'avur*) the glory of your honored and sanctified name" (line 37). The focus has moved from humans to God, but by using the root *avar* here, too, the poem recalls the previously explored aspects of the divine-human relationship. Even while discussing God's holiness, the echoes of our relationship with God remain.

One final text (Mishnah Yoma 1:3) offers yet a further a perspective on *Un'taneh Tokef*. On the morning before Yom Kippur, the high priest is made to stand in the eastern gate of the Temple while the elders "cause to pass" (*ma'avirin*) before him cows, sheep, and goats so that he will know the difference between them when he performs the atonement ritual the following day. Here the implications of *avar* are taken to a new level. This passing is done to familiarize, not to judge. Extrapolated to the heavenly scene, the people of the world pass before God not in judgment but as a way of renewing a relationship between unfamiliar parties. In this metaphor, the High Holy Days are about closing a gap in the connection between God and people, not about a judgment based on a checklist.

The core of *Un'taneh Tokef* is actually the re-examination of our varied relationships with God on the annual judgment day. The poem's biblical allusions juxtapose images of God judging us, supporting the weak among us, and anticipating our collective redemption. Our fate is at once deserved and random. Our passing before God can be our end or our (re)birth. By looking at *Un'taneh Tokef*—and, indeed, prayer in general— in light of its literary allusions and nuances, we open up new possibilities in our relationship with God.

12

The Poetics of Prayer

HOW UN'TANEH TOKEF MEANS WHAT IT MEANS

Dr. Reuven Kimelman

The *Un'taneh Tokef* is to Rosh Hashanah what *L'khah Dodi* is to Shabbat. Its imagery captures the spirit of the day more memorably than the classical Rabbinic liturgy to which it has been added.

Un'taneh Tokef has affinity with the three sections of the *Musaf* service: *Malkhuyot, Zikhronot,* and *Shofarot.* Like *Malkhuyot,* it begins and ends on the motif of God's eternal rule over all. Like *Zikhronot,* it refers to the book of records that chronicles our lives, it notes there is no forgetting by God, and it shows how judgments are made and destinies determined. Like *Shofarot,* it mentions the blast of the shofar and alludes to the revelation at Sinai.

Instead of introducing them, however, it introduces the *K'dushah*. This is because its insertion was ascribed to Rabbi Amnon of Mainz who died as an example of *k'dushat hashem* (martyrdom) for his refusal to apostasize by converting to Christianity. The juxtaposition is based on the strophe that transitions the *Un'taneh Tokef* to the *K'dushah*: "And sanctify your name through those who declare the sanctity of your name" (line

Dr. Reuven Kimelman is professor of classical Judaica at Brandeis University. He is the author of *The Mystical Meaning of Lekha Dodi and Kabbalat Shabbat* and of the audio books *The Moral Meaning of the Bible* and *The Hidden Poetry of the Jewish Prayerbook.*

36). "Those who sanctify your name" refers to those who recite the *K'dushah*, which begins, "We will sanctify your name," as well as to those who are martyred as *k'dushat hashem*. The request is based on the theology of Ezekiel. God must sanctify God's name by redeeming Israel, lest their exile be attributed to God's inability to redeem the people, entailing a desecration of the divine name.

The insertion of *Un'taneh Tokef* after *uv'khen* ("And then [*uv'khen*] to You may our recitation of the *K'dushah* ascend, for You our God are king") evokes its appearance in Esther 4:16: "*Uv'khen* [and then] I will go in to the king ... and if I am to perish, I will perish." Esther's entrance in trepidation to the quarters of the king of Persia sets the stage for our entrance in trepidation into the presence of the king of kings.

Un'taneh Tokef graphically presents Rosh Hashanah as a day of divine coronation and judgment. The coronation theme derives from the creation of the world, the judgment theme from the creation of humanity. According to the Midrash, Rosh Hashanah commemorates Adam's birthday as well as his day of judgment and pardon. But how was Adam pardoned if he was banished from Eden? The answer is that the original penalty of death on the day of the crime was stretched to a divine day consisting of a thousand years (as computed in Psalm 90:4). This led to a reduction in sentence, not an acquittal. As an auspicious day for reduced sentencing, Rosh Hashanah was selected as our day of judgment.

Un'taneh Tokef enhances its dramatic effect by simulating the opening of Job, where the scenes shift back and forth from heaven to earth. The first scene sets up a contrast between a day based on dread and God's kingship based on kindness. This contrast between the awesomeness of the day and the kindness of God sets the tone for the whole poem. The scene itself spells out how all our deeds and intentions will be adduced in the divine court, where God, who knows all, is judge, accuser, and witness. God recalls specifically what we tend to forget, presenting the book of records where we ourselves have signed off on our every deed.

The next scene ascends to heaven. There, even the angels are terrified at the upcoming judgment. It begins with the blast of the shofar, but not the one we are used to from Rosh Hashanah. Some say it is the eschatological shofar of Isaiah: "And in that day, a great shofar shall be sounded; and the strayed who are in the land of Assyria and the expelled who are in the land of Egypt shall come and worship Adonai on the holy mount, in Jerusalem" (27:13). Because of the upcoming shuddering of the angels, others prefer the allusion to the shofar of Amos: "Were a shofar to be sounded in a city would the people not shudder?" (3:6). In either case, it is strange that what gets heard is not the shofar but "a thin whisper of a sound" (line 7). This alludes to 1 Kings 19:12, where God appears to Elijah on Mount Sinai not in the wind, the earthquake, or the fire, but in "a thin whisper of a sound." He then hears a voice addressing him, "What are you doing here, Elijah?" (19:13).

Here, too, God is not in the blast of the shofar, but in the thin whisper of a sound that asks (on this day of judgment), "What are you doing here?" The allusion to the voice that Elijah heard and to the shofar conjures up another verse that combines the two, namely, Exodus 19:19: "The blare of the shofar grew louder and louder. As Moses spoke, God would respond to him in a voice." Reading the Moses allusion through that of Elijah makes the divine voice that Moses heard at Sinai the thin whisper of a sound that Elijah heard there. The *Shofarot* section in the *Musaf* also begins by referring to the revelation at Sinai, citing Exodus 19:19. Accordingly, when the great shofar is sounded, attune your ear to hear the thin whispering voice of God.

The next scene moves back to earth, where all humanity passes in review before God either as the angelic hosts or as a flock of sheep or as soldiers in formation. Whatever its original meaning in the Mishnah (Rosh Hashanah 1:2), the term in *Un'taneh Tokef* refers to angels or sheep, since angels were just mentioned and sheep are about to be mentioned. This section ends with the verdict being signed and delivered. Precisely at the moment when it seems that all is over, the next strophe surprisingly proclaims that though the verdict is inscribed on Rosh Hashanah, it is not sealed until Yom Kippur. What a relief! There is still time to make amends.

The drama now becomes excruciating. The opening line continues the rhyme scheme of the previous two, asking with regard to those who were initially inscribed (and possibly sealed), "How many will pass on and how many will be created?" (line 15). Twelve doublets follow, the first seven referring to life and death, the last five to the quality of life. All begin with "who will." The first is a transition; it repeats the content of the previous line, albeit structured as the upcoming strophes. The next deals with timely and untimely death. Then come five strophes illustrating ten modes of premature death. Their large number expressed in staccato shakes us up with what is at stake. The next five are structured antonymically, shifting from the positive to the negative. (Some recent versions have reversed the order of the penultimate and/or ultimate one to end on a positive note.) They deal with our physical, mental, psychological, material, and social situation by spelling out the vagaries of our stability, serenity, suffering, income, and status. They are linked by final rhyme, beginning rhyme, or the consonance of letters. Together they warn us that even the lives that are spared can be rocked by trial and tribulation. How vulnerable is our life, how fragile our existence.

Confronted with such a fatalistic vision, we ask why we were just granted an extension from the inscribing of Rosh Hashanah to the sealing of Yom Kippur. The startling answer is: "And *t'shuvah, t'fillah*, and *tz'dakah* [repentance, prayer, and charity] help the hardship of the decree pass" (line 21). Not only is everything not foreordained, but we have a hand in the outcome.

This signature line of the *Un'taneh Tokef* represents a revision of several Rabbinic antecedents. According to one Talmudic opinion (Rosh Hashanah 16b), "Four things rip up [*m'kar'im*] a person's decree: *tz'dakah*, crying out, change of name, and change of deed"; some add "change of place." According to the Jerusalem Talmud, (Ta'anit 2:1, 65b), "Three things abrogate [*m'vatlin*] the harsh decree: *t'fillah, tz'dakah*, and *t'shuvah*." Later midrashim combine this last statement with the changing of name, deed, and place. *Un'taneh Tokef* introduces three changes. It puts *t'shuvah* first, it changes the verb from *m'vatlin* ("abrogate") to *ma'avirin* ("pass"), and adds *ro'a* ("hardship") to "the decree."

What is gained by these changes? By placing *t'shuvah* first and keeping the number to three, it evokes the famous triad of *Pirkei Avot* 1:2: "The world/age stands on three things: Torah, *avodah* [service], and *g'milut chasadim* [acts of kindness]," as if to say that the outcome of the judgment stands on three things: *t'shuvah, t'fillah*, and *tz'dakah*. *T'shuvah* replaces Torah, but the other two are comparable, just more specific. By prioritizing *t'shuvah*, it paves the way for its prominence in the next section. The second change weakens the force of the verb. The decree is just mitigated, not abrogated. An allied expression, *ma'avir rishon rishon* ("who removes sins one by one"), found in the Talmud (Rosh Hashanah 17b) and in the *machzor* (such as in *El melekh yoshev al kisei rachamim* of the Yom Kippur liturgy), denotes mitigation. Although there is disagreement on how the mitigation is computed, all agree that it results in a reduction of the number of counts a person is charged with, especially as a first offender, either by combining the charges or by eliminating the initial ones. Still, the charges are not dropped; they are only reduced, as in the case of Adam in the midrash.

The problem is that replacing the verb *m'vatlin* ("abrogate") with *ma'avirim* ("pass") makes the word "decree" difficult. Decrees are torn up or abrogated, not made to pass or mitigated. The solution was the addition of *ro'a*, since the harshness or the misfortune that results from a decree can be mitigated. It is mitigated through *t'shuvah*, *t'fillah*, and *tz'dakah*, either because they can lead to a reconsideration of the original judgment of Rosh Hashanah or because they provide the resilience to bear the ups and downs of life.

How so? Repentance starts with our relationship with the self, prayer addresses our relationship with God, and charity works on our relationship with others. In other words, repentance is inner-directed, prayer is God-directed, and charity is other-directed. The first involves the mind, the second the tongue, and the third the hand advancing from thought to word to deed. Adversity is most disruptive when striking those bereft of religious and social support systems. All the more reason to recite *Un'taneh Tokef* in community. Putting ourselves in order, repairing our relationship with God, and working on improving our relationship with others help us overcome our isolation. By enhancing our capacity to withstand the vicissitudes of life, we gain the confidence to believe that this too will pass. Repentance means we care enough about ourselves to strive for our ideal self. Prayer means we care enough about God to make ourselves worthy of God's assessment. Charity means we care enough about others to help them in their need. Otherwise, faced with tragedy, we might give up on ourselves, on God, and on others.

The next section answers the question why God is so forbearing by presenting the divine perspective. The divine perspective that is presented on *t'shuvah*, however, paradoxically undermines the very idea of a verdict's irrevocability, as it says: "You wait until the day they die, accepting them immediately if they return" (line 24). As our maker, God knows what we are made of. Like a mother, who, knowing her children's shortcomings, will always receive them back, so God is forgiving till the very end.

The final section depicts graphically exactly how fragile and transient human life really is. It goads us to anchor life in the permanent and eternal, in God, since "You are king, the living and everlasting God" (line

31). It also addresses God, underscoring the gap between the human and the divine, intimating that God should be tolerant of our shortcomings and charitable in divine judgments. This brings us full circle to the opening lines, where God's throne is "established in love" (line 2).

13
Death without Dying

Rabbi Lawrence Kushner

The core teaching of *yontif* is pretty straight forward: We're all gonna die. But three things, the *Un'taneh Tokef* assures us, will avert (*ma'avirin*) that terrible decree. Doing them may not make us immortal, but they—and here the language is unequivocal—will buy us yet one more year of life. As it is commonly understood, "On Rosh Hashanah it is written and on Yom Kippur it is sealed: *t'shuvah*, *t'fillah*, and *tz'dakah ma'avirin*/(avert) the terrible decree" (line 21).

Surely Rabbi Amnon of Mainz, the traditionally ascribed author of the *Un'taneh Tokef*, like any thoughtful person, must have noticed that there is no correlation whatsoever between righteousness and mortality. Any fool can see that very good people often die very young. So how can a prayer based on such a preposterous premise retain such popularity over the ages? And, just what is it anyway about *t'shuvah*, *t'fillah*, and *tz'dakah* that can claim to avert a decree that cannot be averted?

I can think of a lot of things the poet might have chosen to emphasize instead for such a holy convocation. I mean, why not, for instance, mitzvot (commandments), *talmud Torah* (study of Torah), and *tikkun*

Rabbi Lawrence Kushner is the Emanu-El Scholar at Congregation Emanu-El of San Francisco and the author of many books on Jewish spirituality and mysticism, including *The Way Into Jewish Mystical Tradition*, *Honey from the Rock; The Book of Letters: A Mystical Alef-bait* (all Jewish Lights); and his most recent novel, *Kabbalah: A Love Story*. He contributed to all volumes of the *My People's Prayer Book: Traditional Prayers, Modern Commentaries* series, winner of the National Jewish Book Award, and to *My People's Passover Haggadah: Traditional Texts, Modern Commentaries* (both Jewish Lights).

olam (repairing creation)? Why not *yirah* (reverence), *ahavah* (love), and *shalom* (peace)? That's a pretty good list. Or for that matter, if we're seriously talking about averting the decree of death, why not a low-cholesterol diet, regular exercise, and Buddhist meditation (which do, nowadays, seem to enjoy unusually high popularity among the people of Israel)? Just what is so special about *this* particular verbal troika of *t'shuvah*, *tefillah*, and *tz'dakah* that it can make such a claim? Let us look at them more closely.

T'shuvah is returning to God. This, our tradition tells us, may be effected through apology, remorse, or restitution, but it always requires a diminution of one's ego and its conquests. Every return makes us less. Adin Steinsaltz says that, in *t'shuvah*, "a person turns himself about, away from the pursuit of *what he craves*, and confronts his desire to approach God."[1] When it's done, we wind up with less than what we thought we wanted. By confessing our shortcomings, our inadequacies, our arrogance, and our self-righteousness, we take up less space. Our egos are smaller.

With *t'fillah*, there is a similar self-diminution. In any genuine prayer, we give our selves back to their source in the Holy One. As Abraham Joshua Heschel put it so poetically, "To worship God is to forget the self…. In prayer we shift the center of living from self-consciousness to self-surrender."[2] We even give our power of speech over to God: "O God, open my lips…." Or, as Dov Baer, the great Maggid of Mezritch, said, in prayer we are like shofarot: if God's breath does not blow through us, we cannot even make a sound.[3] It's not about what *you* want; it's what God wants that matters.

Tz'dakah, of course, is the easiest. It is the tangible giving away of our money, skill, and time—in a word, our very substance. When you're done "giving" *tz'dakah*, you are physically diminished. To be sure, you will probably be spiritually increased, but there is also no doubt that you'll be poorer. There will be less of you.

All three share this common denominator of a loss of self—not self-abnegation, self-denial, self-deprecation, or self-renunciation (as in the punch line to the old *yontif* joke, "Look who thinks he's nothing")—but a voluntary, loving lessening of our selves. *T'shuvah*, *t'fillah*, and *tz'dakah* all require increasingly smaller egos.

In Hasidism, such a deliberate loss of self, dissolution of ego, is called *bitul hayesh*, literally "nullifying being." The goal is simply letting go of one's ego. Indeed, this may be the *summum bonum* of all spirituality:

to die *into* God. But to do that you must first get yourself out of the way so that there can be room for God. In the words of the Talmud (Arakhin 15b), "God says, 'My I and your I are not able to live in the same dwelling.'" (It always comes off sounding a bit like a line from an old Gary Cooper western where the sheriff says to the bad guy, "Ain't room enough in this here town for your ego and Me.") Or, to turn a more contemporary phrase: it's your ego, stupid!

In the words of the Hasidic master Yehiel Mikhal of Zlotchov, we become "like a drop that has fallen into the great sea and … is one with the waters of the sea and it is not possible to recognize it as a separate thing at all."[4] Our aim, in other words, is to literally lose our selves in the divine All. Yes, that does sound a bit like death. (We recall again the core *yontif* teaching.)

This brings us back to the verb *ma'avirin*, usually rendered as "avert." But that is not its only meaning. The root of *ayin vet resh* (*avar*) seems to mean something like "to cross over, to get to the other side, to go beyond, or to transcend." We speak of a transgression as an *averah*, a going over to the other side—of the Force! The Jewish *Book of the Dead, Ma'avar Yabok,* takes its name from the "ford at the River Yabok," which Jacob, our father, had to "cross over" in order to meet Esau and earn his destiny.

Maybe the verb *ma'avirin* doesn't mean "to avert," that is, "to annul" the terrible decree (of our death). Life experience and common sense tell us that is not an option. Maybe it means to *go beyond* our terror of death by beating it to the punch and giving our egos away, even though we're still alive! To be sure, our suffering and our demise won't go away. But, mysteriously, through renouncing our fantasies that we are gods, through renouncing our egos and their appetites, through making ourselves as [the divine] Nothing, we can be liberated from our terror. In the words of *Adon Olam, b'yado afkid ruchi,* "into God's hands I commit my soul."

Dov Baer of Mezritch said, "the work of the pious is greater than the creation of the heavens and the earth.[5] For, while the creation of the heavens and the earth was making something *from* Nothing, the pious transform something *back* into Nothing. Through everything that they do, even with mundane acts … they transform something into Nothing."[6]

Indeed, despite the gruesome machinations of his death, Rabbi Amnon does seem "beyond" it all. Despite his torments, we envision the man going to his death, on *yontif,* with a beatific and untroubled smile. The words of poet Stephen Mitchell speaking of Job also apply to Rav Amnon: life is "the breath-thin surface of a bubble, and everything else, inside and outside, is pure radiance. Both suffering and joy come then like a brief reflection, and death like a pin."[7]

Amnon's death testifies to his life teaching: Through the selflessness of *t'shuvah* (I return my *self* to its source), *t'fillah* (I pour out my *self* before God), and *tz'dakah* (I make myself the gift), we too can *ma'avirin,* transcend the terror of our own death. Now, you get a roomful of people to all try to think that way for a day and you've got yourself a day that is, in the words of the prayer, "holiness … full of awe and dread" (line 1).

On his deathbed, Rabbi Simha Bunam of Przysucha said to his wife, "Why are you crying? My whole life was only that I might learn how to die."

14

Laminated in the Book of Life?

Rabbi Ruth Langer, PhD

*U*n'taneh Tokef is one of my favorite *piyyutim* of the High Holy Day liturgy. Its particular power probably results from a series of personal intersections I've had with it, points in my life where it has come to particular attention—attention that allows it to transcend the literal meaning of the words on the page.

As far as I can reconstruct, the first time I thought seriously about *Un'taneh Tokef* took place in the course of a rather heated argument with my grandfather. This was memorable, because as a child, I would never have argued with him. It is probably because Grandpa was generally the silent person in the room, listening intently and saying little. Now this was a "grown-up" conversation and marked something of a turn in our relationship. I was a rabbinic student, living with my grandparents while interning with Dr. Walter Jacob at Congregation Rodef Shalom. I had attended High Holy Day services there my entire childhood but must have encountered the prayer only the one time I insisted on staying with my grandfather for the afternoon service. *Un'taneh Tokef* appears only then in volume 2 of the *Union Prayer Book*, and its interpretative translation dodges the theological problems of the prayer's discussion of divine

---

Rabbi Ruth Langer, PhD, is associate professor of Jewish studies in the Theology Department at Boston College, where she also serves as associate director of its Center for Christian-Jewish Learning. She received her PhD in Jewish liturgy and her rabbinic ordination from Hebrew Union College–Jewish Institute of Religion.

justice.[1] I don't recall reciting it or hearing it sung that day. But now I was preparing to lead High Holy Day services from *Gates of Repentance*, at that point still rather newly published. There the poem appears in full in every morning service preceding the *K'dushah*, with a literal translation and even an introduction that draws special attention to it.[2] I needed to practice its haunting and, for me, rather difficult melody.

In our argument, I defended the prayer's poetry and music. My grandfather criticized its theology and recalled with pride that at age twenty-six he had called for its abolition at the Union of American Hebrew Congregations (UAHC) convention.

My grandfather, Marcus Lester Aaron, was not your average Reform Jew. Deeply influenced by the rabbi of his youth, Dr. J. Leonard Levy, and himself a man of deep spirituality, principle, and intellect, he had sought to become a rabbi but, as an only son, was required to go into the family business. He compensated by a lifetime of lay engagement and learning, serving on local and national boards of Reform Jewish institutions until he literally could not attend the meetings. So when we disagreed in 1983, he spoke from a lifetime of dedicated and thoughtful service to the Jewish world. He still stood by his words from 1927, where he pointed out theological inconsistencies between Reform thinking and the received prayer texts:

> We speak in our weekly service of bowing in submission to God's "inscrutable will," and yet we speak in our Atonement service in the most definite terms of the methods of Divine judgment: "On the first day of the year it is inscribed and on the Day of Atonement it is sealed: How many shall pass away and how many shall be born; who shall live and who shall die...."And then comes language, more beautiful in thought and of greater moral significance, but equally curious in judicial legalmindedness: "But Penitence, Prayer and Charity avert the evil decree." None of us, I dare say, would venture to quarrel for a moment with the emphasis on penitence, prayer and charity; but the exposition of the methods of the Divine judgment in which that emphasis occurs sounds quaint and strange, and appears as a survival of a rabbinic scholasticism which the modern mind has outgrown.[3]

My grandfather asserted that liturgy is to be read solely through the lens of rationalism and scientific advancement. If a prayer does not make total sense when we dissect it, we should not feel forced to contort ourselves to come to an understanding of it. Within limits, we should feel free to abandon it. It is possible and even probable that this discussion influenced the elimination of the words he cites in the English of the 1945 newly revised edition of the *Union Prayer Book*, volume 2.[4]

I argued then (in the 1980s), and I maintain today, that we can approach liturgy on numerous levels and that rational understandings of its theology should not be the only legitimate criterion. Elements of its performance, our memories and associations with past performances, its music, and the beauty of its poetry all play into our relationship with a prayer text. Not only that, but in the wash of words that is Jewish liturgy, we leave ourselves the freedom to allow some words to pass us over and others to stand out. Depending on what we bring to prayer, on our shifting personal and communal situations, different parts of the liturgy will have different power for different people at different times. To eliminate this possibility is to flatten our communal experience.

An example of this occurred in the mid-1990s. My grandfather was no longer alive, but I was now a mother. My daughter was in kindergarten, learning for the first time formally about the High Holy Days. She reported that on Rosh Hashanah, God opens the book of life, and on Yom Kippur, God "laminates" it. Obviously, we laughed. But in her age-appropriate concrete thinking, she had translated the traditional imagery into something familiar. She could never have comprehended the abstract philosophy behind my grandfather's objections. Indeed, I submit that concrete thinking does not disappear from our society after kindergarten and may be found even among adults. For those not compelled by abstract philosophical ideals, it is precisely the concrete imagery of *Un'taneh Tokef* that may bring them effectively into the annual stocktaking that the High Holy Days demand. Those who are abstract thinkers can be taught to abstract from the poem itself and understand its imagery not as literal descriptions, but as an evocation of a theological ideal.

But even for abstract thinkers, the concrete imagery sometimes makes sense. A decade ago, my husband spent the summer undergoing chemotherapy and radiation in preparation for radical surgery after the holidays. "Who will live and who will die, who at their end and who not at their end" (lines 15–16) was no longer a metaphor. It could not have been more real. We had done all that we humanly could. He had the highest-quality medical care available; friends around the world had been offering *Mi Sheberakhs*, prayers for his recovery. The outcome of the surgery and the cure of his cancer, though, required God's participation, too. We recited *Un'taneh Tokef*, among other prayers that season, with full attention to its literal meaning as it applied to our known and very particular circumstances. We participated in "prayer, penitence, and charity" too, from a desire to leave no stone unturned. Ten years later, I can say with gratitude that we did "avert the evil decree" (line 21).

Thus, I look at *Un'taneh Tokef* (and many other prayers) as texts that operate at many levels and in many ways. Its melodies themselves bring me to a spiritual depth and prepare me to join in the recognition of God's sanctity in the *K'dushah* that follows it. There are years when the literal meanings of some of the poem's words are important; there are others when the general theology expressed is more my focus. I try to remember to leave room for other people's needs too. Did God really declare Hurricane Katrina some eleven months in advance? I myself prefer not to know. The purpose of the prayer is to turn us to deepen our prayer, penitence, and charity at that season so that, by the closing of the "heavenly gates" at the end of Yom Kippur, we stand purified before God, renewed, and ready to face the coming year, strengthened and inspired to be the best people we can be.

15

Un'taneh Tokef through Israeli Eyes

Rabbi Dalia Marx, PhD

Only when I spend the High Holy Days outside of Israel do I realize that there is something unique and incomparable in the way they are experienced back home, especially in the case of Yom Kippur. I don't just mean the car-free streets and the dramatic quality of the day's eerie stillness. Ask Israelis for the first thought that pops into their minds when they hear the words "Yom Kippur," and at least half of them will say without hesitation, *Milkhemet Yom Kippur* (the Yom Kippur War). Even now, almost four decades later, the war that began with the surprise attack coordinated by Egypt and Syria on the afternoon of Shabbat Yom Hakippurim, October 6, 1973, remains a traumatic and painful memory in the Israeli psyche. In no other war was the existential threat to Israel so tangible. The fragility of the young state was never felt as substantially and concretely as in that Yom Kippur War, the fourth great war in Israel's history.

Rabbi Dalia Marx, PhD, is a professor of liturgy and midrash at the Jerusalem campus of Hebrew Union College–Jewish Institute of Religion and teaches in various academic institutions in Israel, the United States, and Europe. Marx earned her doctorate at the Hebrew University in Jerusalem and her rabbinic ordination at HUC–JIR in Jerusalem and Cincinnati. She is involved in various research groups and is active in promoting progressive Judaism in Israel. Marx writes for academic journals and the Israeli press and is engaged in creating new liturgies and midrashim. She expresses her thanks to Hagai Ben-Gurion and Pinchas Leiser for their help and for their valuable notes concerning this commentary.

The memories of men rushing headlong out of synagogues, grabbing their kit bags, speeding to their military units, and leaving anxious spouses and bewildered children behind will remain engraved in the shared consciousness for a long, long time to come. I remember well the look my parents exchanged as the emergency siren interrupted the serenity of the day. My father ran to the attic to get his military gear and then magically disappeared to join his unit by the Suez Canal. Even when he eventually came back safe and sound and life went back to normal, my childhood at age seven was never again complete. Something essential was lost forever.

The 1973 war symbolized the end of an era, the sudden evaporation of the euphoria that the Six-Day War had occasioned only seven years earlier (1967). The words of *Un'taneh Tokef*—"Who will live and who will die, who at their end and who not at their end, who by fire and who by water, who by warfare and who by wildlife" (lines 15–17)— acquired newly relevant meaning. Yom Kippur became a day of self-examination (*cheshbon hanefesh*) in ways one could never have imagined.

Ancient Words, Contemporary Music

The best entry into the Israeli experience of Yom Kippur is through a setting of *Un'taneh Tokef* by Yair Rosenblum (1944–96), a celebrated Israeli composer, known best for the songs he wrote for military bands (like the popular *Shir L'shalom*, "Song for Peace"). In 1988 he was invited to serve as musical director for the sixtieth anniversary of Kibbutz Beit Hashitah, where he remained for three years. During his stay there, Rosenblum was exposed to a memorial ceremony that had taken place in the kibbutz every Yom Kippur evening since 1944 (on Yom Kippur Day, the kibbutz just held a public gathering to discuss internal and national questions). The ceremony's eventual crystallization in the eighties featured two kibbutz members, Shula and Hanoch Albalack, singing traditional Yom Kippur liturgical poems (*piyyutim*).

Touched by the memorial service, especially the treatment of the eleven kibbutz members and sons who had lost their lives in the Yom Kippur War, Rosenblum composed a new setting for *Un'taneh Tokef* blending motifs from Ashkenazi and Sephardi traditions with Israeli folk music. It was first performed by Hanoch Albalack in 1990. The composition was intended as an intimate tribute to the Beit Hashitah victims lost in the war. No one could imagine that it would eventually become virtually an official piyyut of the High Holy Day season.

Rosenblum's *Un'taneh Tokef* exemplifies the relatively recent phenomenon of grassroots cultural and religious revival. Arye Ben-Gurion, the founder of the collective kibbutz archives and a well-known pioneer in reclaiming Jewish traditions and refashioning them for contemporary Israeli needs, recorded it. The tape passed from hand to hand and received widespread initial recognition even before it got to the radio. Additionally, a moving documentary film (directed by Yehuda Yaniv) chronicling the mourning ceremonies at Beit Hashitah reconstructed the song's composition and its initial performance.

During the film, Rosenblum repeatedly expressed his fear that the work would not be accepted by the ideologically secular kibbutz members. But, surprisingly, the musically complex and theologically challenging *piyyut* was greeted warmly, not just in Beit Hashitah (where it became the concluding and most elaborate part of the Yom Kippur ceremony), but throughout Israel. Rosenblum's *Un'taneh Tokef* is now a standard component of radio broadcasts and ceremonies marking the High Holy Days. More surprising is the fact that through the secular media, his *Un'taneh Tokef* has radiated beyond the kibbutz world into synagogue services, some of them Orthodox, as part of their Rosh Hashanah and Yom Kippur liturgy.

The Theology of Rosenblum's *Un'taneh Tokef*

Rosenblum's piece embodies at least three realms of meaning: the Jewish, the Israeli, and the human, corresponding to the historical, the local, and the existential.

The Jewish (or historical) realm derives not just from the liturgical text itself but from the medieval account of the sufferings of Rabbi Amnon of Mainz, a tale taught in every Israeli elementary school and accepted by many as historical truth. The torments of Jews throughout the generations, as embodied by his anguish, are present whenever the *piyyut* is heard.

The Israeli (or local) realm is informed by the context of Rosenblum's work: the trauma of the Yom Kippur War. It couples the emotional proximity of the lofty yet ambivalent experience of the Day of Atonement for non-Orthodox Israeli society with specific memories of the war. Not so incidentally, the term *Yamim Nora'im,* "Days of Awe," can be understood in modern Hebrew as "days of terror" or "of horror."

Yet what gives Rosenblum's piece its fullest measure of significance is its treatment of the human (or existential) realm, its resonance with the fragile and uncertain nature of the individual. The composer excludes the final and most accentuated passage of the *piyyut,* a comforting affirmation of God's infinite greatness, "But You are king, the living and everlasting God" (line 31), and ends instead with disturbing images of the existential human state: "[Man is] like shattered pottery, like withered grass and like a faded blossom" (lines 28–29). Interestingly enough, Rosenblum composed his piece in the later years of his own life, when, according to some, he knew he was suffering from an incurable disease. His *Un'taneh Tokef* thus stands also as a personal requiem of a man who was reminded of his numbered days on earth.

Un'taneh Tokef and Religion in "Secular" Israeli Society

I can think of few liturgical pieces as popular as this one in Israeli society—a remarkable fact, given how challenging the text and music are. The choice of Rosenblum, a "secular" composer, is significant here.

Since the establishment of the State of Israel (actually, already from its early political Zionist roots), there had been a clear separation between the "religious" (the Orthodox [*dati*] and ultra-Orthodox [*charedi*]) and the "secular" (*chiloni*). The notion of being religious but not Orthodox has therefore always been hard for most Israelis to fathom, even today, and all the more so in the early nineties. The "secular" majority entrusted the "religious" (the only form of religion imaginable then) with the task of preserving Jewish values, education, and texts (with the exception of the Bible, which played an important role in Zionist narratives). This implicit agreement left no room for the creation of alternative (non-Orthodox or ultra-Orthodox) forms of Israeli Jewish religion.

The Zionist *chalutzim* ("pioneers") deliberately and consciously left the realm of the synagogue, as a matter of ideological conviction, but they had been sufficiently educated in traditional Judaism to know what they were leaving. By contrast, their children and grandchildren usually lack the knowledge necessary to make informed choices. This is not to say that Israelis are uninterested in religion and spirituality; on the contrary, the rate of young Israelis who experience Eastern and other forms of alternative religion is very high. But the bifurcation of society into "religious" and "secular" had the consequence of depriving native-born Israelis of their legitimate Jewish roots. They may be aptly compared to the fourth son of the Passover Haggadah, who does not even know what to ask.

The last two decades (and especially since the assassination of Israel's Prime Minister Yitzchak Rabin in 1995) have witnessed a growing Israeli interest in Jewish texts and heritage. I do not mean the phenomenon of becoming a *ba'al t'shuvah* (becoming "religious"), but rather a bold and fresh consideration of a new Israeli form of religion that is not Orthodox or ultra-Orthodox through informal or semi-formal study and even through experimental worship groups. This identity search is still a rather elitist phenomenon, touching the lives of intellectuals and the affluent in particular, but it is expanding to wider circles. However, new musical compositions and new settings for classical *piyyutim* and liturgical texts become more and more popular in the wider Israeli scene. The centrality that *Un'taneh Tokef* has acquired within even secular Israeli society is an example of this phenomenon.

Rosenblum's decision to omit the last passage of the *piyyut* ("But You are king, the living and everlasting God"; line 31) might suggest that he saw the prayer as a fully secular statement of life's uncertainties and the gloomy fate of the individual. But I don't think that is the case. Rosenblum did omit explicit treatment of God, but he confronted the poem's central claim of the entire world being judged, along with the theological concept of providence. He did not omit the central sentence, "And repentance, prayer, and charity help the hardship of the decree to pass" (line 21)—which is nothing if not a religious claim.

Rosenblum reclaimed the traditional text but tore it loose from its traditional context. I am not sure that the listeners of this piece always realize it, but it seems to me that beyond its artistry, this may explain the popularity of the composition in nontraditional (secular and liberal religious) society. But it has made its way also into many traditional synagogues, evidence of something altogether novel for Israel: the impact of the so-called "secular" upon the "religious."

Un'taneh Tokef is a remarkable illustration of the way Israeli Jews are struggling to make peace with their past, to understand their present, and to guarantee their future by reclaiming traditional texts in new and innovating ways.

16

The Litmus Test of Belief

Rabbi Rachel Nussbaum

Although the month of Elul is my busy season as a rabbi, I really love this time of year. For me, Rosh Hashanah and Yom Kippur are accompanied by meaningful customs, beautiful melodies, and a sense of new possibility. For a number of my community members, though, I know that the High Holy Days pose a real challenge and have the potential to feel alienating. For many, the key challenge is that the observance of these holidays (more than many others) is focused around prayer. Moreover, the High Holy Day liturgy is filled with anthropomorphic images of God that conflict with the belief system of contemporary Jews. This time of year, I am often asked: Why should I say words that I don't believe to be true?

The problem is that many of us learned to read the liturgy far too literally. Perhaps if we reframe how we approach it, we can remove the stumbling block posed by this litmus test of belief.

The words of the *Un'taneh Tokef* serve as a great case in point. This medieval *piyyut* (liturgical poem) has come to play an integral role in the *Musaf* service of Rosh Hashanah and Yom Kippur, and it contains some of the most classic (but also potentially alienating) images of God. For example, the prayer opens with the image of each individual standing

Rabbi Rachel Nussbaum is rabbi and executive director of the Kavana Cooperative in Seattle, Washington. She was ordained at The Jewish Theological Seminary of America. She was recently awarded an Avi Chai Fellowship for her innovative approach to Jewish community building.

before God in a courtroom, while God, the presiding judge, decides who will live and who will die in the coming year. The God portrayed here knows all and has the power to "remember everything that has been forgotten" (line 5)—much like Santa Claus in the song, who "knows when you've been bad or good, so be good for goodness sake." If taken literally, this image induces a feeling of panic in me. Because we are all human and therefore imperfect, no one can be assured that the judge will rule favorably. I can understand why—if presented only with the false dichotomy between reading this prayer literally or not showing up—many Jews would prefer staying away.

If we can learn to read the liturgy less literally, though, then the words of the *machzor* become poignant in a positive and potentially transformative way. A first step is the realization that the *machzor* presents not one image of God or of the relationship between God and human beings but, rather, a composite sketch, a collage of many images. These images are far too diverse to be understood literally, so we are invited to inhabit each metaphor temporarily and to think about what each of them can teach us about God, ourselves, and the world. In doing so, the language of the liturgy provides us with a road map for the human journey through self-reflection, *t'shuvah* (repentance), and self-improvement.

Read in this way, *Un'taneh Tokef*'s fearful image of God as judge takes on a different valence. If we understand it as a metaphor, we can ask what effect it will have on us—emotionally, psychologically, and behaviorally. If even the angels are gripped by fear and trembling on this day (as the text of the prayer contends), then it makes sense that we, too, are supposed to experience a sense of fear or awe on Rosh Hashanah. Yes, Rosh Hashanah may be a celebration of a new year, but it is also a day to be taken seriously. The courtroom setting, together with the fact that the book of memories bears all of our signatures, helps to emphasize that we bear full responsibility for all of the actions that have been recorded over the past year. Hopefully, this realization will motivate us to scrutinize our deeds in a deeper way.

From there, *Un'taneh Tokef* quickly moves on to a second image: God as a shepherd. In comparison to the judge-defendant relationship, the shepherd-flock metaphor is softer, as it necessarily implies a level of caring. Whereas a judge is supposed to be impartial and detached, a shepherd has a vested interest in the well-being of his sheep. This shepherd cares about each creature, causing each one to pass beneath his staff individually. If we can inhabit this image fully, we might feel noticed, cared for, protected, and nurtured. Feeling safe in this way, we can challenge ourselves more deeply, with the power to change more profoundly.

The third section of the prayer opens with the statement that on the High Holy Days it is decided and sealed "how many will pass on and how many will be created, who will live and who will die" (line 15), and it continues with a long list of the (mostly bad) ends that might await us. As a child, I remember being terrified by the idea of horrible fates (plagues, strangling, and more!) being sealed at this time of year. Today, I read this section far less literally. I understand it as building on the ideas that precede it: having been pushed by the courtroom scene into a state of fear but rescued by the shepherd image, which assures us safety and well-being, we may be able to do what we cannot achieve on the other days of the year: contemplate our own mortality concretely enough to imagine our own deaths.

This brush with mortality, however fleeting, is terrifying, so the liturgy leads us back from the brink with the affirmation, "You do not want the dead to die, but for them to return from their path and live … accepting them immediately if they return" (lines 23–24). We reassure ourselves that all will be well, because God understands that we are only human and wants to keep us alive and protect us.

The prayer concludes with a set of images that increasingly emphasize impermanence. In contrast to God, who is "boundless" and "endless" (line 32), we human beings are "like shattered pottery, like withered grass and like a fading blossom, like a passing shadow and like a vanishing cloud, and like blowing wind and like sprouting dust and like a dream that will fly away" (lines 29–30). The text transitions through stages—from pottery to grass to shadow and ultimately to dream—a succession of steps that is increasingly ethereal. Emotionally, the idea that is reinforced here is that we are all small and insignificant in the greater scheme of things. Although it wouldn't be healthy to think this way all the time, when coupled with the courtroom image in which our behavior and our decisions matter deeply in the universe, this last set of images provides a beautiful counterpoint.

The end of the prayer gradually transitions us into going even a step farther in confronting the fact of our own mortality, as we try to imagine the world without ourselves in it. In our "real lives," it generally requires something very jarring—for example, a near-tragedy, or the death of a friend or loved one—to push us to think in this way. The beauty of *Un'taneh Tokef* is that we are coaxed to this place in a series of sequential steps that lead us on a gentle journey through the emotions of fear and then security, vulnerability and then reassurance, until we arrive at a place where we can contemplate the unfathomable.

I believe that the structure and diverse images of the High Holy Day liturgy were crafted to challenge, support, and push us, so that in a very short period of time, we get to reorient, and even transform, our lives. Experiencing the succession of prayer-book images and the emotional responses generated by each one leads us to a reconsideration of our lives. We are not supposed to believe literally in the words we are saying. We are to read prayer in the language of metaphor and poetry, so as to open ourselves up to the very human experiences of reflecting on our lives, confronting our limitations, and changing and growing each year.

17

Meditations on the Poetry of *Un'taneh Tokef*

Rabbi Margaret Moers Wenig, DD

Descriptions of God are speculation, imagination, projection, fantasy, philosophical proposition or pure poetry. Some are banal. Some are hate-filled. Some are so sublime they move us to tears. Some lead us to insights about ourselves. Some transport us beyond our parochial perceptions to act on behalf of others. Notions of God represent our greatest hopes or fears about the power that lies far beyond us or both beyond and within us.

Great writing about God is great art, as "true" as great literature, music, painting, and dance are "true," addressing something deep within us, something that truly matters. I experience *Un'taneh Tokef* as great art.

One can never do a piece of music justice when "translating" it into words. Commentary on a poem is only rarely as sublime as the poem itself. With that caveat, I will attempt to put into words what this work of art means to me.

"This is the day of judgment"[1] (line 9): We are judged. Our children judge us. Our parents judge us. Prospective partners, current partners,

---

Rabbi Margaret Moers Wenig, DD, teaches liturgy and homiletics at Hebrew Union College–Jewish Institute of Religion in New York and is rabbi emerita of Beth Am, The People's Temple.

and ex-partners judge us. Students and teachers, customers and clients judge us. When we interview for a job, audition for a role, apply for a grant, or bid on a contract, we are judged. Outside standards hold us accountable. Sometimes we live up to them. Sometimes we don't. Sometimes we don't know what the standards are until we have violated them. Sometimes we don't learn we've violated them until years later when a child remembers a hurt we unknowingly inflicted, a friend brings up an unintended betrayal, or people we worked with recount a business decision that turned out to have been a serious mistake. We are judged.

*"Your throne will be established with love [*chesed*] and You will reign from it in truth [*emet*]" (lines 2–3):* Chesed and *emet* are opposites. In a secular court of law, judge and jury endeavor to interpret the law and discern the facts. Love has no place in a court of law. Intimate, long-term relationships, however, would never survive such scrutiny. Life partners, parents, children, and friends learn the raw truth about each other. If they wish to remain in relationship, they have to find compassion for one another's failings.

"And You will remember everything that has been forgotten, and You will open the book of memories" (line 5): Our lives are an open book. Nothing remains a secret. Secrets have a way of seeping through the cracks and bubbling to the surface. It is only a matter of time before we find ourselves exposed, as naked as the day we were born. Lies, half truths, obfuscations ultimately fail to convince. Better we should live our lives assuming that all our deeds, phone calls, e-mails, text messages, and financial transactions are known, recorded, remembered, and on permanent display in the Library of Conscience.

"And it will be read from: everyone's signature is in it" (line 6): We write the stories of our lives. We are given certain genes. We may be born into poor or wealthy families; during peace or wartime; to nurturing, neglectful, or even abusive parents. But how we respond to those circumstances, how we play the hand we have been dealt, is up to us. God merely reads what we ourselves have written.

Moreover, our choices do not disappear into thin air. They leave their mark. Our deeds matter. As insignificant as they may seem at the time, our deeds have a lasting—sometimes irreversible—impact. People may remember what we have done long after we have forgotten.

"And a great shofar will be sounded and a thin whisper of a sound will be heard" (line 7): Revelations may come to us when we listen to

Beethoven's "Ode to Joy," Maria Callas's *Tosca*, Moshe Ganchoff's *chazzanut*, or Louis Armstrong's trumpet; or when we behold Mount Rainier, the Guggenheim Museum at Bilbao, or Central Synagogue in New York. But revelations also arrive in less dramatic ways: in the slow movement of Beethoven's Fifth Piano Concerto, the dwarfed trees above the Arctic Circle, the call of a bird, the cry of an infant, a realization that grows over time—even in the silence of a corpse.

"Truly You are judge ... " (line 3); "As a shepherd searches for his flock" (line 11): Judge and shepherd play different roles. The shepherd who "has his sheep pass under his staff" (line 11) is the same shepherd who "makes me lie down in green pastures, who restores my soul" (Psalm 23).[2] The shepherd's job is to protect his sheep from predators and accidents, thirst and starvation, and to find and rescue them if they wander off and become lost.

How can one be both judge and shepherd? Parents who impose expectations upon us may also care for us. A teacher who grades us may also encourage us. An employer who could fire us may stop us from doing something foolish, steer us back on course, and never tell a soul.

"On Rosh Hashanah they will be written down, and on Yom Kippur they will be sealed[3] ... [But] t'shuvah, t'fillah, *and* tz'dakah *help the hardship of the decree pass" (lines 14, 21):* What could sound more final than a diagnostic test result, a divorce decree, a death certificate? And yet even the most final of "judgments" may not be the last word. *T'shuvah, t'fillah,* and *tz'dakah*[4] help the hardship of the decree pass. They don't tear up, annul, cancel, avert, or rend the decree—they temper it. They won't cure a disease or restore a loved one to us, but they may attract people to our sickbed or to our house of mourning who make us smile, laugh, or even cry with joy. They may restore to our lives a sense of connection, purpose, or peace—like rehab, which doesn't eliminate an addiction but teaches us how to live with it, doesn't erase the damage we have done but insists we own up to it and attempt to repair it. I have seen people turn their lives around. It's not easy. But I have seen it: Remaining sober or clean. Reconciling with estranged children or parents. Getting back on one's feet after emotional or financial devastation.

Have you ever seen a desert after a rain? Or a lava flow? On the Big Island of Hawaii are two volcanoes. Their eruptions destroyed everything in their wake—forests, homes, roads—and left great swaths of black lava hardened into a ropy or a razor-sharp jagged surface. The barren landscape is frightening to behold. What power! But on the wet side of the island, the rainy side, vegetation pushes through the black swaths of death. And as the years pass, more green appears. Underwater, the hardened lava has become home to numerous varieties of coral, which shelter and nourish thousands of beautifully colored fish. Rain could not stop the flow of the deadly lava, but rain could ultimately turn the barren volcanic landscape into a foundation for life. Like rain, *t'shuvah, t'fillah,* and *tz'dakah* can bring new life to a barren landscape.

"You … write down their sentence" (line 13); "[You are] quick to forgive" (line 22): When a human judge issues a verdict, it may be appealed. A convict may be released for good behavior before serving a full term. More merciful than an earthly court, God holds the divine judgment in abeyance, awaiting our repentance until the day of our death.

God sets no statue of limitations on *t'shuvah.* Asking for forgiveness, even years after the fact, may go a long way toward mollifying a person we have deeply hurt. Showing a sincere willingness to change may soften the hardened heart of those who loved us once. And if they are not mollified, they should be, for that is how God would react to a penitent soul: "slow to anger and quick to forgive" (line 22). That is the way we should react as well. Yes, we judge, we bear grudges, we recall hurts, we may even hoard them. We may be completely justified. But if those who have hurt us do genuine *t'shuvah,* no matter how long it takes them, it is our job to let go of the anger we long harbored.

"You will decide the end of all creatures" (line 13); "You do not want the dead to die" (line 23): No one lives forever. Some things are simply not in our hands. We may have a genetic predisposition for breast cancer or manic-depressive illness or heart disease. But we have also been given minds to study diseases and sometimes find treatments and cures, to anticipate and sometimes avert accidents, to predict weather and sometimes to mitigate the impact of earthquakes and floods.

"Their origin is from dust"⁵ (line 27); "You are … everlasting" (line 31): No matter how healthy or careful or righteous we are, we will all die. But some elements of the universe preceded us and will outlast us: energy, light, change, atoms, force, mass. So, too, elements of culture endure: love, hate, fear, gratitude, longing, satisfaction. Ideals, too, live on: freedom, responsibility, goodness, justice, truth. These are "everlasting," or as enduring as anything we can imagine.

"Your name suits You" (line 34); "You named us after You" (line 35): Something of us, too, endures. What we teach the next generation may be taught for generations after. One deed of loving-kindness may send ripples into the future. We are part of an ongoing chain of humanity, of Jewish tradition. Our lives are fleeting, but we may write books, establish foundations, compose music, generate ideas, found or revitalize synagogues that will nurture generations long after we have died.

Despite our failings and our inescapable mortality, at our core resides something enduring and worthwhile. Perhaps it is "the faith of those despised and endangered that they are not merely the sum of damages done to them … [but] a connective link in a long, continuous way of ordering hunger, weather, death, desire and the nearness of chaos."[6]

Our work may have a greater impact than we will ever know. (Bach was less well known during his lifetime. Van Gogh sold only one painting while he was alive.) We should act with the conviction that we may impact the world for generations to come.

"Act for the sake of" (line 35): The poem closes with an urgent appeal to God. Looking back over the entire poem, perhaps all the imperfect verbs are not statements of present fact (as they are commonly translated) or of a future of which we are certain but, rather, appeals to God for a future for which we fervently hope. Perhaps the poet is not asserting but pleading: "*May* the limits of our lives be set by You, God, rather than by the negligence or cruelty of fellow human beings. *May* we be judged by You, rather than by critics or competitors who judge us falsely or without mercy. *May* the quality of our lives reflect our worth, rather than the vagaries of chance."

Un'taneh Tokef rings true to me as an artistic wrestling with impermanence and death, with deeds and their consequences, with power and powerlessness, with fear and reassurance, with mistakes and second chances.

18

Who by Fire

CONTEMPORARY PERSONAL
AND LITERARY REFLECTIONS

Dr. Wendy Zierler

I am in my kitchen preparing for Rosh Hashanah. In the background, a CD is playing: Shlomo Carlebach and his daughter Neshama singing a duet of *Kivakarat Ro'eh Edro* ("Like a Shepherd Who Checks His Flock"). Neshama is leading the song, and her father is responding, echoing her lead. I have heard and sung along with this melody many times in my own synagogue, which has adopted several Carlebach melodies for the High Holy Day liturgy. Being that it is an Orthodox synagogue, however, I have never once heard these melodies led by a woman, let alone by a daughter whose famous father has long since passed away, a stark reminder that we are all "like a passing shadow and like a vanishing cloud" (line 29). How could he be so alive in my kitchen, singing so generously and eternally with his daughter, whose name means "soul," and not be alive at the same time? Have I ever in my life heard anything so beautiful and heartbreaking? All at once, this familiar prayer has been made new.

Dr. Wendy Zierler is associate professor of modern Jewish literature and feminist studies at Hebrew Union College–Jewish Institute of Religion, New York. She is the author of *And Rachel Stole the Idols* and the feminist Haggadah commentary featured in *My People's Passover Haggadah: Traditional Texts, Modern Commentaries* (Jewish Lights).

Two days later, on Rosh Hashanah itself, I am at services with my eldest daughter, who, for the first time, is trying to stay in shul and learn the *t'fillot*, rather than wander in and out of the sanctuary. I repeatedly compliment her on her stamina and spiritual resolve. We reach *Un'taneh Tokef*; we begin to sing along together. I am swept away by the melody, by the poignant experience of harmonizing with my own daughter, when I feel a sudden tugging on my arm followed by a whisper in my ear, "The melody is nice, but the words!—really depressing!" I laugh, almost out loud. "It is depressing," I say. "But also very moving." I wonder how to explain to my daughter the power of this motley, mortality-ridden, question-filled prayer.

It is my scholarly habit to search for the contemporary meaning of classical Jewish texts in works of modern literature that rework them. If modern, even secular, writers choose to invoke a prayer in their work—one whose theology and metaphors are premodern and perhaps alienating—it must have enduring relevance and beauty for them too. I am always struck by the way in which modern literature and art can reimagine ancient sources. And so I go looking for contemporary renditions of *Un'taneh Tokef*.

I begin with a novel: *Who by Fire* (2008) by Diana Spechler. In the middle of the novel, a character named Ash, who has fled his troubled, secular Jewish family for the structured life of an Orthodox yeshivah in Jerusalem, spots what he thinks is a suicide bomber in the Old City and launches into an extemporaneous prayer that culminates with a reference to *Un'aneh Tokef* that furnishes the title for the novel:

> Dear God, please don't let the worst happen: That terrorist might hear the soldier's running footsteps behind him; even if he hasn't made it to the Kotel [the Western Wall, still standing from the destruction of the Temple in 70 CE], he might get nervous and detonate. I envision a sudden orange fire, and I think of the prayer we say on Rosh Hashanah and Yom Kippur: *Who by water, and who by fire; who by sword, and who by beast.* Every year after Aleena disappeared, my mother would cry when we got to that part of the service. It's about God having already decided who will die that year, and how. I remember the way my mother's knuckles would go yellow against her prayer book, and I would look up and her and know what she was thinking.[1]

The Aleena mentioned in this paragraph is Ash's younger sister who disappeared when she was a child, who is believed to have been kidnapped and murdered, but whose body has never been found. Her disappearance lingers on as an excruciatingly unanswered question in the novel, a source of ongoing psychic entropy from which each member of the family seeks, in his or her own way, to escape. Ash's invocation of *Un'taneh Tokef* in this context of his mother's continuing dread for his sister's safety and his own sudden fear of a detonating bomb reads like a desperate assertion of divine order and power in the face of human powerlessness. Here is a God who definitely makes up his own mind about how and when we will die, filling us with fear but also with solace that at least there is a God and, thus, that there is more to life than our many unresolved questions.

But what are the words "Who by fire and who by water" (line 16) if not questions? For me, it is this alternation between order and disorder, assertion and inquiry, that furnishes the power of *Un'taneh Tokef*. On the face of it, this *piyyut* is chock-full of clichés about God and faith that at once shore us up with their very regularity and familiarity and at the same time make us worry and tremble. God as king, judge, shepherd, accountant, scribe, chronicler—all of these worn metaphors crammed together in one poem have the liturgical effect of sandbags propped against a dike that will not hold or contain the floodwaters. But can they hold?

Leonard Cohen's famous 1974 song "Who by Fire," another, earlier adaptation of *Un'taneh Tokef*, underscores and enlarges the interrogative point that lies at the very heart of the prayer by posing questions not merely about the various tragic ways that a person might die, but also about the times, seasons, and personal and psychological circumstances that define a person's life and death, as well as about the very existence of God and divine providence.

Cohen's poem/song mimics many aspects of the "who by fire" section of *Un'taneh Tokef*. Like the prayer, it is rhythmic and rhymed and built around pairs of opposites—sunshine and nighttime, "high ordeal" and common trial—a structure that lends both poems a sense of solidity and structure. (Indeed, both Cohen's poem and the "who by fire" section of *Un'taneh Tokef* recall the structure of the "To everything there is a season" poem in chapter 3 of Ecclesiastes, a tidy series of opposites that affirm the order of the universe in contrast to Ecclesiastes' countervailing complaint about the vanity of human life. Cohen's song begins to sound an ironic note in the first stanza, however, when he imagines death in the "merry merry month of May," that moment of vitality in the springtime of our lives, when we are filled with hopes for all that we "may" be and do. All is not possible, however, even for those in power. Who, then, holds real power? "And who shall I say is calling?" Cohen refrains, as if answering a phone call in which no one else is on the other end of the line. Who can one call to answer these questions?

Reputedly Cohen wrote his song in response to the Yom Kippur War, during which he spent time in Israel, first trying to join the Israeli army and ultimately entertaining the troops. There is nothing in the lyrics, however, that suggests this specific historical focus. The song works because it strikes a universal, modern chord of mortal despair.

The connection between "who by fire ... who by warfare" of *Un'taneh Tokef* and the Yom Kippur War, however, is real. In 1990, Yair Rosenblum (1944–96), the famous composer of *Shir L'shalom* ("Song for Peace"), which was sung at the Tel Aviv peace rally where Yitzchak Rabin was assassinated, wrote a setting for *Un'taneh Tokef* in memory of the eleven soldiers from the secular Kibbutz Beit Hashita who fell on the same day in the Yom Kippur War. For many secular Israelis, Rosenblum's rendition has become their main means of identification with Yom Kippur. Here is an example of how *Un'taneh Tokef* continues to resonate even for a population that accepts none of the *piyyut*'s theology, providing a liturgical occasion to pose tough national questions and bewail painful losses.

Even more recently, in January 2009, poet and editor Eran Tzelgov published his own *Piyyut Layamim Hanora'im* ("Hymn for the Days of Awe") in response to the military operations in Gaza. Like Cohen's song, Tzelgov's protest poem builds on the "who by fire" section of *Un'taneh Tokef*, offering a chronology of dates and names of wars and violence between Israel and the Palestinians.[2] Like the shepherd who counts and enumerates and takes note of each sheep in his flock, the poet counts off a list of past transgressions:

> Who by water
> Who by fire
> Who by my hands
> Who under my hands
> Who in Forty-Eight[3]
> Who in Five Fifty-Six[4]
> Who in Retribution Acts[5]

Who in Sixty-Seven, in Sixty-Eight, in Sixty-Nine,
    In Seventy, in Seventy-One, in Seventy-Two,
    In Seventy-Three
Who in the year of my birth
Who in Seventy-Five, in Seventy-Six, in Seventy-Seven,
    in Seventy-
Eight, in Seventy-Nine, in Eighty, in Eighty-One
Who in Sabra and Shatilla
Who in Eighty-Three, in Eighty-Four, in Eighty-Five, in
    Eighty-Six
Who in the first Intifada with broken arms and legs,[6]
Who in Eighty-Eight, in Eighty-Nine,
Who by Ami Popper[7]
Who in Ninety-One,
Who in my name[8]
Who in Ninety-Three, in Ninety-Four, in Ninety-Five
Who in Kfar Qana[9]
Who in Ninety-Seven, in Ninety-Eight, in Ninety-Nine
Who in the Al-Aksa Intifada
Who by "targeted prevention"[10]
Who in Two Thousand and One
Who by 1.5 tons of explosives[11]
Who in Two Thousand and Three, in Two Thousand and
    Four, in Two Thousand and Five
Who this time in Kfar Qana[12]
Who by cluster bombs[13]
Who in Two Thousand and Seven
Who on the Hanukah of "Cast Lead"[14]

Who's next in line

Both the passage from the Spechler novel that opens this exploration and Tzelgov's poem that caps it portray a predetermined, repetitive, mortal reality. But whereas in Ash's conception, God decides our fate and that is that, Tzelgov's poem serves as protest, a call to "secular," national *t'shuvah*, which in many ways accords with the radical turn that occurs in the second part of *Un'taneh Tokef*.[15] Tzelgov's poem begins with the idea of *t'shuvah* or change in its move from generic questions of the prayer to self-questioning, as signaled by the repeated use in lines 3 and 4 of the words "my hands." If we want to reorient our thinking and depart from old ways, we need first to shift the focus of our thinking and ask new, even painful questions.

Reordering, reconfiguring, and recasting are part and parcel of *Un'taneh Tokef.* "And repentance, prayer, and charity help the hardship of the decree pass" (line 21). The shift in the usage of the verb *a.v.r.* from the beginning of the prayer to the way it appears in this sentence highlights this point. Earlier in the prayer, human beings are seen as passing (*ya'avrun*) impotently (depressingly!) under God's staff. The word used there, *ya'avrun* ("they will pass") shares almost the same vowel and conso-nant sounds as *yibarei'un* ("they will be born") but represents the opposite meaning. You pass (*ta'avir*) before us, God, and count us, decreeing our fate. When we say *t'shuvah, ut'filah, utz'dakah ma'avirin et ro'a hag'zerah,* however, we claim the verb *a.v.r.* for ourselves, in active, causative form. Like the three Rabbinic principles upon which the world stands, here is a three-fold formula for how we can begin to ask other questions, ones that can help determine the way we live, if not the way we die, for other than the inevitability of death, nothing else in life is inevitable.

PART III

Un'taneh Tokef and the Limitations of the Human Condition

19

Stark and Inescapable

Merri Lovinger Arian

The power of the *Un'taneh Tokef* is profound, perplexing, and persuasive in its ability to place us exactly where we need to be placed during these *Yamim Nora'im* ("Days of Awe").

How mindlessly we move through our daily existence. We proceed with an innocence, assuming a certain predictability and pattern to the events that might unfold. At best, some of us proceed with intentionality, yet even so, a certain naivety is likely to accompany us along the way. Those of us fortunate enough to be engaged in work that we find meaningful approach our tasks with the hope of creating or sustaining a vision that we believe will make the world a better place to live in. And those of us blessed with family and friends who support us with their love and comfort try as best we can to sustain and nurture those relationships. But still, how easy it is to forget how blessed we are, how easy to lose sight of our embarrassment of riches.

Yet how little it takes to be reminded of just how vulnerable we really are. That dreaded phone call in the middle of the night: an elderly parent who fell and pushed her Lifeline pendant and is now awaiting the arrival of the paramedics. And you wait on the other end of the phone for a call back to see what condition she is in. Or a phone call from your doctor, who needs to see you about some blood results from your last

Merri Lovinger Arian is on the New York faculty of the Hebrew Union College–Jewish Institute of Religion and its School of Sacred Music. In addition, she serves there as Synagogue 3000's consultant on liturgical arts, supervising rabbinic and cantorial students in the art of leading and creating worship collaboratively.

physical. "Not to worry," she advises. "It's probably nothing, but we should follow up." How quickly your perspective changes. Somehow you forgot to notice the calm, but when the waves begin to churn, they are all you can think about.

The *Yamim Nora'im* implore us to take notice. These are the days of awe, and dread, and hope, and longing, and solitude, and community, and memory. We need, once a year, to be shaken. We need to notice the empty seat of a sister, a father, a neighbor, or even a child who never again will be able to join us in High Holy Day worship. And similarly, we need to acknowledge our gratitude for those who are with us, those who have found healing, and those who bring completeness and meaning to our lives.

And we need to recognize our journey over the past year. The High Holy Day liturgy offers us countless opportunities to revisit our actions and numerous opportunities to offer thanks and ask for forgiveness. But *Un'taneh Tokef* is different. This prayer makes us stare into the face of our mortality. And stare we must. The imagery is stark and inescapable. "Who will live and who will die? ... Who by fire and who by water? ... Who by hunger and who by thirst? ... Who by strangling and who by stoning?" (lines 15–18). And even those words can ring hollow year after year ... becoming mindless mantras of misery. Until there is a September 11 or a Hurricane Katrina. And then it is no longer "merely" poetry. It is at that moment when, like the angels, we "recoil and [are] gripped by shaking and trembling" (line 8).

But how does this kind of fear-invoking liturgy find its place amidst the majesty and holiness that typify the High Holy Day experience? As we listen to the soulful, often heart-wrenching tones of *Kol Nidre*—notes that plead with us to once again revisit our wrongdoings over the past year—or the sweet, lullaby-like lilt of *Avinu Malkenu*, which holds and caresses us as a parent might her child, surely we experience a real sense of holiness. Our smallness in the face of the universe becomes apparent. These prayers cannot help but lead us to re-examine who we are and how we might be better. Yet all of this is accomplished with a poetic, prayerful, and artistic subtlety. Why during the *Un'taneh Tokef* do we need to be hit over the head?

It is here, in this particular prayer, that we are warned that what we do really matters. Our actions have consequences, and those actions will be remembered. When we act from our smallest self, the self about whom we are least proud, we hope to go unnoticed. But in truth, nothing goes unnoticed. "Truly You are judge and prosecutor and litigator and witness" (lines 3–4). We must take the stand and own up to our own failings. For many it is difficult to buy into a belief system where our actions or words are rewarded and punished, as the literal text of the prayer might imply. But the message of accountability, the need to own and be responsible for our actions, is what is at the core of this prayer. The words of the *Un'taneh Tokef* remind us of this all too often forgotten truth. Subtlety simply will not work. This is the time that we need to hear it straight. Like a child who endlessly tests his parents to see just how far he can go, we, too, test those limits. And we come to synagogue on the High Holy days to "fess up," to acknowledge our limitations, and to pray for guidance so that we may do better next time. The message needs to be made painfully clear.

"To everything there is a season, and a time for every purpose under the heavens" (Ecclesiastes 3:1). This is the time, and the purpose is clear. We need these stark reminders. We need to be held accountable. When we truly confront this liturgy, and when we truly hear the message not couched in any soft subtlety, then *nashuv*, "we can return," renewed and hopeful, empowered to face the New Year as the Holy One would want, as one made *b'tzelem Elohim*, in God's own image.

20

At the Edge of the Abyss

Rabbi Sharon Brous

"Life changes fast. Life changes in the instant. You sit down to dinner and life as you know it ends."[1] Joan Didion wrote these words after her husband died suddenly one night at dinner.

I read Joan Didion after my dear friend died a couple of years ago from a massive brain tumor that had been discovered about forty hours earlier. She was thirty-one years old, pregnant with her second child, just finishing her PhD, and struggling, like so many of us, to balance her professional aspirations with her instinctive need to be a good mother, wife, and friend.

Rabbi Eliezer taught, "Repent one day before your death." His students, baffled, asked him, "But how can we possibly know when we'll die?" Rabbi Eliezer replied, "All the more reason you should repent today, just in case you die tomorrow" (Talmud, Shabbat 153a).

The great spiritual challenge of the High Holy Days is to recognize the fragility of life, the brevity and capriciousness of human existence—but not in some distant, theoretical way. The challenge of the High Holy

Rabbi Sharon Brous is the founder of IKAR, a Jewish spiritual community in Los Angeles that integrates spiritual and religious practice and the pursuit of social justice. Listed among the *Forward*'s fifty most influential American Jews and *Newsweek*'s leading rabbis in the country, she lectures and writes frequently about new trends in American religious life, next-generation engagement, and social justice. She lives in Los Angeles with her husband and three children.

Days is to confront the radically unpredictable trajectory of our lives and live as if every single day truly might be our last.

Many of us struggle to overcome the terror of death through avoidance and repression—we simply couldn't function were we to live with its awareness. But our tradition compels us to recognize that *afar anachnu,* "All we are is dust" (Psalm 103:14)—the end is inescapable. The only legitimate choice is to face death's inevitability with a dedication to living a certain kind of life.

The centrality of *Un'taneh Tokef* in the liturgy of Rosh Hashanah and Yom Kippur reflects the Rabbis' understanding that an awareness of our deep vulnerability is the very essence of the religious and spiritual life. "Life changes fast. Life changes in an instant." There's simply no time for denial or escapism.

After the death of a child in our neighborhood, I called one of my rabbinic colleagues who was supporting the bereaved family. "What can I do to support *you?*" I asked. "Go home and hug your kids," he said. And I did. For an instant, I felt the weight, the privilege, and the burden of having a love so rich in the world. I understood the preciousness and the capriciousness of life.

That is precisely what *Un'taneh Tokef* is designed to accomplish. Our tradition, in all its wisdom, demands that we obliterate the false protective shelter and, knowing that each moment might be our last, fight for a life of meaning *today.* The High Holy Days force us to shift from denial of death to purposeful engagement with life.

Un'taneh Tokef climaxes with the words *Ut'shuvah, ut'fillah, utz'dakah ma'avirin et ro'a hag'zerah,* "And repentance, prayer, and charity help the hardship of the decree pass" (line 21). We can't dictate our fate. We can't hide from death. But there are three things that we can do to bring meaning into the radical uncertainty of our lives.

T'shuvah ("repentance"): You don't have to be a static, stagnant being, dwelling perpetually in the mistakes of years past. You can choose to make *t'shuvah,* affirming that life is dynamic and people change. Find the courage to ask for forgiveness from the people you have hurt. Find the strength to forgive those who have hurt you and the audacity to forgive yourself. Open your heart and embrace the people around you—most importantly those you most often take for granted. Hug your kids.

T'fillah ("prayer"): You don't have to be alone. You are part of a story that is bigger than you, where the critical currency is God and the soul, not money, power, or celebrity. Let the majesty of nature distract you. Open your heart to pain. Let the world take your breath away. Connect to something beyond the physical, the tangible, the utterly graspable. Allow yourself not to understand and yet to appreciate anyway. Live in mystery.

Tz'dakah ("charity"): Stop digging yourself further and further into your own dramas, as if the privileges of freedom and prosperity come with no responsibility to others. Open your eyes and give a damn! Let your heart break over illness, poverty, loss, and violence. Affirm the power of love! Bring healing and comfort! Stake your claim in the world!

T'shuvah, t'fillah, and *tz'dakah* will not save us from cancer; they cannot protect us from terror. In fact, an alternative early version records the assertion as, *Ut'shuvah, ut'fillah, utz'dakah m'vatlin et ro'a hag'zerah,* "And repentance, prayer, and charity *nullify* the decree." But this version did not survive—the Rabbis simply couldn't stomach the false promise that doing good things would grant long life. They couldn't bear the implication that those who die must have done something wrong. They wouldn't delude us into believing in some magical formula that would ensure a long and healthy life.

And yet they insisted we are not powerless in the face of life's capriciousness. We cannot ensure long life, but we *can* find meaning, purpose, and celebration in the life we have. So they settled on *Ut'shuvah, ut'fillah, utz'dakah ma'avirin et ro'a hag'zerah,* "And repentance, prayer, and charity help the hardship of the decree pass." The decree cannot be changed. But we retain the power to make for ourselves a life worth living.

This is the great challenge of a Jewish religious consciousness: on one hand, we are to remember that our lives can be taken from us at any moment; on the other, we are to affirm our unique human capacity to effect change in our lives and in the world and to love with every ounce of our being. The annual High Holy Day encounter with death is designed to unsettle our routines, break us free from stagnation, and shock our system out of its instinctive selfishness and indulgence. It compels us to ask, "If my life ended now, would it have been worthwhile?"

I know for my friend who died of the brain tumor, the answer to that question was *yes.* To love with all your heart, to believe with unflinching faith, to sing without inhibition—this is a life worth living. Is ours?

The horror of death's inevitability lets us at least begin to touch the beauty and the profundity of life. Though we cannot live forever, we can choose to make a life worth living.

21

The Answer Is "Me!"

Rabbi Edward Feinstein

> On Rosh Hashanah they will be written down, and on
> Yom Kippur they will be sealed:
> … Who will live and who will die, who at their end, and
> who not at their end?
> Who by fire and who by water, … who by earthquake
> and who by plague, …
> Who will rest and who will wander, Who will be tran-
> quil and who will be troubled…. (lines 14–19)

I sat in shul for years reading these words before I realized the answer. The answer to each of these questions is "Me."

Who will live and who will die? I will.

Who at their end and who not at their end? Me. Like every human being, when I die, it will be at the right time, and it will also be too soon.

Fire, water, earthquake, plague? In my lifetime, I've been scorched and drowned, shaken and burdened, wandering and at rest, tranquil and troubled. That has been my life's journey.

Rabbi Edward Feinstein is senior rabbi of Valley Beth Shalom in Encino, California. He is an instructor in the Ziegler Rabbinical School of the American Jewish University and the Wexner Heritage Program. He is the author of *Tough Questions Jews Ask: A Young Adult's Guide to Building a Jewish Life* (Jewish Lights) and *Capturing the Moon;* and the editor of *Jews and Judaism in the 21st Century: Human Responsibilities, the Presence of God, and the Future of the Covenant* (Jewish Lights).

Of course, I prefer to deflect this truth. I would much prefer to let the prayer talk about someone else, perhaps the fellow in the next row. It has taken a lifetime to reveal that defense as a lie. The prayer is not about someone else. It's about me. It is a frightfully succinct summary of my existence. So now I read it again, but in the first person, and it makes me shiver:

> I will live and I will die, at the right time, and before my
> time,
>> I will wander but I might yet find rest, I will be
> troubled but I may achieve tranquility.

This is the central truth of the High Holy Days. This is what makes them *Yamim Nora'im,* days of terror. We are vulnerable. We are finite and fragile. The facts of human existence that matter most are out of our control. Not one of us decides when we will be born. Neither do we determine when we will die. Health and sickness, wellness and brokenness are not of our choosing. We invest ourselves in the lives of others, we love them and need them, but we cannot protect them from the world and its accidents.

That terrifying truth of the human condition is forced upon us on these holidays. All year long we may pretend that we are in control. All year long, we may strut about surrounded by the tokens of our power and influence. Our titles, our uniforms, our credentials, our wallets provide an illusion of control. But the holiday skillfully strips us of all that. We stand shoeless, wrapped in a *kittel* (a death shroud), hungry, weary, dizzy. We feel viscerally the fragility of being human. And we face the truth.

> A midrash: When God contemplated creating the human being, God consulted the angels of heaven.
> The angels of compassion said, "Let him be created, for he will perform acts of loving-kindness"
> And the angels of peace said, "Don't create him! He will fill the world with conflict and strife."
> The angels of justice said, "Let him be created, for he will pursue the right."
> And the angels of truth said, "Don't create him! He will be false and deceitful."
> So what did God do?
> God threw truth into the earth and created the human being.

There is some incompatibility between human beings and truth. For human beings to exist, truth must be buried. It must be repressed. There are certain truths we cannot know, dare not discover, if we are to live normally. So it is most of the year. But on these holidays, we are commanded to unearth the truth and face it. We are commanded to know what the rest of the year we would rather avoid. Because only in so doing will we strip away the excuses, the rationalizations, the sturdy walls of defensiveness that keep us stuck in the ruts of mediocrity. Only the acid of this truth is strong enough to dissolve all that keeps us from becoming who we are meant to be.

> *B'rosh hashanah yikatevun, u'v'yom tzom kippur yechatemun.*
>
> On Rosh Hashanah they will be written down, and on Yom Kippur they will be sealed. (line 14)

Who is "they"?

In the conventional reading of the prayer, God is imagined as judge, auditor, grand inquisitor. The great book of life is opened, and our actions for the year are examined. God decides if this year we are worthy of a renewed grant of life. God decides if this will be a year of plenty or poverty, of sickness or health, of rest or toil. God decides, and God's decision is recorded. But before the decree is sealed, we have three appeals: repentance, prayer, and charity. The decision can be litigated. Vigorous appeal just might change God's mind.

Most Jews read the prayer this way. Even those who have long abandoned traditional theologies still harbor fearful images of God deep within. After all, we were all once small children, completely dependent upon the goodwill of all-powerful adults. That sense of being judged for life and death still lives deep inside ourselves.

But this reading is disturbing. It connects our fate to our behavior, and it puts our destiny into God's hands. Was my mother's cancer really God's decision? Did she deserve it? Was it punishment for some infraction? What about the victims of tsunami, plague, Holocaust? Were they victims of God's unrelenting judgment? Did they not pray hard enough or repent vigorously enough?

If this were the prayer's only meaning, I would stop saying it. I'm sure many Jews have. But I choose to read it differently. The decree is not my individual fate. It is the human condition itself. It is the fragility, the vulnerability of being human—the blunt truth that we do not control the fundamental facts of our own existence. But that's not the end of the prayer. There is a powerful conclusion:

> *Ut'shuvah, ut'fillah, utz'dakah ma'avirin et ro'a hag'zerah.*
> And repentance, prayer, and charity help the hardship of the decree pass. (line 21)

This may not have been the original wording. An alternative and, possibly, the original version is derived from a statement in *Genesis Rabbah* 42:13 and found in variant manuscripts of the prayer[1]:

> *Ut'shuvah, ut'fillah, utz'dakah m'vatlin et hag'zerah.*
> Repentance, prayer, and charity cancel the decree.

This version corresponds more closely to the conventional interpretation: if we make use of this threefold appeal, God will actually *cancel* the decree! In comparison, our version seems compromised. *Ma'avir,* "help make it pass," is so much weaker than *m'vatel,* "cancel." Repentance, prayer, and charity mitigate the decree's severity—that's all. The decree stands. Because the human condition doesn't change. What God has given us are three tools for ameliorating and, thereby, transcending the harsh facts of human life.

T'shuvah ("Repentance")

Viktor Frankl was a noted Viennese psychiatrist who was taken first to Theresienstadt and then Auschwitz. Assigned to a labor detail, he was able to observe his fellow prisoners. He wondered what it was that enabled certain inmates in the concentration camp to maintain a sense of hope and inner strength while others lost their will to live. In his classic book *Man's Search for Meaning,* he affirms the truth that while we may not decide the conditions of our existence, we always possess the freedom to interpret those conditions and the freedom to choose our response. I may not choose what happens to me in life, but my character—the accumulation of my responses—is always mine to control. There are people who melt at the slightest disappointment or setback. And there are those who have suffered immeasurably and yet maintain an air of optimism and hope. Our response is not an autonomic reflex. It is freely chosen. We always possess the freedom to shape the interpretation of our experience, to decide what it means to us. We possess the freedom to construct a life narrative and to fashion a response. And we can always change our responses. We therefore bear full responsible for our character. This freedom and responsibility for our own character is the definition of being human. Our behavior is not shaped by inborn animal instinct. Even when life brings loss and pain, we can choose to sink into bitterness, rage, and suicide or to transcend tragedy and rise to a life of purpose and hope. We can live in self-absorption, nursing the resentments of victimhood, or we can reach out to the other in love and caring. This freedom lifts us above the fragility of life to a level of meaning. This is *t'shuvah.*

T'fillah ("Prayer")

> They were still newcomers to our community when his father died suddenly. After the funeral, he refused my request to hold a minyan at his home. "Nobody knows us, Rabbi, no one will come." But I persisted, and he relented. When I pulled up to the house that evening, more than a hundred people crowded his home. Families from his kids' school, kids from the youth group, people they met during the High Holy Days all filled his home with prayers for comfort and healing and life renewed. He was waiting for me on the lawn, his eyes filled with tears. "You were right! How did you know they would come?"

We cannot alter the fundamental facts of the human condition. But we need not suffer them alone. We hold hands, we share tears, we lift our voices and cry together. And in so doing, we lift one another up, out of the darkness. In prayer, we transcend loneliness and alienation and discover the warm consolation of loving community. This is *t'fillah.*

Tz'dakah ("Charity")

We cannot alter the fundamental facts of human existence, but we can make the world a bit more gentle. Hence *tz'dakah*—literally, "charity," encompassing all other acts of *tzedek*, "righteousness." These acts accumulate. They have undetectable resonance, echoes. An act of goodness might ripple across the world to heal an aching soul far beyond our horizon. And our acts touch us. The first Lubavitcher rebbe, Shneur Zalman, taught that there are moments in every spiritual life when we lose faith, lose touch with the divine, lose hope. What does one do at such moments? Perform one selfless act of goodness, he taught. At that moment, you will feel the presence of God in your fingers. In your act of caring, you will feel God's caring. In your act of healing, you will feel God's power to heal. This is *tz'dakah*.

Human life is fragile, vulnerable, and finite. We possess three divine gifts that enable us to transcend the limitations of the human condition: We are free to shape our character. We are able to share our common suffering and celebration in prayer and in song. We are equipped to heal and to help one another and to bring a measure of peace to the world. We bravely affirm the meaningfulness of human existence and our faith that God is present among us.

22

The Dance between Fate and Destiny

Rabbi Karyn D. Kedar

What we most want to know is by definition unknowable. Life, death, health, accident, conflict, fortune—the very flow of life—appear arbitrary. What is true, fair, and just is irreconcilable with what baffles us and confounds us. Why do some people suffer; why do some find love while others are left lonely; why do some give birth and others remain childless; why do innocent children die? What evil motivates acts of terror and genocide? And so, in the hushed moments of the High Holy Days, we are filled with fear, anger, and confusion.

And then, just as we are about to close our eyes, or our spirit, the tones and sounds of the liturgy change. A declaration is made: this day is "full of awe and dread.... And angels will recoil and be gripped by shaking" (lines 1, 8). The rhythm and meter become a drumbeat heralding the truth of our humanity. To live is to be vulnerable. To be human is to be mortal. We proclaim that truth simply, profoundly, unequivocally. Some of us argue, others rage. Some declare that there is no justice, no true judge. The rhythmic beat is undeterred by our reactions of denial, anger, indifference, or piety: "who will live and who will die ... who by hunger and who by thirst ..." (lines 15, 17).

Rabbi Karyn D. Kedar is the senior rabbi at Congregation B'nai Jehoshua Beth Elohim in Deerfield, Illinois. She is the author of several books, including *The Bridge to Forgiveness: Stories and Prayers for Finding God and Restoring Wholeness; Our Dance with God: Finding Prayer, Perspective and Meaning in the Stories of Our Lives;* and *God Whispers: Stories of the Soul, Lessons of the Heart* (all Jewish Lights).

It is true. Some will live. And some will die.

Un'taneh Tokef: The force of this day demands that we lift the veil of illusion and see fate and destiny like ministering angels dancing between this world and the next. *Fate* is the ordained path of our lives, the stuff that happens beyond our power to know and to control. *Destiny*, however, is how we respond to fate by the choices we make. We can choose to live with intention, choose the company we keep, choose to make our lives a great learning of the mind and spirit through consideration, introspection, dialogue, perseverance. We cannot control what happens to us. We absolutely can control our reaction to what happens. This is the dance of fate and destiny, the very essence of the human condition. Our life is not judged by events but by our reaction to them; our character and good name are formed from the fortitude, tenacity, and courage that it takes to live an elevated life.

And so, we declare that on these High Holy Days the universe spins, fate and destiny dance, and some will live and some will die and some will be tranquil and some will be troubled. Through song and word, hunger and exhaustion, we are brought to a ledge; we are vulnerable. Fly or fall—we choose. And then, in simple language, with the rhythm of a breathless heartbeat, we are given a spiritual imperative, and with this imperative are instructions on how to fly, how to persevere through difficulty and trauma, and how to exercise destiny rather than fall to the harshness of fate.

Three words form the spiritual foundation of destiny: *t'shuvah, t'fillah,* and *tz'dakah*—to reach within, to reach beyond, and to reach toward others. This becomes a spiritual imperative, a practice and a discipline. It is not only a way to act but also a way to see the world. Our lives are elevated through introspection (*t'shuvah*), the philosophical and theological discourse of prayer (*t'fillah*), and the compassion and generosity that *Un'taneh Tokef* calls "charity" (*tz'dakah*). We are beckoned to live and to engage in a life of meaning, of purpose. We are elevated by service, through a conversation with the choices that lie before us on our path. We are challenged by the awesome power of this day—not to fall, but rather to fly. Not to become bitter, cynical, defeated. Through repentance, prayer, and charity we learn, and then we teach, the great lessons that come from adversity, and our destiny becomes a tapestry designed and woven by the choices made every moment of every day. Reaching within, and reaching beyond, and reaching out toward others is a disciplined rhythm for daily life, spiritual preparation that will give us meaning and purpose.

Repentance is an intentional and consistent self-examination of what is right and what is wrong, an accounting of sins of speech, of deed, and of avoidance. It comes first because it provides us with self-awareness and the belief that change is possible. It commits us to growth and understanding. It makes us more human and, therefore, more compassionate. It humbles the lofty sense of self, softening our spirit and strengthening our resolve. *T'shuvah* literally means "return." Return to the person we were created to be, return to the path of a higher more meaningful existence. There is optimism. There is purpose. There is hope.

And just as we turn inward, we yearn to reach outward, beyond the walls of self. To engage in something greater, to believe in more than our own self-musings. And so, the next spiritual imperative is prayer. Prayer engages us in the question of faith. A simple utterance gives word and voice to what we do not and cannot understand. In prayer, we yearn for reconciliation between what is and what is possible. Prayer is the touching, ever so gently, of what is holy and eternal and good. Prayer is the imperative to offer words of gratitude even in the face of derision and adversity. Prayer is wonder. Sometimes our prayers offer comfort and context. Sometimes they pose or answer questions. And sometimes prayer gives us the forum to shake a fist at the heavens and shout at the anguish of our lives—not acceptance and resignation, but conversation. The fact that we are called the children of Israel is theological more than historical. Our ancestor Jacob fought with the Invisible One, wrestling with fate and destiny and becoming wounded in the struggle. And so we have learned that sometimes prayer and struggle are the same. And like a fight with an angel, with forces unknown and beyond our control, we dance, wrestle, and ultimately embrace the idea of divinity in life. All this is prayer, and whether it is as rigorous as a solitary fight at dawn or as quiet as a "thin whisper of a sound" (line 7), we can experience a shift in perspective—steadying us, guiding us, tugging at our sensibilities by allowing us to admit that we are not infinite and that we are not all. And though it may hurt to live, it is good to be alive.

There is reason. There is purpose. We need faith.

While *t'fillah* (prayer) addresses what cannot been seen, *tz'dakah* (charity) addresses what should not be ignored. By reaching beyond self, we gain concern for others. *Tz'dakah* arises from the awareness that, no matter how deep our suffering and pain, there are other people who need us. Life is a communal activity beyond self-interest, not a solitary act of self-preservation. When we are in pain and confronted with mortality, the imperative of *tz'dakah* becomes a gift. We are not the center of our universe. Giving is the way to reach beyond our circumstance and enter into the world of legacy, an existence that transcends our mortality. We must give away our money. We must give away our time. We must give away our kindness. It is right and just.

There is meaning. There is purpose. We need love.

This day of holy power confronts us with what we cannot know and cannot control. We confess and acknowledge our mortality, plainly and graphically. We look for a context, a net to catch us if we should fall, a vocabulary to make sense out of that part of life that is non-sense, a way to believe that ultimately, despite it all, life has meaning and purpose. We do not know why people die in fiery plane crashes or are swallowed up by swollen oceans, why some find fortune and others suffer poverty, why some find love and others live in loneliness, or why babies get ill. We just know that these things happen. All the time. The holy power of this day is its spiritual imperative to repent, to pray, to give.

We must reach within ourselves and examine who we are and who we are to become.

We must reach beyond ourselves, touching boundaries beyond our understanding.

We must reach out toward others—those we know and those we don't, those we love and those who are strangers. This day is full of awe and dread, for we see clearly that mysterious dance between fate and destiny. And as the angels tremble, we mortals yearn for meaning, for purpose, and for love.

23

Empowering Human Beings to Challenge Fate

Rabbi Asher Lopatin

U n'taneh Tokef is usually seen as a prayer extolling God's complete and utter divine power. It comes, after all, immediately after the phrase "because You are our God and our ruler." God is the great mover of the world, the supreme judge who determines fate.

We, therefore, read the second paragraph as a long list of God's decisions for the year ahead, a set of fearful possibilities that sum up the High Holy Day mood of repentance and soul searching. The paragraph is terrifying; just reciting it—not to mention hearing it chanted in the heart-wrenching tones of tradition—confirms our deepest fear that the world is beyond our control, a combination of absolute divine power and equally absolute human weakness.

But in a post-Holocaust era, which, despite all our protestations, has nonetheless seen Cambodian and Rawandan atrocities and the continuing Darfurian genocide still going on before our very eyes, it is tough to just accept these decrees without shouting out: Enough dying! Enough

Rabbi Asher Lopatin is the rabbi of Anshe Sholom B'nai Israel Congregation, a modern Orthodox synagogue in Chicago, and is a founding rabbi of the multi-denominational Chicago Jewish Day School. With his wife, Rachel, and their children, he plans to make aliyah in 2011 to a new, pluralistic community in the Negev.

starvation! Enough burning and drowning! Doesn't our generation have to say at last, We won't assent to hundreds of thousands of people being starved, raped, murdered, and chased from their homes in this or that place around the world! We will not just look on and say, "We leave it to God to determine who will live and who will die; who will have clean and safe drinking water, and who will not." Did we really believe it when we said, after Auschwitz, "Never again"? With continuing genocide even now, how can any moral human being dismiss what happens in the world as fate beyond our control, the inscrutable decree of a just and awesome God? We should know by now that if we take that approach, one genocide will inevitably follow another—endlessly. Such a trivializing of our role in history betrays the memory of the Holocaust. Instead of affirming "Never again," it says, "Again and again—what can you do?"

When someone dies, says Moses Isserles (in his sixteenth-century gloss to the *Shulchan Arukh*, based on a Talmudic statement, Bava Kamma 38a), we are prohibited from saying, "Oy, what can you do?" What a startling assertion! One would expect the opposite—who are we, after all, to challenge God's decree of death? Why shouldn't we say, "*Neb'ch*, we'd like to have it otherwise, but what can you do? God is in charge." Yet Isserles denies us that right. It's not in keeping with a Torah that demands 613 activist mitzvot to say that our lives don't make any difference to what goes on in this world.

Yet "What can you do?" is exactly what *Un'taneh Tokef* seems to be saying. What can we mere mortals do in the shadow of the all-powerful God who controls our destiny? We can pray, do *t'shuvah*, and give *tz'dakah* (exactly what the High Holy Days call for), but ultimately, God is the doer. Honestly, I am frustrated by the vision of human powerlessness implicit in this traditional read of *Un'taneh Tokef*. I refuse anymore to read it that way.

I salute Moses Isserles for telling us that we are not allowed to say, "What can you do?" because we *can* do something. We are not helpless. We can start by reading *Un'taneh Tokef* as empowering humankind to take responsibility for what happens on earth, especially for the wars, catastrophes, and economic woes that other generations might have just dismissed as the work of the gods or, worse, the work of God.

But how can a prayer about God's all-determining judgment affirm human responsibility and action? It can. With a more careful look at the text, the human element becomes clear.

Un'taneh Tokef opens with a description of God's judgment—a judgment so unavoidable that angels quake in fear. But think about it: how does *Un'taneh Tokef* actually describe God's actions here? Contrary to what we would expect, and in blatant disregard, actually, of God's presumably absolute determination of our fate, we have to say that God is not really acting on God's own. Rather, God is reacting to human actions. God is sitting on a throne reading the books that describe what we humans have done. These books even contain our signatures—as if God is excited to have autographed copies to leaf through. This is a powerful God whose script, however, is written by us! Yes, these weak and flawed human beings are the characters who, God expects, will take action in this world. The God of *Un'taneh Tokef* has spent the last year stepping back from the world in order to let human beings act independently, and those actions become the book of the world, signed by the people responsible for them. That is what God reads on these High Holy Days—an account of the extent to which we have filled the vacuum of God's self-imposed absence by becoming our own agents of change, morality, and spirituality in this world.

For all God's greatness, the High Holy Days focus on us—what we have done, what we are planning to do. In fact, the very "holiness of the day" (line 1) with which *Un'taneh Tokef* opens is determined by us. Nowadays, for historical reasons, we have a fixed calendar to go on, but originally, the court in Jerusalem declared the arrival of the new moon based on the testimony of witnesses who saw it arrive the night before. Rosh Hashanah and Yom Kippur are holy, but only when the human court declares them so. It is human action, not divine determination, that makes the initial difference. Given all this, how can we imagine God expecting us to say, "What can you do?" God expects us "to do" right over wrong. Whatever we do, or fail to do, gets recorded and judged. God, in a sense, is the great motivator and cheerleader for human action because we know, according to *Un'taneh Tokef,* that God is watching.

It is specifically the angels in *Un'taneh Tokef* who are nervous, because according to Jewish tradition, they cannot act on their own. They react to human action on one hand and to God on the other. They have no means to acquire merit. But we human beings have every opportunity of being meritorious in the eyes of God—if we work to stop the next genocide, to cure the next disease, to limit the next epidemic, and to ensure ample food and water for people around the world. Only human beings do mitzvot—not angels, not even God. We may fail, but we may also succeed.

The list of potential deaths that *Un'taneh Tokef* lists does not employ the name of God—not even once! It just says these things— some good, some terrible—will happen. Our tradition clearly stipulates, "Reward is not given in this world." So these momentous events, which are in the world—who will live and who will die—cannot be rewards or punishments. But even by the traditional reading of *Un'taneh Tokef,* they can hardly be capricious acts of an all-powerful God and, by extension, a list of reminders of human powerlessness and a world out of control. What about the first paragraph, where God is totally consumed with human actions on these days of judgment? It is, recall, our own actions that God reads to determine how God should act in the year ahead.

Granted, humility is important; we have limitations as human beings, and God has God's own reasons for doing things in this world. I do not mean to say that each of us absolutely controls our individual fate from year to year. I mean only that we are not absolutely powerless, at least over the future of the world as a whole. We should read *Un'taneh Tokef*'s list of deaths as God's acknowledgment that human actions make a difference. "Who by fire, and who by water" (line 16) is, at least to some extent, an outcome over which we human beings have control and must take responsibility. We determine, ultimately, if there is peace on this earth, if people are safe from rapacious fires and floods, and if they are safe from the ravages of economic cycles. We determine who is respected and who is not— champions of morality or of superficial success—and the models, therefore, that future generations will emulate. Especially in the face of trauma, we humans must reclaim our will and determine whether we are at the end of our rope or if we have the inner strength to do more mitzvot in this world.

The legend of Rabbi Amnon writing *Un'taneh Tokef* on his deathbed portrays a man who considered himself a failure for not holding fast enough to his faith and who had just minutes more to live, but who nonetheless wrote a prayer that would transform the Jewish world forever. Yes, fate might have been knocking, but Rabbi Amnon summoned up the courage to do one more giant mitzvah: to compose this prayer and ever after change the script that God would read. *Un'taneh Tokef* empowers human beings to insist that fate alone need not determine "who will live and who will die" (line 15). The great message here is that we are responsible for changing this world. We cannot let anyone, not even God, take away that responsibility and that holy role.

24

Who by Common Trial

Catherine Madsen

Elias Canetti once wrote in a notebook, "Shallow religions: those we feel no fear behind." He did not specify which religions these were. Like any useful aphorism, the suggestion teases the imagination with particulars: Was he speaking anthropologically, theologically, liturgically? Was he reacting to modern efforts to lighten the mood of Western religions? He was a Jew who never practiced Judaism; did certain expressions of Judaism seem to him particularly complacent? He wrote this in London in the mid-1950s; was he thinking of the comfortable Anglican status quo? We are left to our own speculations.

Canetti might have added that there are fears and fears; the mere presence of fear behind a religion is not enough to guarantee its profundity. There are, so to speak, shallow fears in religion, fatalistic and paralyzing fears. In Christianity as I once experienced it, "Where will you spend eternity?" was one of them: the creeping dread that on Judgment Day you will be rejected, you will appear before Christ as he sends the sheep to the right and the goats to the left, and he will look at you and say he never knew you. The *feeling* of that fear is not shallow; it can be terrible and despairing. But it is the displacement of an existential fear onto a schematized one.

For some Jews, the *Un'taneh Tokef* seems to project the same kind of fatalistic fear: the pages of the Book of Life are stacked against us, and

---

Catherine Madsen is the author of *The Bones Reassemble: Reconstituting Liturgical Speech*; *In Medias Res: Liturgy for the Estranged*; and a novel, *A Portable Egypt*. She is a lay leader at High Holy Day services at the Jewish Community of Amherst, Massachusetts, and bibliographer at the National Yiddish Book Center.

we are marked for life or death according to an unattainable moral standard. But the same existential fear lies beneath it. It is the fear of being and remaining what we are: the fear of having our one life, as we have handled and mishandled it, stand without alteration in the universal record. Serious Christians eventually discover that the aversion to doing wrong is a more powerful and effective deterrent than the fear of damnation; to have done something shameful that cannot be repaired, and to know it, is all the damnation you need right here on earth. For Jews, the prolonged moral reckoning of the month of Elul and the Days of Awe is meant to gather and intensify the whole year's consciousness of moral failure, to link it explicitly to our mortality, and to bring us through this crisis not to fatalism but to responsiveness.

Modern religious thought, often preoccupied with questions of belief, has largely lost the sense of ritual enactment. Confronted with a highly dramatic liturgical structure based on an obviously imaginary scenario, many people will simply dismiss it as they dismiss biblical literalism or the fairy-tale elements in art. What, you expect me to believe that we parade before God every year like sheep before a shepherd to be judged? What, you expect me to believe that God created the world in six days? What, you expect me to believe that God allowed Satan to afflict a righteous man on a bet? What, you expect me to believe that a king divided his kingdom among his three daughters according to how much they loved him? But if we place the *Un'taneh Tokef* beside *King Lear*, it is immediately clear that these frame stories are starting points, inductions. Their importance is not in their plausibility; of course they are imaginary. Their importance is in their subsequent handling by a powerful imagination.

In Judaism the day of judgment happens not at the end of time, not even on the day of our death, but once a year. In Leviticus 16:29–34, God proclaims an annual day of atonement in rather practical terms, as though atonement will naturally be needed at regular intervals: as though a structure must be built to accommodate our need for judgment, and even to limit it to manageable proportions. By this point in the Torah it is clear that God's need to judge us must also be kept within bounds. Modern Jews are well aware of being compelled to judge ourselves, and believe vehemently that this need must be kept within bounds; "judgmental" is a favorite pejorative. We are not so well aware that the need must still be met. We all earn death, over and over; as modern Jews we may not want our religious authorities to tell us so, but as feeling individuals we know it inwardly. Even children, as soon as they know they can make mistakes, feel the graveward pull of their shame. No parent who has lost a young child will call that death deserved, and only an ideologue would say that Jews have earned everything they have suffered. Yet the sense of falling short, of having done permanent wrong, of being dust, is not cancelled by the evil done to oneself. Our own sins must still be met with seriousness, with ordeals and conditions. They require catharsis, not dismissal.

In another sense, death is not a moral question at all; we die not because we are sinners but because we are mammals. Yet as conscious mammals we are oppressed by a haunting, indeterminate foreknowledge of our end. Our sense of earning death by our moral failures presupposes that we will die anyway—even that, since we will die anyway, we might as well believe we have earned it. In the *Sh'ma koleinu* on Yom Kippur we pray *Al tashlicheinu l'et ziknah*, "do not cast us off in the time of our old age"; that cry cuts though the whole elaborate structure of confession and forgiveness, the sins neatly arranged in acrostic order, the fasting and the abstaining. Whatever our sins, whatever our atonements, the natural, gradual weakening of the body proceeds. In the whisperings of middle age we begin to feel it: the twinge that lasts for an instant, the limp that lasts a few days, the joint that gradually goes from bad to worse, the minor infirmity that entails major retrenchments of all our eating, drinking, sleeping, and lovemaking habits. *Of course* God will cast us off in our old age: that is what death and its preliminary infirmities amount to. It is unclear what our moral failures have to do with it.

Obsessive-compulsive ritual—probably the earliest kind known to the human brain—is founded precisely on inaccurate belief, on magical thinking. You avoid stepping on the crack so as not to break your mother's back: what other control do you have over your mother's well-being? When ritual grows up, it retains the inaccurate belief, rather as our brains retain all their previous structures right back to the reptilian, but makes that belief the scaffolding for an emotional and intellectual elaboration as different from it as calculus and engineering are from compulsive counting. The agonizing verse of Job and *Lear*, the piteous images of human fragility in the *Un'taneh Tokef*, appear within their inductive frameworks with painful vividness, in the way that a scene of miracle or martyrdom appears within the ornamental border of an illuminated page. The poetry is in the pity. The fantasy of the Book of Life and God's judgment is memorable, but the extraordinary aspect of the prayer is its emotional impress: *Any of us might die of anything, any time. When? Now or later? With or without warning? Who by stroke and who by cancer, who by famine and who by plague, who by collision and who by explosion? We are grass, glass, shadow, cloud, Adam.* If liturgical language is performative speech, the *Un'taneh Tokef* is as performative as anything you will ever hear.

Certainly it is imaginary; how else but through imagination do you talk about death in the community where you spend your life—with the people you know, the people you do business with, the people who help you, love you, employ you, exasperate you? Indirection and fable are forms of delicacy; they create an atmosphere in which painful subjects can be raised without speaking of specific deaths that have wounded the people you know. The *Un'taneh Tokef* was written in a time when fear and sorrow were closer to the surface of public life than they are now, but in private life we still know that security is a thin veneer. God suspends the earth over the void, says a *piyyut* in the Yom Kippur *Shacharit Amidah*; the *Un'taneh Tokef* shows us the thread on which it hangs.

We are moral creatures; we are vulnerable creatures; vulnerability wins. This is the realest thing anyone will ever tell us in ritual. Surrounded as it is by a liturgical padding of the accustomed, the incomprehensible and the massively dull, the prayer is the lightning flash that reveals the naked contingency of our lives. Without the padding of dullness we could not endure it. In that stark light we see also the contingency of each other's lives—poor bare forked animals—and grasp that we can come to each other's aid. Our moral failures may or may not bear directly on the time and manner of our death; the constant possibility of death does bear directly on our moral achievements. *T'shuvah, t'fillah,* and *tz'dakah* will not save us, but they will for a little while save others from the end that awaits us all.

25

A Text in Context

Rabbi Jonathan Magonet, PhD

The High Holy Days tend to sneak up on us. Once a year, as if from out of nowhere, we are confronted with a couple of days of synagogue attendance. The transition is sudden and the adjustment often difficult. It is not supposed to be that way, however, since both Rosh Hashanah and Yom Kippur are preceded by an entire preparatory month of Elul. This full penitential season offers a unique opportunity for self-reflection, at the heart of which is *Un'taneh Tokef,* as a sort of climax to it all.

To get at my own relationship with this "prayer of prayers," I need to provide some personal history—history, however, that I shared with others, as the postwar, post-Shoah generation of Europeans.

My childhood in a typically nonpracticing but nominally Orthodox shul in London seemed designed to alienate us all from Judaism. The High Holy Days were just another enforced attendance at a service with little meaning and excruciating boredom. I would still begrudge my once-a-year synagogue visit had I not made the transition from medicine, the career mapped out for me by my parents, into the unexpected personal journey toward the rabbinate. The decision came out of a number of years setting up Jewish youth conferences around Europe for my own postwar generation and personally facing the ghosts of the Shoah by working with Jews and Christians in Germany. As a new rabbinical student, I had to explore as an adult the Jewish liturgy that I

Rabbi Jonathan Magonet, PhD, is emeritus professor of Bible at Leo Baeck College, where he was principal (president) from 1985 to 2005. He is coeditor of three volumes of *Forms of Prayer* (the prayer books of the British Movement for Reform Judaism) and editor of the recent eighth edition of the *Daily, Sabbath and Occasional Prayers* volume.

had found so off-putting as a child. The final turning point in my attitude was the invitation in the 1970s to work on a new edition of the *siddur* of the British Reform Movement. "You write songs," said my future coeditor of the full set of prayer books, Rabbi Lionel Blue, "so you can translate the poems!"

We were a new generation of rabbis, born during or after the war, graduates of the newly founded Leo Baeck College in London, trying to define for ourselves our own religious identity. We had inherited a mixed bag of traditions shaped largely by refugee rabbis from the Continent who had developed our movement after the war and been our teachers at the college. In their hearts, they still belonged to a Jewish world and scholarly culture that no longer existed. We felt that we needed a prayer book that spoke directly and personally to our own generation, unmediated by the identity crisis of our teachers.

The new Sabbath and daily prayer book that appeared in 1977[1] was enormously successful in that regard. But now we had to revise the High Holy Day *machzor*, unchanged since the beginning of the century and including blessings for "our Sovereign Lord King George" as well as other long-deceased members of the British royal family.

Un'taneh Tokef was absent from the *machzor* we inherited, as also was *Kol Nidre*, though some congregations had pasted the texts into their old books, alongside stickers offering a prayer for the State of Israel and updating the monarchy to Queen Elizabeth. We were faced with a book with a seemingly haphazard mixture of psalms, traditional prayers, and often incomprehensible liturgical poems (*piyyutim*). So, as editors, we had carte blanche in tackling the task. But here the difficulties really began.

Even more than the Shabbat and daily liturgy, the High Holy Days belong to a medieval, hierarchic world. We stand in judgment before "our father, our king," a stern ruler with the power of life and death over us. Even translating central words like *melekh* as "king," or even "sovereign," does not convey the awe and dread the term meant originally, especially for us living in the United Kingdom, a democratic country with a disempowered "constitutional monarch." So being faithful to the literal meaning of much of the liturgy was neither true to the intent of the original nor to the reality of our own world. We had to bridge these two very different cultures in such a way as to provide for two-way traffic between the experience of the past and the needs and perceptions of today.

Before tackling the formal services, I set about compiling an anthology of traditional and contemporary materials addressing such key High Holy Day issues as responsibility, sin, guilt, self-judgment, repentance, forgiveness, and atonement. This collection, initially published separately as a paperback called *Returning*, helped define the themes that we would have to explore as we set about developing the services themselves. For those who wanted to prepare themselves for the High Holy Days, we included in the *machzor*[2] itself daily study materials for the whole month of Elul, as well as passages for daily use during the Ten Days of Repentance.

Yom Kippur is like a play in five acts or a symphony in five movements, each with its own contribution to the experience of the whole. We tried to clarify the structure to give a sense of a journey through the day. The five "acts" or "movements" are the five separate services of Yom Kippur (plus *Yizkor*, the short memorial service). Each service has at its core the *Amidah*, the one constant feature, like the "motor" running through the day. But each service becomes unique because of the elements added to it, petitionary prayers called *s'lichot*, and the twofold confession (*Vidu'i*). Here was the place to chart the stages of the journey through the day.

We came to see the five services as forming a pattern: The opening *Kol Nidre* service offers the first tentative attempt to admit our personal failure to live up to the promises we make to ourselves, to others, and to God. Structurally, it corresponds to the closing *N'ilah* service, when all pretense has been stripped away. As we stand before the closing gates, even words will fail us; we will have only the final cry of the shofar to express our emotions.

Thus:

Kol Nidre (introduction)—*N'ilah* (conclusion)

Working inward, we saw the morning service as focusing on our nature, identity, and task as Israel, and the challenges posed to us as a community and a people. If this service looks inward, the corresponding afternoon service faces outward, with the book of Jonah exploring our relationship to the outside world, the "Ninevehs" to which we would soon return. This leaves the *Musaf* (additional) service right in the center of the pattern—the deepest part of the day. Appropriately, *Un'taneh Tokef*, the day's climactic poem, occurs in *Musaf*. That is,

Kol Nidre (introduction)—*N'ilah* (conclusion)
Morning (particularistic)—Afternoon (universalistic)
Musaf (includes *Un'taneh Tokef*)

Ironically, the very name "additional" suggests that it is merely tacked onto the morning service. It is the moment when the shuls empty out for a "non-lunch" break. But it becomes very different if we see it as the heart of the five services and of the day itself, the deepest point to which we descend on our inward journey and from which we will later return to our daily life.

Un'taneh Tokef dramatizes the central challenge of Yom Kippur. Taken in isolation, the passage raises enormous questions. Is it really true that our fate for the coming year is sealed during the High Holy Day period and that it is determined by our past behavior? At this point, every prayer book editorial committee faces the need to provide its own translations of difficult passages. What, in fact, does the complex medieval Hebrew want us to believe?

The central statement, as traditionally translated, "But penitence, prayer, and charity avert the severe decree" (line 21), seems patently at odds with our daily experience. In the light of the Shoah, when so many good and pious people were murdered, it approaches blasphemy. The imagery within the passage itself, the brutal ways in which life can be ended, is shocking in its directness. But it is matched by the deeply moving portrayal of our transient existence. We understood the Hebrew to say that human life is

> fragile like a cup so easily broken, like grass that withers,
> like flowers that fade, like passing shadows and dissolving
> clouds, a fleeting breeze and dust that scatters, like a dream
> that fades away.[3] (lines 28–30)

The same service includes the passages describing the rite of the high priest on Yom Kippur, with its powerful imagery of the casting of lots and the fate of the two goats, one sacrificed to God, one led off into the wilderness. The very randomness of this choice also speaks to the arbitrariness of life. At this deepest point in the day, then, we are invited to ask ultimate questions about the significance and worth of our own personal lives. Dressed in the white *kittel,* which may one day be our own shroud, this one day a year is the time for such contemplation, as if from the grave, detached from the pressures and realities of daily life. In such a context, *Un'taneh Tokef* lends emotional and imaginative support to facing our own mortality.

Again, we faced issues of translation. How does one present these difficult texts? Our solution was to soften the sense of predestination by introducing interpretations at two crucial points. The conventional translation, "On the first day of the year it is inscribed, and on the Day of Atonement the decree is sealed, how many shall pass away and how many shall be born, who shall live and who shall die," became

> On Rosh Hashanah we consider how judgment is
> formed
> on Yom Kippur we consider how judgment is sealed,
> for all who pass away and all who are born, for all who
> live and all who die....[4] (lines 14–15)

The second change was the phrase *et ro'a hag'zerah* (conventionally "the severe decree"), which we rendered as follows:

> Yet repentance and prayer and good deeds
> can transform the harshness in our destiny.[5] (line 21)

This translation/interpretation offers the potential of a practical transformation of our lives through our conscious change in behaviour—at the very least, a psychological strengthening of our ability to cope with the challenges that confront us.

There are few places in our liturgical year or ritual life when we can address so directly our human transience, independent of the emotional upheaval accompanying a bereavement or similar tragic experience. Yom Kippur is a time out of time, a great spiritual gift. The liturgy should provide the intellectual, emotional, and aesthetic materials that support a prolonged meditation on our personal mortality and, hence, the meaning and purpose of life.

All components of Yom Kippur, but especially *Un'taneh Tokef,* offer a trustworthy framework that leads us, step by step, into these depths and then conducts us safely back out into daily life.

26

The Power of Vulnerability

Rabbi Or N. Rose

As I read the words of *Un'taneh Tokef* this summer, I find myself focusing on the issue of human vulnerability.

This has everything to do with events in the life of my family over the last several months.

Eight months ago, my wife underwent a bilateral mastectomy after being diagnosed with a gene that causes breast cancer. She took the test because both her mother and her grandmother had breast cancer.

Three months ago, my mother-in-law was diagnosed with breast cancer again, after living in remission for more than twenty years. She recently had her remaining breast removed and is now undergoing chemotherapy.

If I have learned anything this year, it is about the precariousness of life. Courageous and strong as people can be—and these two women are both certainly bold—we are also all like "withered grass" and "faded blossoms" (line 29). Painful as it is to admit, some of us will not be here next year, and others of us will be diminished physically or otherwise. Whether "by fire or by ... water" (line 16), in old age or in youth, frailty and death will be a part of our lives in the coming year.

I must say that I struggle with the theological worldview presented in *Un'taneh Tokef.* While I would like to believe in a God who sits in perfect

---

Rabbi Or N. Rose is an associate dean at the Rabbinical School of Hebrew College. He is the coauthor of *God in All Moments: Mystical and Practical Spiritual Wisdom from Hasidic Masters* and coeditor of *Righteous Indignation: A Jewish Call for Justice* and *Jewish Mysticism and the Spiritual Life: Classical Texts, Contemporary Reflections* (all Jewish Lights).

judgment over the world, rewarding the righteous and punishing the wicked, I am having difficulty doing so. Much as I yearn for a divine parent, shepherd, or sovereign, I do not experience such a being in my life or at work in the world. While I continue to listen carefully for the sound of God's "thin whisper" (line 7), I am as confused as ever about who or what this God is.

Despite my theological uncertainty, I know that we are not ultimately or exclusively in control of our fates. For all of our efforts at mastery in our personal and professional lives, the complex and unpredictable forces of existence are greater than any individual can fathom, let alone hold sway over. While this realization can lead to despair and apathy, it can also free us to focus our attention on those areas of life over which we do have control and to which we can respond meaningfully. Accepting our limitations, embracing our vulnerability, in other words, can actually lead to empowerment and transformation.

Of course, discerning when and where to act is itself a complicated matter. The Protestant theologian Reinhold Niebuhr gave eloquent voice to this challenge in his now famous Serenity Prayer: "God, give us grace to accept with serenity the things that cannot be changed, courage to change the things that should be changed, and the wisdom to distinguish the one from the other."

I view the High Holy Days as a great gift in this regard. Our ancestors have bequeathed to us a compelling ritual framework in which to do the hard work of self- and communal assessment, knowing that this task should be done regularly but is often ignored or taken up only in fits and start at other points during the year. How often do we actually take the time to ask ourselves the "big questions" of life? And if we do so, how sustained are these reflections?

The process of soul searching during Rosh Hashanah and Yom Kippur involves both a retrospective and a prospective dimension. We look back over the past year; examine our thoughts, feelings, and actions; and evaluate as honestly as possible our successes and failures. We also look forward, attempting to learn from the past, seeking to integrate new insights as we prepare to begin a new year.

This dynamic is captured skillfully in the 1999 *Kol Haneshamah: Prayerbook for the Days of Awe* (Reconstructionist), which includes two interpretive versions of the *Un'taneh Tokef* on facing pages (pp. 345–46). The first, by Rabbi Jack Reimer, asks us to focus on the past:

Let us ask ourselves hard questions
For this is the time for truth....

Did we fill our days with life
Or were they dull and empty?

On the opposite page, Rabbi Stanley Rabinowitz calls us to think about the future:

Who shall be truly alive, and who shall merely exist;
Who shall be happy, and who miserable?

Central to the teachings of the *Yamim Nora'im* is the message that we *can* change. Despite missed opportunities, poor decisions, or bad habits, growth is possible if we are willing to do the work.

The author of the original *Un'taneh Tokef* makes this point dramatically in his declaration that "*t'shuvah* and *t'filah* and *tz'dakah*" can ameliorate God's negative decrees issued against those the divine finds spiritually or morally wanting. I do not take this statement literally, because I do not know a God who issues positive or negative decrees, and I know too many righteous people who have suffered terribly despite their best efforts at serving God and humanity.

But I do believe that repentance (*t'shuvah*—including genuine acts of apology and forgiveness), prayer (*t'fillah*—including expressions of gratitude and of lament), and charity (*tz'dakah*—including monetary giving, but also other acts of *tzedek* [justice]) can enrich the quality of our lives.

Influenced by several early Hasidic teachings on the High Holy Days, I have come to believe that during this season of introspection we need to take the divine books of "remembrance" mentioned in *Un'taneh Tokef* and other related sources off the heavenly bookshelf, carefully review the relevant sections, and begin writing the next chapter of our lives. While there is much that we do not know and cannot control, this is a time to take stock and to recommit ourselves to becoming the people we ought to be. In facing our vulnerability, in coming to terms with our limitations, we have the opportunity to enter into a process of discovery and discernment that can lead to healing and renewal.

27

Mortal Matters

THE FAITH OF
UN'TANEH TOKEF

Rabbi David Stern

*U*n'taneh *Tokef* gets our attention. On Rosh Hashanah and Yom Kippur, days when we can feel inundated by words of prayer, somehow the stanzas of this medieval liturgical poem stand out, heard above the clamor of the day and the congestion of all its companions on the pages of the *machzor*.

Why? Because for many Jews, *Un'taneh Tokef* is profoundly moving, or troubling, or both. It rarely leaves us bored. It speaks of life and death, mystery and agency, limitation and hope, our mortality and God's eternity. And unlike other prayers in the *machzor* that in fact address many of these same issues (but which we find forgettable), *Un'taneh Tokef* raises these crucial questions about the meaning of our lives with the poetic force of a two-by-four. It is a literary achievement of bluntness, urgency, and transcendence.

The poem's imagery is unforgettable, its litanies profoundly disturbing: "On Rosh Hashanah they will be written down, and on Yom Kippur they will be sealed: ... who will live and who will die, who at their end and who not at their end, who by fire and who by water ... who by earthquake and who by plague" (lines 14–18).

Rabbi David Stern is senior rabbi of Temple Emanu-El in Dallas, Texas.

I confess, I do not understand these words literally. I do not believe in a divine Puppet Master who makes a list of all the grisly ways His or Her children will perish in the coming year. But I do believe this: the troubling litany serves as a vital symbolic reminder that there are events in the world that are simply beyond our control. Not that those events are moral judgments about our lives, not that our tragedies are our punishments, but that their occurrence is sealed—sealed off from our control, sealed off from our best intentions and our best efforts. We will be struck by diseases that we have done nothing to invite. Hurricanes and flash floods and human evil will wreak their havoc, shattering the foundations of our homes and our most treasured assumptions.

The *Un'taneh Tokef*'s litany of what shall be written and sealed is a series of clipped-phrase hammer blows pounding home the reality of our own mortality, the finitude of our power and prerogatives. The hammer strikes at all sorts of fantasies we manage to cling to (and sometimes depend upon) throughout the year: our self-sufficiency, our status, our unswerving virtue, our immunity from circumstance. "Who will live and who will die": each blunt couplet exposes our treasured myths of infinite reach and unshakable mastery as seductive fictions. Life is glorious—but it is also fragile, tenuous, and contingent.

In the synagogue during the Days of Awe, that deeply sobering acknowledgment can be a powerful blessing. In the scales of secular society, human limitation is measured as defeat. Out there, our finitude seems to diminish us, and being humbled suggests humiliation. But Rosh Hashanah and Yom Kippur allow us to see our human limitations as a source of wisdom, not of weakness. Like Yom Kippur itself, with all of its evocations of death and mourning, the *Un'taneh Tokef* confrontation with mortality is a gift. The virtual deathbed creates real opportunity: for unsparing self-examination, for a radical adjustment of perspective, for rising above the press of daily demands to a place where we ask ultimate questions. It doesn't mean that the losses aren't real, the limitations sometimes painful. It does mean that only once we recognize those limitations can we reckon with the promise we have.

But it's fair to ask, Can human action have meaning in a world of radical contingency? A world of uncontrollable events and devastating diseases? A world where human will, human wisdom, and human choice confront profound constraint?

The powerful, paradoxical *Un'taneh Tokef* answer is—yes. Even as *Un'taneh Tokef* reminds us of what we cannot control, it beckons us toward human responsibility for all that we can. In the first paragraph, the poem refers to God as *chotev v'chotem*, "author and sealer" (line 4). But never does this poem (or our tradition as a whole) grant God sole authorship of the book of our lives. The prayer goes on to say instead that God opens the book, but *chotam yad kol adam bo*, "everyone's signature is in it" (line 6). Each of us signs the book of our lives with our deeds. God writes, and we write. God seals, and we seal.

That is why immediately following the litany of human limitation comes the most powerful statement of human responsibility in our liturgy. In a great and saving act of liturgical chutzpah, having tattooed us with the reality of events beyond our control, *Un'taneh Tokef* summons us to agency: *ut'shuvah ut'fillah utz'dakah ma'avirin et ro'a hag'zerah*—as the Reform Movement's *Gates of Repentance* renders it, "Repentance, prayer and charity temper judgment's severe decree."

T'shuvah, our ability to repent and effect change in our own lives; *t'fillah*, our capacity to reach out to God; *tz'dakah*, our facility for reaching out to others—none of these makes us immune to life's harsh blows. They are not acts of magic that constrain or control the deity, and they do not wish or whisk away the profound challenges of our lives. (A similar formulation in Talmud Tractate Rosh Hashanah speaks of certain actions having the power to "tear up" the divine decree—not so here.) But even though the verb *ma'avirin* can be translated as "temper," or even "avert," the object of *ma'avirin* is not the decree itself, but the decree's harshness (*ro'a hag'zerah*). Repentance, prayer, and charity do not prevent misfortune—to say so would simply be to return to the fantasy of human mastery that the earlier litany demolished. But they do temper the harshness of life's circumstances by asserting our redemptive capacity for response.

In his masterwork *Man's Search for Meaning*, Viktor Frankl describes in devastating detail the grim humiliations he suffered at Auschwitz: the stripping of clothes and possessions and dignity. Life was provisional, tenuous, indeterminate. The nod of a Nazi head or the point of a gloved finger—utterly beyond the control of the prisoner—yielded life or death. And then Frankl's core insight: "Everything can be taken from a man but one thing—the last of the human freedoms—to choose one's attitude in any given set of circumstances, to choose one's way."[1]

As Frankl writes, "Human freedom is not freedom from conditions, but freedom to take a stand toward the conditions."[2] We do not choose our suffering, or the diseases that afflict our loved ones, or the crises that beset our families. But we do choose our way: whether to find new meaning in our moments or to stay stuck, whether to be present for the ailing or to let our own discomfort trump their need, whether to find healing in our homes or to hunker down in self-justification and denial.

As daunting as the list of "who will live and who will die" might be, the truth is that the events that we can control constitute most of our lives. We do a lot of signing of that book, day in and day out. And we come to synagogue during the Days of Awe in part to read what we have written in the year past: the words spoken in haste or in anger, the selfishness that narrowed our lives, the times when we were so busy with the press of daily life that we failed to perceive the needs of the people we love the most.

Our problem is that we listen to only half of the *Un'taneh Tokef*'s message. We convince ourselves that God, or fate, or destiny wrote the whole book. We say that there is nothing we can do, and we are wrong. For all that is sealed, for all that hurts us and is beyond our control, there is infinitely more that is within our reach to change. The destiny of the world's hungry is not yet sealed. The number of American citizens who will live in poverty or without health care this year is not yet sealed. The number of Jews who will complete another year feeling that Torah is somebody else's book, Shabbat somebody else's holiday; the number of families that will crumble because the drumbeat of professional accomplishment drowns out their ability to hear one another—those are not yet sealed either.

When it comes to the book of our lives, God is *chotev v'chotem*, but our *chotam yad* is on every page—we are God's coauthors, and we have collaborated before. Remember the story of the tablets Moses receives at Mount Sinai. The first set, the Torah teaches, is inscribed by God and given to Moses. That is the set that Moses shatters when he sees the people committing the sin of the golden calf. Moses then returns to the mountaintop, where a second set of tablets is created—but this set Moses and God create together. And it is the second set—the set that bears the mark of human contribution—that endures.

That is the story of our lives, because if we think that God takes care of everything alone or that we can take care of everything alone, then our lives will be shattered with the first dark night. It is the tablets of divine-human partnership that endure—more worldly than the first and less pristine. So often, we want our lives to be that original unsullied set, but our lives do not cooperate. The first set is broken. Our lives—messy, hectic, uneven, shot through with laughter and pain—are that second set of tablets: no less sacred, and in fact more whole than the first; no longer untouched by the human hand, now touched by the human heart. With the second set of tablets, we accept that we are not alone, we accept the reality of the broken pieces of our lives, and we accept the responsibility to create a new path of wholeness and of hope.

The conclusion of *Un'taneh Tokef* poses a crucial question: do we feel diminished or comforted by the juxtaposition of our mortality with the eternality of our God? The last line of this final section (omitted in *Gates of Repentance*) guides us and serves as a three-word seal on the whole poem: *ush'menu karata bishmekha,* "You have linked our name with your own" (line 35). Our mortality gains significance because it exists under the aspect of God's eternity. Our acts of compassion matter because they transpire in the context of God's goodness. God is, in the words of Rabbi Samuel Karff, a "Conserver of value."[3] The faith of *Un'taneh Tokef* is that the acts of mortal beings have timeless significance even in a world that sometimes breaks our hearts. That truth, too, has sacred power on our most holy days.

28

Turning Fate into Destiny

Rabbi Avraham Weiss

One of my heroes is Danny Heumann. Danny was a strapping young athlete until more than twenty years ago, when he suffered a tragic accident that left him a paraplegic. I'll never forget Danny's call just days after Natan Sharansky arrived in Israel. "Sharansky is free," Danny said. "When will I be free?" Danny, of course, meant free from his wheelchair.

We all have our own wheelchairs (may we be spared the real one); we all have our limitations. How do we overcome these challenges? How do we deal with adversity? *Un'taneh Tokef* offers a way.

The centerpiece of *Un'taneh Tokef* is an affirmation that "on Rosh Hashanah they [our futures] will be written down, and on Yom Kippur they will be sealed" (*b'rosh hashanah yikatevun, uv'yom tzom kippur yechatemun* [line 14])—a promise that is usually understood to refer to this world.[1] *Tosafot*, however, refers it to the world to come (*olam haba*),[2] a position based possibly on the statement of Rabbi Yaakov as found in the Talmud, "There is no reward for precepts in this world" (Kiddushin 39b). The reason may be that if there were absolute reward and punishment,

Rabbi Avraham (Avi) Weiss is the founder and president of Yeshivat Chovevei Torah, the Modern and Open Orthodox Rabbinical School in New York. He is also the senior rabbi of the Hebrew Institute in Riverdale. Most recently, he founded Yeshivat Mahara"t, an Orthodox school ordaining women to become spiritual leaders. Rabbi Weiss was named one of the fifty most influential rabbis in America by *Newsweek* magazine. He is the author of *Spiritual Activism: A Jewish Guide to Leadership and Repairing the World* (Jewish Lights).

we'd be stripped of our freedom of choice. Who wouldn't give ten dollars to charity knowing they'd receive fifteen in return? And who would sin knowing punishment would immediately follow? Hence, there is no reward and punishment in this world, only in the future world.

Un'taneh Tokef follows, however, with the paragraph that begins, "How many will pass on and how many will be created" (*kamah ya'avrun, v'khamah yibarei'un* [line 15]), and then delineates different ways of dying: "who by hunger and who by thirst" (line 17), for example. Clearly, this paragraph refers to this world. But if there is no reward and punishment in this world, on what are these outcomes dependent?

Un'taneh Tokef may be suggesting that the ways we live and die are a function of *mazal*, normally translated as "chance," but (as we will see) denoting here a divine decree that is not related to what we deserve. In the words of Raba: "[Length of] life, children, and sustenance depend on *mazal*, not merit [*lo bizchuta talya milta, elah b'mazala*]" (Talmud, Mo'ed Katan 28a). Since there is no reward and punishment in this world, we can hardly assume that we get what we deserve while still inhabiting it. As explained above, *mazal* in the Talmud is not the random happening of events, but the fate we're dealt by God that is often incomprehensible to us, although understood by God. This is certainly the case in *Un'taneh Tokef*, where the "who shall pass away" paragraph is preceded by the paragraph in which God is described as the shepherd who lovingly judges and carefully watches over each of us individually.

In recent years, the paragraph outlining different ways of dying has gained new meaning for me. As I say the words, "Who at their [timely] end and who not at their [timely] end" (line 16), I think of Andrew Zucker and Ariel Jacobs, who left their homes on the morning of 9/11 and never came back. Their wives gave birth soon after. "Who by water" (line 16) could be Katrina, and "who by warfare" (line 17) brings to mind Daniel Pearl's final moments. (The Hebrew text *u-mi ba-herev* literally means "and who by sword," recalling even more vividly the horrific beheading of Daniel Pearl.) "Who by hunger and who by thirst" (line 17) suggests Darfur. And "who by stoning" (line 18) recalls the towers, those giant buildings made of endless stones, falling down. All this suffering is not a function of wickedness, but of *mazal*.

But we can influence *mazal*. In the words of the Talmud:

> "I will complete the number of your days" (Exodus 23:26)
> refers to the years of the generations. If one is worthy, one
> is allowed to complete the full period; if unworthy, the
> number is reduced; so Rabbi Akiva. But the Sages said: If
> one is worthy, years are added to one's life; if unworthy, the
> years of one's life are reduced. (Yevamot 49b)

In other words, the *mazal* with which we are born is somewhat elastic.
While it cannot be absolutely cancelled, it can be altered to some
degree.[3]

In simple terms, if we want to know how long we'll live, if we'll be
prone to depression or if our children will have learning disabilities, a
good start is to check out our pedigree. We are all born with *predispositions* to a certain fate—but predispositions, against which we can take
precautions. How can we improve our physical well-being? By seeking
medical attention, and by eating and exercising properly. How can we
cope with depression? By cultivating emotional and spiritual inner
peace. How can we help children with learning disabilities? By being
patient and by giving time, money, and love to them. Although unable
completely to *cancel* our fate, we can at least *alter* it to some degree.

This may be the key to the *Un'taneh Tokef*'s crescendo, *ut'shuvah,
ut'fillah, utz'dakah ma'avirin et ro'a hag'zerah* (line 21). This phrase is
often translated as "Repentance, prayer, and charity *cancel* the evil
decree." Were this the case, however, the Hebrew would read, *m'vatlin et
hag'zerah hara'ah. Ma'avirin* means "to cause to pass over" or "get through,"
not "to cancel." As the translation in this book indicates, *ma'avirin et ro'a* is
descriptive: it means that repentance, prayer, and charity temper, or
remove, the sting or harshness of the decree. In other words, we have it
within our power to reshape, although not totally to change, our fate.

Adversity, then, is not a function of punishment, but of *mazal,*
which we can impact somewhat with our deeds. Rabbi Yosef Dov
Soloveitchik said it well when he distinguished fate (*goral*) from destiny
(*yi'ud*). Fate (is God) capriciously cast(ing) us into a particular dimension
of life that we cannot control. Destiny "is an active existence in which one
confronts the environment into which he or she is cast." According to
Rabbi Soloveitchik, "One's mission in this world is to turn fate into destiny, an existence that is passive and influenced to an existence that is
active and influential."[4]

Esther Wachsman, mother of Nachshon Wachsman, who was murdered in a terrorist attack in Israel, pointed out that after her son was killed, she was overwhelmed with grief. She could move forward only by reminding herself that she had a choice of either being a victim of her fate, or initiating a new destiny.[5] Rabbi Harold Kushner echoes her insight by distinguishing *why* bad things happen to good people from *when* bad things happen to good people. "Why" is a philosophical question about a past event, for which there may be no good answer, and we do not control our past. "When" is a pragmatic question about the future, over which we have some control.

Rather than ask "why" when confronted with adversity, it may be more beneficial to ask, "Now that this evil has happened, what can we do about it?" Not only should we ask "What can we do about it?" but we should also ask, "What does God do about it?" God gives us the power to overcome, to do things we never thought we could. Recognizing the strength God gives us to move forward, we may be better able to face the question of why the struggle occurred in the first place.

Sometimes I think there are no great people in this world—only great challenges. Faced with these challenges, God from above helps us do the impossible. And as God is limitless, so are we, created in the image of God, given the strength to reach toward limitlessness.

Which brings me back to my friend Danny. Danny always said he would marry and walk to his *chuppah* (the wedding canopy, or just a word for "wedding" proper). How overwhelmed I was when he introduced me to his wife-to-be. And just a few years ago, I had the honor to perform his wedding. I'll never forget the doors in the back of the hall opening, and there was Danny standing—although paralyzed from the shoulders down, he had learned to walk, strapped to his crutches. Watching him jump and push himself down the aisle, I offered the prayer, "Danny don't fall, Danny don't fall." And when he arrived, he lifted his hands in victory and received a standing ovation. To some degree, he overcame his wheelchair; Danny was free.

Is there anyone who has not experienced life's adversities—sickness, aging, business and family issues? The price of being human is inevitable adversity. What is critical, however, is to remember that when we are confronted by challenges, God gives us a hidden gift—the power to overcome, the power to soften the harshness of the suffering.

Perhaps it's all summed up in the motto "Never allow that which we cannot do to control that which we can." This may be the meaning of *Un'taneh Tokef.* Whatever our fate, we can have some impact upon it and turn fate into destiny.

29
Death Rehearsal

Rabbi David J. Wolpe

Each Yom Kippur we face our deaths. As the cantor intones the minor-key masterpiece of *Kol Nidre,* the congregation prepares. Step by step we are led closer to imagining our end. Finally, the process culminates in that disturbing, electrifying prayer, the *Un'taneh Tokef.*

Un'taneh tokef (line 1): Literally, "We give power." We give the prayer power, and the day power, when we realize what is at stake. What gives Yom Kippur its awesome authority? The recognition of its central message—you are mortal. You do not have forever. Repent now. Repair now the broken relationships of your life. Return to the wholeness of your full self. There is little time to craft a self in this world before life is taken. Begin today, because death looms above all life.

"A great shofar will be sounded and a thin whisper of a sound will be heard" (line 7): The call to prayer is the shofar, whose piercing, plain-tive notes grab our attention. But on the heels of the shofar is this whisper of sound. The message of prayer is in the stillness and silence of a whisper. God does not speak in thunderous pronouncements, but in a small, insistent tone. God will not take away our choice by forcing us to listen. We can ignore that voice if we choose, the voice heard in a whisper, in the frail prodding of law and conscience. On Yom Kippur we attune our ears and our hearts to really listen to God's call, so easily ignored, but so overwhelming once we attend to it.

"Who will live and who will die?" asks the *Un'taneh Tokef* (line 15). Each year on Yom Kippur, in each synagogue, we look around and notice

---

Rabbi David J. Wolpe is rabbi of Sinai Temple in Los Angeles. His most recent book is *Why Faith Matters.*

the absences, the familiar worshipers who are gone. The question becomes real, and its truth begins to strike us: we do not know who will live and who will die. Mortality is wanton, capricious; it could claim anyone. It could claim me.

"Who by fire and who by water, who by warfare and who by wildlife, who by hunger and who by thirst, who by earthquake and who by plague, who by strangling and who by stoning?" (lines 16–18): Substitute modern terms. "Who by heart attack and who by car crash? Who by AIDS and who by cancer? Who by neglect and who by despair?"

Gradually the message begins to force itself upon us. Every stratagem of poetry and ritual is employed to teach us something we already know—that we will die. But although we know it, we do not feel it. We hide.

We are not the first to hide. Recall the story of the greatest king of Israel. In the Bible, David is vital, alive—the most vibrant of all biblical figures. He is a warrior, a lover, a sinner, a poet, a harpist, a forerunner of the messiah. Throughout the book of Samuel we see in David a man filled with the zest and brio of life. Yet when we open the book of Kings, David is an old man; shivering in bed, he cannot even keep himself warm. The first verse of the book reads, "King David was now old, advanced in years" (1 Kings 1:1). One chapter later, the Bible reads, "David was dying" (1 Kings 2:1). The Rabbis notice a significant difference in those two verses. When he is old, he is still called King David. When he is dying, he is simply David.

We hide behind power and position and title in this world. But when we face our own death, we do not face it as a king, or a rabbi, or an employee, or a parent. We face it as David, as the essence of each individual soul. Death brings you face-to-face with who you are.

We can delay that confrontation with our souls until the instant of death. The *Un'taneh Tokef* urges us to feel it now, confront our mortality, see ourselves, and face God.

Traditionally on Yom Kippur we dress in white, not only for purity, but also to remind ourselves of the shrouds in which we will be buried. Like corpses, we need no food, for we have no bodily discomforts or desires. While our spirits cry out, our physical being is as if dead.

"And repentance, prayer, and charity help the hardship of the decree pass" (line 21): The decree is death. Nothing can avert the decree itself. It comes to all, great and small, kings and humble shepherds. But a life of closeness, of *t'shuvah,* of kindness, envelops us in a loving community. With that community, a conscience that is clear, and a relationship to God that is close, the ache is eased somewhat. The end comes, but softly.

"Their origin is from dust and their end is to dust: At their peril gathering food, they are like shattered pottery, like withered grass and like a faded blossom, like a passing shadow and like a vanishing cloud, and like blowing wind and like sprouting dust and like a dream that will fly away" (lines 27–30): Finally we come to understand our fragility, and we seem left with nothing but despair. The prayer has beaten down our resistance and we understand. Alone, mortal, we are nothing. What are we to do with the inevitability of death?

"But You are king, the living and everlasting God…. You named us after You; act for the sake of your name. And sanctify your name through those who declare the sanctity of your name" (lines 31, 35–36): That is to say, "May our name be linked with yours." We are fading, but God is forever. On Yom Kippur, if we recognize our plight, we find in ourselves the need for God and the path to God. Then we have joined the only thing in the world that does not fade away. We have linked ourselves with immortality. The finality of death is no more.

Above the clamor of the everyday and the din of history, the message of *Un'taneh Tokef* shines: There is so little time. When the shofar blows, let the shudder of mortality awaken your soul. Come out of hiding, and seek the eternity promised by our covenant with God.

PART IV

Un'taneh Tokef and Its Call for Sanctity, Transformation, and Renewal

30

The Power of the Thin Whisper of Silence

Rabbi Ruth Durchslag, PsyD

In the *Un'taneh Tokef* we are reminded to heed *kol d'mamah dakah*, what we translate here as "a thin whisper of a sound" (line 7), but which equally might mean "a voice of silence," a voice we hear after the blast of God's shofar. How odd to be instructed to hear a voice of silence, especially after the blast of the shofar. Why the juxtaposition of noise and silence, and what, exactly, does this voice of silence have to say?

To understand these lines in the *Un'taneh Tokef*, we can look at what our tradition has to say about stillness. The tradition of silence goes back to the giving of the Torah at Sinai (Exodus 20). Revelation was a moment of intense spectacle. Immediately preceding the giving of the Torah, smoke enveloped the mountain "like the smoke of a kiln" (Exodus 19:18). The mountain trembled. There was lightning and thunder, and God appeared in a blaze of fire. As God descended the mountain, the Israelites heard the blare of the ram's horn, the blast of the shofar. The tale is dramatic, powerful, and riveting, capturing the majesty and importance of this defining moment in our past. Certainly

---

After twelve years as a successful clinical psychologist, Dr. Ruth Durchslag decided to become a rabbi. She is passionate about bringing Judaism to alienated and disaffected Jews who have never found a way into organized Jewish life and reaching out to anyone seeking personal meaning within Jewish tradition. Toward that end, Rabbi Durchslag is forming a new worship community in Chicago that focuses on alternative life-cycle rituals and worship as paths to spiritual growth.

the Torah's description of revelation seems complete. What more could there be to say?

Apparently there was something missing. *Midrash Rabbah* 29:9 maintains that after the giving of the Torah "no bird twittered, no fowl flew, no ox lowed ... the sea did not roar, the creatures did not speak, the whole world hushed into breathless silence." Silence. Silence, the Rabbis say, was the missing element in the Torah's tale of revelation. Though the Israelites heard the words of Torah from Moses, only in the fullness of silence could they experience them in their hearts.

The voice of silence recurs in the story of Elijah (1 Kings 19). Elijah is commanded to leave his cave to stand before God. As God passes by, God sends a forceful and mighty wind. The mountains split, and rocks shatter. There is a fearsome earthquake, and after the earthquake the land is engulfed in flames. What more could God need to make Elijah recognize God's power and majesty? The text is clear. God is not in the mighty winds, the earthquake, or the fire. Rather, God is a *kol d'mamah dakah*, "a thin whisper of a sound." God is in the voice of silence. The thunder and fire and wind capture Elijah's attention, but it is only when Elijah listens to the silence that he can hear the voice of the divine.

In our time, too, we have examples of the power and importance of silence. Each year throughout Israel a horn is sounded on Yom Hazikaron (the Day of Remembrance for the soldiers who have been killed in battle) and on Yom Hashoah (the day commemorating the Holocaust). Immediately following the blast, Israelis cease what they are doing. Quiet permeates. Traffic stops. People get out of their cars and stand quietly in the road. Discussions cease mid-sentence. TVs go dark, and radio announcers interrupt their broadcasts. For two minutes the world is completely and utterly still. As at Sinai, the only voice to be heard is the voice of each person's soul.

The words of the *Un'taneh Tokef* are a verbal equivalent of the shofar. They are searing, provocative, disturbing. "And let us acknowledge the power this day's holiness" we read, "for it is full of awe and dread" (line 1). The prayer demands our attention, shaking us out of our complacency. We are reminded of the inevitability of our mortality. God sees and remembers all that we do. God is witness and judge to the narrative of our lives. On this day, God authors the narrative of our deaths.

And yet the prayer offers a tantalizing reprieve. We are reminded that *t'shuvah*, *t'fillah*, and *tz'dakah*—repentance, prayer, and charity—can transform the harshness of God's decree. Changing our ways may gain us a few more precious hours, a few more days, or a few more years. But change is so incredibly difficult. How many times have I promised myself I will pray a little more, be a little more generous, or seek forgiveness quicker, only to have my good intentions dissipate in the demands of the day? Each year at the High Holy Days we ask the question, how can we change?

The *Un'taneh Tokef* provides a clue: "A great shofar will be sounded and a thin whisper of a sound will be heard" (line 7). The key to change is to be still and hear the whisper after the noise: the whisper of self, the whisper of the divine. How, in a world of tumult, can we find a way to stop and heed the call of our inner voice? What, for each of us, is the blast of the shofar?

For me, it was becoming seriously ill. Until three years ago I thrived on a life of noise. For as long as I remember, I filled my life with chaos, looking to become whole by jumping higher and running faster. And then, three years ago, God stopped me in my tracks. Literally. One day I was healthy, thriving, and working out at the gym. The next day I woke up and couldn't use my arms and legs. For the next two years I was partially paralyzed, suffering from chronic fatigue, and spending most of my time in bed. My illness forced me into a life of stillness. It was, for me, my moment of revelation. It was not until I was forced to engage silence that I was truly able to hear.

In the years since my illness, I have learned the power of tuning in to my self. In my meditation and healing practices I look to silence as a way to become more whole. It is in silence that I am better able to listen to my truth. When I am still, I see more clearly how I have wronged others and am able to be less judgmental when they wrong me. It is in silence that I connect most powerfully to the divine. For me, change, true change, does not come from verbal declarations or vows. Change comes when I quiet the chatter of my mind and tune out the noise of the world. It is then that I hear most clearly the call to compassion, compromise, and concession. Change and my deepest caring come when I am quiet and tune in to my heart.

It is deeply challenging to hear the voice of our hearts. Most of us live our lives tuning out our heart-song. Our culture institutionalizes and condones escaping from ourselves. We worship noise and distraction. We are hesitant to look inside. Fearful of finding pain, fear, or emptiness, we cut ourselves off from the silence of self and the voice of the divine. That is why we need the blast of the shofar on these High Holy Days—especially if our lives have not been jolted by illness, death, or some other "shofar" of our own—why we need a day of *t'shuvah,* a day dedicated to returning to our essence, to reclaim ourselves and our lives. A reminder, perhaps, that it is only when we look inside that we can truly see. And only in the silence will God meet us where we look.

31

Evoking Fear, Prescribing Hope

FROM SUFFERING TO SERVICE

Rabbi Elyse D. Frishman

*U*n'taneh tokef k'dushat hayom ..., "And let us acknowledge the power of this day's holiness, for it is full of awe and dread" (line 1) The verb *un'taneh*, from the root *n.t.n.*, meaning "give," is difficult to translate. The standard translation, "let us acknowledge," is accurate but misses some of the deeper nuance. To *acknowledge* is an act of ego; this prayer is anything but the ego's expression. It is more an act of submission, not as resignation, but as submitting ourselves to a spiritual awakening. A better understanding would be, "*And let us give ourselves over* to the power of this day's holiness."

Judaism teaches us to distinguish the ordinary from the holy. This doesn't mean that ordinary things are unalterably separate from holy ones; rather, the ordinary can become holy. When we enter a crowded room, for example, we notice people superficially—what they're wearing, their hairstyles. An ordinary perception. But standing with a person and talking together while looking into one another's eyes, our perception

---

Rabbi Elyse D. Frishman is editor of *Mishkan T'filah: A Reform Siddur* and rabbi of The Barnert Temple in Franklin Lakes, New Jersey.

shifts; that person is seen differently, more deeply. This is a holier perception. Noticing the beauty of nature is ordinary behavior. Acting to preserve that beauty, the behavior becomes holy.

Our tradition therefore teaches the art of transforming the ordinary
into the holy. We don't merely see, we perceive. Not merely eat, but taste.
Not lust, but love. Animals exist in the realm of the ordinary. Angels live
in the domain of the heavens. Humans have the capacity to live in both
realms, *kodesh v'chol,* "sacred and ordinary." We are the only creatures
who can elevate the ordinary to the holy.

The society we yearn to shape isn't just utilitarian or self-serving. We
imagine utopia, a messianic *shalom,* the peace of absolute wholeness, where
all aspects of life become interconnected in complete harmony. Imagine the
jumbled pieces of a puzzle; the task is to organize them into a perfect fit. We
realize that the pieces can't be joined randomly. When the larger picture
emerges, the pieces themselves make sense because they cohere with one
another. So, too, with our life efforts. We're part of a larger puzzle. We go
through life seeking our proper place in the whole, locating others, for
example, whose place seems bound up with our own. Life's meaning
emerges only when we surpass mere self-sufficiency and link ourselves
properly with others. Each of us thereby influences the whole.

When we live in a manner that reflects this perception of our place
in life, we realize holiness. When we act according to our own little piece
and nothing more, we are ordinary.

"Let us give ourselves over to the power of this day's holiness, for it is full
of awe and dread." The "awe and dread" seem to lie in the fact that, for
better or worse, for life or death, each person's fate is being determined
now, by God. How difficult to move beyond the fear this induces.

Hebrew has two terms for "fear": *pachad* and *yirah. Pachad* is mortal fear: a madman wields a knife before you and you cower, afraid for
your life. *Yirah* is awe, reverence: gazing at the starlit heavens and realizing your insignificance. *Pachad* generates an action from the self's insecurity: survive! *Yirah* generates the humility to understand your place and
purpose in the larger scheme of things: behave! *Un'taneh tokef* is meant to
awaken *yirah,* spiritual insight into our behavior.

But it also evokes *pachad,* because when our spirit awakens, it
encounters the limitations of its vessel, the mortal body. Death is first

mentioned in the story of Adam and Eve, when God threatens the man if he eats from the tree of knowledge. God creates the woman to help him, the man does eat—and doesn't die. But immediately after eating, both woman and man become self-aware. Their first act, like God's, is creative: they sew the first set of human clothing. But their second is to withdraw from God's presence, overwhelmed and terrified by the consciousness of their insignificance and of God's power—even God's anger. God demands, *Ayekah?* "Where are you?" The man responds, "I heard your voice in the garden, and I was awestruck because I was naked and I hid myself" (Genesis 3:9–10).

But the man wasn't naked! He was clothed! He was naked only in the sense that he was self-aware and consciously separate—from the woman and from God. Eating and absorbing the fruit of knowledge had distinguished him as an individual. In that moment, he made the fateful choice not to lose himself in mystical union with God. He chose, instead, to remain fully human. *Yirah* before God is mixed with *pachad* at the twin possibility of death, on one hand, and losing one's bodily individuality through mystical union, on the other.

From the anthology of midrash *Yalkut Shimoni*, Isaiah 429:

> "If one sees a pot in his dreams, he should expect peace."
> What does a pot have to do with peace? Two of the most opposite things in this world are fire and water. They cannot exist together. The water will extinguish the fire, or the fire will evaporate the water. Yet if you put a pot between them they both can exist. The pot brings *shalom* between these two opposing substances. The pot symbolizes the ability to make *shalom*.

Shalom means "wholeness"; it enables separate items to function purposefully together. Like fire and water, our soul and God cannot blend; God's fire would absorb us. The body comes between us and God; the body is the pot that contains the soul. Our existential puzzle is that we are God's creation, so we seek oneness with God. Yet to be self-aware requires distance from God, a formal separation. God, too, is struck by the separation and is tempted to bemoan *Ayeka?* "Where are you? What happened?" Yet human separateness is part of the original divine plan to which God adheres in the end; it is God's sacrifice for us, much like a parent who must withdraw to allow her child to mature. Mortality requires that separation—the enclosing of our soul within the vessel of the body, separate from God. As long as we live, however much we seek to become one with God, we may not fully do so without the vessel disappearing, and our individuality disappearing with it. Only when life ends does the vessel crack and the soul slip away into God's embrace. How can we not feel *pachad* at the ever-present possibility of that inevitable time? *Un'taneh Tokef* evokes that *pachad*.

But the *pachad* is misplaced; there is really nothing to fear, since at death, the soul, which exists within the soul of God, returns, while the singular soul remains. Our true essence can never disappear. Entropy defines the ongoing deterioration of matter: the body is always dying. But Judaism upholds the eternality of the soul.

Perhaps this is why the imagery of the first paragraph of the prayer strips away bodily individuality: like sheep in a flock or, as some would have it, like soldiers in a regiment (line 10). God notices not each human body, but each soul. This is what matters to God. But however eternal the soul may be, we naturally fear for our lives, which we must lose before the soul returns to its source.

Distinctly human tasks can save us from that mortal fear—by reviving and revealing our spiritual light. *Un'taneh Tokef* proclaims, "And repentance, prayer, and charity help the hardship of the decree pass" (line 21). These do not *avert* the decree; they mitigate its harshness and evil. Why? Each stems from humility rather than insecurity. Each frees us from the burden of self-importance. No person can bear the full responsibility of ultimate control and power.

"Repentance, prayer, and charity": Centuries before this prayer was written, Simon the Just taught, "The world is sustained by three things: wisdom, humility, and compassionate deeds [*torah, avodah*, and *g'milut chasadim*]" (*Pirkei Avot* 1:2). We may want to do good deeds, but how do we know what is expected? Seek wisdom through Torah. But we will not pursue Torah meaningfully without humility, which teaches our place in the universe. True humility, then, leads to wisdom, which, in turn, leads to doing for others. And doing for others releases us from the *pachad* of fearing for ourselves.

All humans suffer. Yet pain is diminished when serving others. Putting our life into a larger context gives perspective and hope. Pain has no meaning, but life does.

Un'taneh tokef k'dushat hayom, "Let us give ourselves over to the power of this day's holiness." Judaism is the art of transforming the ordinary into the holy by acting for others, not for ourselves. We learn to paint from insecurity rather than from certainty, to reveal the beauty, the meaningful, the good, and the holy that emerge from our challenges, not our self-satisfaction, nor even the fear of losing our physical selves altogether. In a season of brutal honesty, *Un'taneh Tokef* does evoke fear, but in order to prescribe hope. That which wounds can also heal. By doing for others, the ordinary can become holy. We can live.

32

The Four Holinesses of *Un'taneh Tokef*

A HALAKHIC UNDERSTANDING

Rabbi Daniel Landes

Few prayers match *Un'taneh Tokef*'s power to overwhelm us. We enter the prayer reluctantly, knowing that it contains harsh judgments about the reality of our lives. We emerge drained but uplifted—and all this as we contemplate our mortality and accept God's judgment. The key to this amazing transformation is that *Un'taneh Tokef* ushers us into four experiences of *k'dushah*, "holiness." *K'dushah*—from the Hebrew root *k.d.sh.*—denotes the status of something being (or becoming) separate. Goods or produce *separated* out for *sanctified* Temple use are called *hekdesh*. There are negative instances too: a priestess serving idolatry who was separated off to be a designated temple prostitute was a *k'deshah*.

But usually, the root *k.d.sh.* is used positively. *K'dushah*, "set aside as holy," derives its power from the absolute separateness of a transcendent God, *hakadosh barukh hu*, "the Holy One, blessed is He." *Un'taneh Tokef* explores the meeting of limited man, tragically immanent, but seeking transcendence. We face the challenge of meeting God despite God's

---

Rabbi Daniel Landes is the director and *rosh hayeshivah* of the Pardes Institute of Jewish Studies in Jerusalem. Pardes brings together men and women of all backgrounds to study classical Jewish texts and contemporary Jewish issues in a rigorous, challenging, and open-minded environment. Rabbi Landes is also a contributor to the *My People's Prayer Book: Traditional Prayers, Modern Commentaries* series and *My People's Passover Haggadah: Traditional Texts, Modern Commentaries* (both Jewish Lights).

k'dushah, God's absolute otherness. Yet that meeting is possible, and through it, we gain a measure of God's transcendence in the form of a transcendent consciousness ourselves. That consciousness enables us to deal with the limitations inherent in our less-than-transcendent lives. *Un'taneh Tokef* provides a theological and spiritual analysis of this experience, and it does so by providing four instances of *k'dushah*, of "holiness": kiddush hashem, k'dushat hayom, k'dushat hashem, and k'dushat hachayim.

Kiddush Hashem: The Holiness of Martyrdom

The first *k'dushah* arises even as we rise to recite this poem, for we cannot do so without being aware of its powerful backdrop, the story of Rabbi Amnon, who accepts martyrdom over apostasy. He chooses *kiddush hashem*, "sanctifying God's name," through giving up his own life. Judaism does not easily acquiesce to this choice. Saving one's life is practically an absolute in Judaism. In order to save one's life, one not just *may*, but *must* violate any of the Torah's 613 commandments save for three: shedding innocent blood, adultery (including incest), and idolatry. "You shall keep my commandments," God says, "and live by them [*v'chai'i bahem*]" (Leviticus 18:5). Through a midrashically constructed codicil to that verse, the Talmud reasons, "[That means] you shall not die by them [*v'lo sheyamut bahem*]" (Sanhedrin 74a).

Why these three exceptions? I believe they are categorical exemplars of violations of basic relationships. We can do many things to violate the man-to-man covenant, but murder is an absolute shattering of it. Adultery, even between consenting partners, destroys the sanctity of the family. As for idolatry, it is true that from time to time we all bend our relationship to God, but idolatry denies the very covenant upon which the Jewish relationship with the divine is predicated.

We now understand Rabbi Amnon's choice of martyrdom. Since acceptance of the triune god is idolatry, it was his only option. By giving up his life, he fulfilled the dictates of the *Sh'ma's* demand to "love Adonai your God … with all your soul [life source; *b'khol nafsh'kha*]" (Deuteronomy 6:5), as the Rabbis say, "even if He takes your life [*afilu notel et nafsh'kha*]" (Berakhot 61b). And this martyrdom is commanded as a public act by Leviticus 22:32, "I shall be sanctified *in the midst of* the children of Israel [*v'nikdashti b'tokh b'nei yisrael*]." For delivering himself up to death, the martyr is known ever after as a *kadosh*, "a sanctified one."

We empathetically relive Rabbi Amnon's decision to embrace this form of *k'dushah*, recognizing that there are values more important than our mortal selves.

K'dushat Hayom: The Holiness of the Day

The second *k'dushah* is found in the third and fourth Hebrew words of the poem: *k'dushat hayom* ("the holiness of the day"; line 1), a term applied to Shabbat and holidays. The term is no mere honorific but has halakhic significance. Only the Sabbath and the biblical holidays are so designated. They are literally considered to be days apart and separate from the profane and mundane days of the week. Post-pentateuchal holidays such as Chanukah and Purim have their own significance and mitzvot, but they possess no holiness. Even the biblical Rosh Chodesh (New Moon), which has special sacrifices and is a time to go to the Tabernacle or Temple, has no *k'dushat hayom*.

Halakhically, the special holiness of Shabbat and holidays expresses itself both in the negative (e.g., the prohibition against performing creative work [*m'lakhah*]) and in the positive (e.g., the obligation to make them joyous, through festive meals). Rosh Hashanah and Yom Kippur too partake in this joy, even though we do not recite *Hallel* on either day; and on Yom Kippur, the Sabbath of all Sabbaths (*Shabbat shabbaton*), we do not eat or *physically* enjoy ourselves, engaging rather in "tenth-day rest" (*sh'vitat esor*), a complete cessation from such pleasures on the tenth of Tishrei, the day of Yom Kippur.

K'dushat Hashem: The Holiness of God

The *k'dushat hayom* of Rosh Hashanah and its magnified expression on Yom Kippur are particularly extraordinary opportunities to experience the holiness of God (*k'dushat hashem*). On Passover we encounter God as the redeemer who has liberated us from Egypt; on Shavuot we experience God as the revealer who has given us the gift of Torah; on Sukkot we encounter God as the sustainer who shelters us in our fragile dwellings under clouds of glory. On the Days of Awe, we confront God the judge, who cares about everything we have done.

And that's the rub. Why should God care so much and bother us so exceedingly? There is an absolute disjuncture between the lowly and immanent human being, on one hand, and the utterly transcendent Holy One (*Hakadosh*), on the other! Doesn't God's obsession with our lowly being somehow disrupt the notion of God's complete transcendence?

The Jewish view is that a God who moves from God's transcendent perch to be our redeemer, revealer, and sustainer also moves to a throne of mercy to be our judge, caring for the most important part of our being—our capacity to distinguish the moral act from the immoral violation. And indeed, God considers only the deeds that (as the *Un'taneh Tokef* puts it) have "our signature," our personal stamp, upon them. It is only from our perspective, of course, that God's judgment seems localized to a single day. Seen from above, there is no such thing as one day rather than another one, since the Separate One does not exist in time—rather, time exists within God. According to the Talmud,

> When the ministering angels gather before the Holy One and say, "Master of the universe, what day is Rosh Hashanah?" He replies, "Are you asking Me? Let Us, you and Me, ask the court on earth." Rabbi Hoshaiah taught: When an earthly court decrees, "Today is Rosh Hashanah," the Holy One tells the ministering angels, "Set up the judicial dais. Summon the advocates to defend and to prosecute. For my children have decreed that today is Rosh Hashanah." (Jerusalem Talmud, Rosh Hashanah 1:3)

So only from a human perspective (from below) do we summon God in all God's transcendence on this particular day to decide our fate. We cannot bear to be left to a cold, blind, and unresolved fate for the rest of our lives. Rather, we demand that our lives shall be morally resolved on the basis of the deeds that *we ourselves* have signed and sealed.

K'dushat Hachayim: Holiness of Life

This leads us to the fourth *k'dushah*, "the holiness of life" (*k'dushat hachayim*). This halakhic term was introduced in the midst of the Shoah to encourage Jews to find ways to survive. But it describes an attitude fully shared by Rabbi Amnon, who accepted, but did not seek, martyrdom. He has us declare, *T'shuvah ut'fillah utz'dakah ma'avirin et ro'a hag'zerah*—as our translation puts it, "Repentance, prayer, and charity help the hardship of the decree pass" (line 21). I prefer the more direct understanding. It is not just a case of "helping." Rather, "repentance, prayer, and charity avert the evil decree."

Some *machzorim* print three explanatory words over the Hebrew words *t'shuvah, t'fillah,* and *tz'dakah,* indicating the change in life that these acts are intended to accomplish. The decree is averted, as it were, because of what these words entail about our future actions—the actions themselves have the force of changing the decree. Over *t'fillah* ("prayer"), we find *kol* ("voice"); when we end our muteness and finally call out to God with our own voice, we are reborn. Over *tz'dakah* ("charity"), we find *mamon* ("money"); when we reach out to others to sustain them via the money that is ours, we change ourselves from being potential beggars to willing sustainers. Sustaining others is a primary divine quality. Psalm 136:25 says of God, "He feeds all life with bread" (*noten lechem l'khol basar*). One reason this is called "the Great *Hallel,*" says the Gemara, is that feeding others is such a supreme virtue. Finally, above *t'shuvah* ("repentance"), we find *tzom* ("fasting"); when we experience the fast as a resolve to utterly change life's direction, we cease being persons who are being judged. All of this is part of *k'dushat hachayim,* the way we sanctify our own lives. *K'dushat hachayim* offers us a chance to start life anew.

Rabbi Amnon's meditation carries us from his decision for *kiddush hashem* ("martyrdom") to the specific experience of *k'dushat hayom* ("holiness of the day," in this case, the Days of Awe). The holiness of these days allows us to summon God in all his *k'dushat hashem* ("holiness of God," which is to say "transcendence") as our judge. Before God as judge, we pledge to sanctify our lives in *k'dushat hachayim* ("holiness of life"). The experiences of *k'dushah* allow us to join God, as it were (*kiv'yakhol*), on a separate plane of transcendence and, from there, to judge and reflect upon the tragic limits of our immanence. Simultaneously, it pledges us to a renewal of life lived in holiness (*k'dushah*), our newly acquired transcendent consciousness. At that point we join with the angels—*darei malah im darei mattah,* "inhabitants above with inhabitants below" (line 39). Together, we joyously proclaim the utter transcendence of God, "Holy, holy, holy" (*Kadosh, kadosh, kadosh*), the very climactic line that *Un'taneh Tokef* anticipates. The *machzor* introduces it, in fact, with the promise *uv'khen l'kha ta'aleh k'dushah,* "And so, let holiness rise up to You." With that joint proclamation of God's holiness, ourselves alongside the angels, we experience transcendence that passes our understanding but provides meaning for life.

33

Trembling with Angels
THE POWER OF REHEARSAL

Liz Lerman

It is not surprising to me that people describe *Un'taneh Tokef* as both prayer and poem. Not surprising because, from my perspective as an artist, most of our prayer experience, especially when done communally, is a companion to the performance practice that makes up the work of my life. We have movements to learn, lines to recite, roles to play, and a host of synagogue-related behaviors that help us through the complexities of arrivals and departures, of fellowship and hardship. And like really great art, if we are very lucky, we have our problem passages that challenge us to some deeper level of thought and dialogue.

Sometimes these passages are difficult because of structure or form, sometimes because of concept or content. Sometimes their difficulties build up over time, until we wake up one day and wonder how we got through them so easily in the past. Sometimes we change our relationship to them because something has happened to a friend, colleague, family member, or ourselves that makes us see everything we do differently.

Un'taneh Tokef is one of those passages.

Liz Lerman is founding artistic director of the Liz Lerman Dance Exchange. A member of Temple Micah in Washington, D.C., she was the Sally Priesand Visiting Professor at Hebrew Union College–Jewish Institute of Religion. She is the recipient of the National Foundation for Jewish Culture Award in Performing Arts, the American Jewish Congress "Golda" award, and a MacArthur Fellowship. Her latest book is *Hiking the Horizontal.*

One of the great delights of being in the performing arts is the concept of rehearsal. By rehearsal I mean a period of time that is set aside for exploration, testing, learning, and repetitive practice. Rehearsals give us a place to make mistakes. I don't mean small little missteps that would be noticed only by an exceptionally trained colleague. I mean full-on experiments that take participants to the furthest edge of possibility, letting them explore unchartered space/time/ideas/spirit and still have the skills to turn away and come back. In fact, I wish we had a better word for "mistake," because the negative implications of the word make us shy away from errors, even though we learn most deeply by experiencing what does not work.

In rehearsal, making mistakes is the point. When everyone in the group agrees to commit fully, to notice and share experience, and to acknowledge problems without blame, ideas can be explored with conviction and with the thrill of risk. Over the years, what has made this really possible for me and the ensemble I work with is that we agree not only to participate fully in the action of our art, but to engage fully in what follows it. Reflection follows experience. We discover new ideas as part of our misgivings. Our highest standards compel us to notice, and then to attempt to improve or fix or implement changes, even as we experience sacrifice, personal realignments, and, often, loss.

I imagine the experience of prayer in just this way. I am rehearsing a set of ideas. I am practicing with my fullest participation something that other people have written and prepared for me. I allow myself to go into it with all my attention and knowledge, recognizing that I can step back, reflect, and rethink—and, in the spirit of the best rehearsals, report to myself what I have learned. Often that learning takes the shape of making changes in myself, in the material, or in the relationship of the parts to the whole.

Maybe with that last thought I have gone too far. Of course I know the language will be the same next year or next week or next day. But I have the distinct pleasure of seeing my relationship to the material in a fresh light, marking this day, this hour, this year as the unique occasion it is.

We are taught from our earliest days that our relationship to the divine comes, in part, from our people's covenant with God. And mostly, throughout my life, I have seen this as an awesome foreshadowing of contemporary notions of collaboration, a nonhierarchical and enlightened way of being in the world. I have always felt grateful and (actually) a little special because of it.

But I have on occasion wondered, Does this make everything a bargain? I do this for You, God, and then You do this for me? I promise to pray, or to act right in the world, or to send You praise, in exchange for your easing the severity of some decree—in this case the nature of my end.

Un'taneh Tokef brings me up short by its implication that this trading occurs in a vast moral arena, that we do good deeds to mitigate God's judgment. "Is it conceivable that we are engaged in one giant bribe?" I find myself musing. Perhaps this idea comes to the forefront because so much of this poem feels parental; despite our covenant, the power relationship here is unequal. When I consider our motivation for doing good, I would rather it be because it is the right thing to do or because it brings us pleasure, or knowledge, or just the good feelings that follow a hard day's work, not because it is a mechanism to convince God of our merit.

In order to confront this dilemma, I turn again to the idea of rehearsal. But now I look at it as a form of training—that part of rehearsals that is less about exploring new ideas and more about the learning that comes from practice and repetition. There is a certain glory in that tedium. The mind rests, or learns to rest, as other parts of our body take hold. Muscles and bone help us partner with those around us. We begin to perceive together the cues that will consistently lead us to the expected behavior we want. And that, in turn, will allow us to perform to our fullest, when the demands are increased by audience, by circumstance, by context, or by what is thrown at us in our daily living.

The dancer in me knows that repeating steps over and over leads to mastery. I don't mean a mastery that is rote technique. I mean a mastery that then allows the steps to be manipulated and altered to express so much more than the mere physical act itself, no matter how powerful that is. And by adding up the steps of our practice, we are able to take on the more difficult tasks that certainly await us.

Seeing *Un'taneh Tokef* this way, I imagine the acts of charity to which it alludes not as bargaining chips, but as the necessary practice steps for difficult pathways that lie ahead. Perhaps not in this year, but in the next, I will need this mastery. With this viewpoint in mind, I can reject the notion that God makes decisions based on my behavior and say, instead, that my behavior will help me handle what will inevitably come. Practice puts muscle and bone into the book of memories.

What would we discover if we fully rehearsed *Un'taneh Tokef*? I tremble like the angels as I contemplate the mere thought of it. First I would devise a series of improvisational structures. Try to imagine a set of agreed-upon rules that would allow us to experience the language fully with our minds, our bodies, our imaginations. We might enter them through personal stories that reflect the subject matter, through underlying physical action, or through small details drawn from our visions. We would, I am sure, find ourselves disturbed by the intensity of the images conjured up by what we experience. But rehearsal would prepare us differently to descend into the material and then to emerge from it and rejoin life again.

I suspect that one outcome would be a different degree of attention to *Un'taneh Tokef*'s list of horrible endings: fire, water, sword, beast, famine, and so on. Our bodies would tell us that people around the world find their ends in exactly these ways. And this realization might prompt a fierce new commitment to end the tortures for which we, at least, are responsible—not because it might be us next year, but because it could be anybody this year.

As we read the prayer, we are most likely thinking of ourselves and our loved ones. Prior rehearsal might connect us to the larger whole of all life everywhere. We might be motivated to rededicate ourselves to any number of actions for the coming year. Rehearsals make theory and practice, reflection and action absolutely next-door neighbors. We are praying with our bodies.

The artist lives for meaning. The postmodern artist lives for multiple meanings. She seeks the many levels of meaning from the same movement, word, or idea, arranging all of them side by side. The ensuing juxtaposition allows us to see beyond what we could ever imagine when viewing only one thing at a time.

What is true of "movements, words, and ideas" in general is true especially of an age-old text like the prayer/poem *Un'taneh Tokef*, which affords us a beautiful opportunity to muse about the meaning of death: the movement back from dust to dust, and the specificity by which we get there. The artist in me prepares to see the words for what they can tell me as I rehearse them, to hear the words for their rhythm and resonance, to re-create the words with new associations that allow me to experience the year I am leaving and to access what is to come.

Rehearsal does not deplete the language or the ideas of the prayer; it enlarges my capacity to sit with their potential—and with my own. Rehearsing the long list of catastrophic possibilities fills my body and my mind with their stark truths. Yes, I discover, I have experienced some of this already. Yes, I see, too, that I must prepare myself through my actions, my thoughts, my relationships, to confront it all with more intensity than before, for I will have to face it personally, no doubt, some day, in some way. But I am rehearsed and ready, whether to share in the fate of my friends, family, country … or to experience it as the individual artist that I am, making meaning out of endings that may well be my own. All I have to do, for now, is commit fully in the moment; I can reflect afterward. By rehearsing prayer and poetry, I rehearse my own life, by which I mean to bring my whole self to this confrontation with full purpose and with room to make mistakes.

34

The Eternal and the Ephemeral

THE STARK CONTRASTS OF UN'TANEH TOKEF

Rabbi Aaron Panken, PhD

Un'taneh Tokef was always that one prayer I simply could not get through as a congregational rabbi. Generally inured to sentimentality, I do not find myself breaking down at the drop of a hat. But this prayer: *this* was the one that was just too thick with meaning to be glossed over or "speed-*davened*" into oblivion. Year after year, my voice would crack, my eyes tear up, and in some years it was all I could do just to get through the parts I read aloud.

It was impossible to stand before all these families I knew and loved and avoid the deep, intimate sadness provoked by the demanding litany of "Who shall live and who shall die ..." (line 15) in all its many variations. It was all too much—knowing the family over here who lost an infant daughter that year, the young woman over there struggling to

---

Rabbi Aaron Panken, PhD, teaches Rabbinic and Second Temple literature and serves as vice president of Hebrew Union College–Jewish Institute of Religion.

survive what had been declared a "terminal" cancer, the dear friends in the back row coping with the deepening dementia of parents, and those many individuals in the sanctuary whose lives were constantly in the throes of human turmoil. To lead these words was to immerse and re-immerse oneself in the anguish enveloping so many of us that day and, inevitably, all of us—eventually. Leading *Un'taneh Tokef* meant giving explicit voice to it all and dipping a toe into the fear and trembling attendant with it.

Beyond the personal, why does this prayer evoke more emotion than almost any other? *Un'taneh Tokef* gives voice to a particular mythical understanding of the universe that feels all too real and easily penetrates all our modern-day armor against sentiment and our best attempts at scientific bravado. It prompts a sustained look in the direction of the most primitive and longstanding of human feelings: vulnerability and helplessness. And for Western, postmodern people, accustomed to advanced health care, a seemingly boundless entitlement to self-determination, and unparalleled access to resources, it hurts to confront these notions.

As Claude Levi-Strauss, the famed anthropologist, wrote, "The purpose of myth is to provide a logical model capable of overcoming a contradiction (an impossible achievement if, as it happens, the contradiction is real)."[1] It is, ultimately, the contradictions contained in this prayer that somehow reach beyond my regular, rational proclivities and tug at something more primal, more raw, and more emotional than what I consciously espouse.

The rhetorical style of the first three paragraphs and their particular choice of words are the true carriers of contradiction. As Levi-Strauss might have explained it, *Un'taneh Tokef* is ripe with "binary oppositions," polar opposites that convey symbolic meaning. Like the distinctions between pure and impure, male and female, or raw and cooked, the dichotomies of *Un'taneh Tokef*, too, are basic human ways of ordering our understanding of the world. A careful reading of the words with an eye toward these oppositions reveals the remarkable number of contrasting pairs, implied or explicit, within the text:

This day	Regular days
God's throne/judgment	God's love
Judge	Prosecutor/litigant
Witness	Author/sealer
Forgotten	Remembered/memories
Great shofar	Thin whisper of a sound
Angels	Humans
Shepherd	Sheep
Written	Sealed
Pass on	Created
Live	Die
At their end (the right time)	Not at their end (prematurely)
Fire	Water
Warfare	Wildfire
Hunger	Thirst
Earthquake	Plague
Strangling	Stoning
Rest	Wander
Tranquil	Troubled
Calm	Anxious
Exalted	Humbled
Rich	Poor
Ephemeral	Eternal

The contrasts do not always align perfectly into good/bad dichotomies (after all, hunger and thirst are both pretty undesirable), but the majority of the pairs do distinguish positive from negative. In all of Jewish liturgy, I am aware of no other prayer that paints from a palette of such stark contrasts, all of them firmly rooted in the human familiarity with pain. Everyone who recites these words, almost by definition, identifies as their subject through their own personal experience. We each fit into some of these categories, if not all of them, at least (thankfully) for now. But they are all alive in our imagination, ever-present and frighteningly possible in our own future.

This array of opposites points to a difficult core truth about human existence: we live in a constant and tense dialectic that is fully resolved only upon our death. Under the ever-present specter of dying, we somehow manage, nonetheless, to lead our daily lives. But those lives unravel with the ever-present possibility of sickness, death, pain, and a myriad of other tragic outcomes lurking just around the bend. We watch as these sad possibilities afflict our friends, our loved ones, and, eventually, us, and we can only hope to be spared as long as possible.

Yet it is not all doom and gloom. Surely hope, too, permeates *Un'taneh Tokef.* That hope is concentrated in two interesting pivot points that cast altogether different light upon the frightening contrasts. Pivot-point one comes in the fascinating line that begs for an adequate translation: *Ut'shuvah, ut'fillah, utz'dakah ma'avirin et ro'a hag'zerah.* The present volume renders it, "And repentance, prayer, and charity help the hardship of the decree pass" (line 21). Older translations provide one version or another of a very different message: "Repentance, prayer and charity cancel the stern decree," in the words of one prayer-book editor.[2]

Note the significant difference between these two translations. The older ones imply that our actions actually have the power to reverse the divine decree that heaps illness, tragedy, and death upon us. Theologically, this is a problematic statement for several reasons: it implies that tragedies come from God, who has a direct hand in all our day-to-day misfortunes; it contends that our actions affect God enough to render a divine decision alterable; and it fails the reality test of simple observation—when we look around and see the righteous suffer, we must wonder why their expansive *t'shuvah*, *t'fillah*, and *tz'dakah* did not absolve them of such punishment.

The translation in this volume captures the essence of the Hebrew statement far better, inserting just enough ambiguity to make this prayer more manageable in a contemporary context. Our actions, the *t'shuvah*, *t'fillah*, and *tz'dakah* that we do, help us live in such a way that when we must suffer life's darkest depredations, we will have ways of coping with them. Our actions do not change the ultimate outcome one iota, but they can alter our attitude, bolster our ability to withstand challenges, help us handle unavoidable misfortunes better, and see life's value amidst chaos and dismay. This represents a far more realistic understanding of the role of God in suffering and does not confuse (as Eugene Borowitz once eloquently put it) "the Senior partner with the junior," or the divine with the human.[3]

A second pivot point comes at the end of the prayer. A penultimate paragraph stresses our ephemeral nature by equating us with fragile objects like potsherds, breezes, and dust. But then, immediately after, the prayer concludes with a paean to the eternal God, who is everlasting and limitless. This contrast of God's transcendent power with our utter powerlessness, God's infinite eternity with our limited transience, leaves the reader with a final distinction that is, perhaps, the most poignant of all. Even if we were to feel highly significant the rest of the year, the High Holy Days' call to repent and return strips away our outer defenses and confronts us with God's piercing, towering, all-knowing judgment. We cannot help but recognize just how exposed, shaky, and unprotected we truly are. After all, no vanishing cloud or dream can ever hope to last as long as an eternal God, and we are just like them.

In the end, this represents a powerful motivator for immediate change. Even if we bury ourselves under layers of protection the rest of the year, *Un'taneh Tokef* proclaims the moment when our souls are bared and we must respond. The very ephemerality that is our weakness now becomes our strength, for we have the ability to be different in the next moment from the way we are now. Our hope rests in the fact that we can change. Further, *t'shuvah*, *t'fillah*, and *tz'dakah* link our transient selves with what is eternal—God and the kind of repaired world God compels us to create.

Therein lies the ultimate contrast in these two pivot points: by reaching out to an eternal and invulnerable God, we, who are temporary and vulnerable, can become a part of eternity; through our limited actions, we become limitless. Such is the beauty of the offering that comes in the words of this challenging prayer. In heeding them, we have the opportunity to exchange limitations and vulnerability for wholeness and confidence. In confronting our fears through *Un'taneh Tokef*—in the cracking of our voice and the tears that fill our eyes—we find hope.

> Their origin is from dust and their end is to dust:
> At their peril gathering food, they are like shattered
> pottery,
> Like withered grass....
> Your years are boundless and the length of your days is
> endless....
> You named us after You. (lines 27–29, 32, 35)

35

Theology or Anthropology?

Rabbi Sandy Eisenberg Sasso

I have always had an ambivalent relationship with *Un'taneh Tokef.* On the one hand, it speaks in opposition to everything I believe about God. On the other hand, when I hear it, my soul shivers. As the prayer is recited, the ark is opened and we stand. The cantor chants. The melody haunts. At one and the same time, I embrace the power of the liturgical drama and shudder at what the words appear to mean.

God stands in judgment, ready to pronounce sentence for the coming year on each and every individual. "Who will live and who will die?" (line 15). If these words are not enough to frighten us, the prayer details every possible torment—fire, flood, famine, earthquake, plague, suffocation. God decides that?

After cataloging all the lurid details of our possible demise, the prayer tells us that we can change the outcome: "Repentance, prayer, and charity can help the hardship of the decree pass" (line 21). The words are supposed to provide relief and motivate us to act more responsibly, more justly, more compassionately. We are asked to believe that how we behave will determine our fate in the coming year. Then even if death should

---

Rabbi Sandy Eisenberg Sasso is senior rabbi of Congregation Beth-El Zedeck in Indianapolis, where she has served since 1977. She is the author of award-winning children's books including *God's Paintbrush* and *Cain and Abel: Finding the Fruits of Peace* (both Jewish Lights). Her first book for adults is *God's Echo: Exploring Scripture with Midrash.*

come, if we've been good, generous, and faithful, it will be less painful, less severe. Not much of a reprieve, if you ask me.

How are we to affirm all this when our experience teaches us otherwise? Good people suffer. Kind people die in floods. Loving people succumb to illness. Faithful individuals perish in natural disasters. And the opposite is also true. The selfish and unfaithful, the cheaters and liars, the hard-hearted and closed-minded, the haters and the intolerant often prosper and go unpunished. The prayer is an affront to all the innocent children who perish needlessly in famine, to all the gracious and generous men and women who die far too young, and to all their families who wonder why and deserve something other than the response of *Un'taneh Tokef.*

Assuming that there must be a good reason for human suffering, that God is behind every natural disaster, is not only bad science; it is bad theology. The God in whom I believe does not send earthquakes and hurricanes or cause crops to fail and wells to run dry, bridges to collapse, and disease to run rampant. To suggest that there must be some redeeming rationale behind tragedy, to accept reality as a matter of divine fiat is not, I believe, an affirmation of faith, but blasphemy.

Is it not enough to confront the pain of death, the anguish of disease, the tragic accident, without having to add to the injury the insult that it was somehow our own fault? Is the physician's pronouncement that our medical condition is terminal accompanied by God's punitive judgment as well? Should we also have to add to our suffering the belief that it was what God wanted? When we need our faith to comfort us most, when we desperately yearn for acceptance, should we instead face divine rejection or a large cosmic *I told you so?*

Is our focus on the holiest days of the Jewish year to be on what God can do *to* us if we are bad and *for* us if we are good? Then Rosh Hashanah and Yom Kippur become a kind of bargaining game, a way of figuring out how to get a better deal from God. Maybe God will give us a break this year if we just give a little more *tz'dakah*, come to services a few more times, say we're sorry more often.

It is all so undemocratic. Our Supreme Court has nine judges. If our case came before them, at least we would have an astute lawyer arguing on our behalf. But here we each stand before God without a defense attorney. We pass before God as a helpless flock of sheep as God decides our end and writes it down. We don't even protest. The acquiescence, the fatalism, just doesn't seem very Jewish.

Where is the Jewish tradition of challenge? Where is Abraham's arguing for the lives of Sodom and Gomorrah, asking, "Shall not the judge of all the earth do justly?" (Genesis 18:25). Where is Job's chutzpah before the divine? Where is Rabbi Levi Yitzchak of Berdichev, who stands before God refusing to accept the suffering of the Jewish people, calling God to account? Where are the centuries of Jewish doubt, the tradition of Jewish questioning? There is an old Yiddish proverb that says, "If God lived in our neighborhood, people would break his windows." The God of *Un'taneh Tokef* appears to be that kind of God.

It is, I believe, this view of God that Yehuda Amichai, the well-known Israeli poet laureate of blessed memory, describes in his poem *The Jews*.[1] He imagines a divorce settlement between the people of Israel and God, who see each other only once a year, on Yom Kippur. The people who once sang the words of the Sabbath hymn *Ein Kelohenu*—"There is no God like ours"—now sing "There is no God of ours." But somehow, "we sing, we still sing."

We sing because our ancestors sang; they imprinted the melodies in our brains, impressed them on our hearts. We sing in spite of it all, in spite of the words, in spite of injustice, in spite of the doubt, in spite of what is written.

But what if we sang because of the words, because of what was written? What would it take for us to sing, in the words of Amichai, as we once did, "There is no God like ours"? For this we need to hear *Un'taneh Tokef*'s other voice.

If the God of *Un'taneh Tokef* is so untenable, so unintelligible, why do I feel ambivalent about the prayer's message? If, on the one hand, its God image is so disturbing, what is the other hand? I believe the part of the prayer that tugs at my soul is not its divine voice but its human one. More than a theological statement, *Un'taneh Tokef* is an anthropological affirmation.

We all feel the tenuousness of life, the uncertainty of the future, our mortality. We make plans, order our lives as carefully as possible, and fill up our calendars, but deep down we know that tomorrow remains a mystery. No matter how cautious we are, how meticulous about our health, how responsible about our investments, we are not in control of everything that happens to us. There are far too many painful surprises, unexpected consequences.

We often say that those things are *bashert*, "meant to be." They are not. Nothing happens the way it does because it was somehow predetermined before we were born or because some cosmic superpower ordained it. Some things happen because of human will and determination. Some things happen because of human neglect, greed, and hate. And some things happen by the chaos wrought by nature, by chance, without any reason. They aren't meant to be. They just are.

When the prayer says, "On Rosh Hashanah they will be written down, and on Yom Kippur they will be sealed: ... who will live and who will die, ... who will be tranquil and who will be troubled, ... who will be rich and who will be poor" (lines 14–20), we affirm not a theological statement but a human one. We don't know what will happen, and the prayer captures our uncertainty.

And then the prayer does something more. It tells us that some things can be changed—"*T'shuvah, t'fillah,* and *tz'dakah* help the hardship of the decree pass" (line 21). We can be kinder, more forgiving, more generous. We may not be able to make our lives longer, but we can make them better, less bitter, more loving. We may find ourselves facing unintended circumstances, confronting situations not of our making. Those circumstances aren't inherently meaningful, but we can make them meaningful; we can give them purpose. It is up to us to confer significance on time, to bring holiness into our lives.

What do I believe? I believe in acts of compassion and deeds of loving-kindness, and I call them godly. I've witnessed extraordinary courage in the face of tremendous trial, and I can't imagine whence it comes. I call that place "God." I've glimpsed people wrestle joy and laughter from the midst of difficulty, and I name that joy "holy." I've watched people struggle for right when everything conspires against it, and I call that impulse to righteousness "sacred." It is not that God is just, compassionate, and forgiving but that justice, compassion, and forgiveness are godly, and we are its agents and vessels. And I would venture to say that is what most Jews believe.

The Rabbis tell us that first the people of Israel must declare the day of Rosh Hashanah and only then does God ascend the throne of judgment. *We* sound the shofar; *we* announce the festival; *we* make the time holy. Without that, Rosh Hashanah is just another weekday.

At the end of the prayer, the tone changes. "[Our] origin is from dust and [our] end is to dust"(line 27). We gather food "at [our] peril" (line 28). Even as we are asked to face our mortality, to remember that we are "shattered pottery ... withered grass ... a faded blossom ... a passing shadow" (lines 28–29), we are reminded that we are connected to something eternal. We are part of a people and a faith that transcend time. "Your years are boundless," God; "the length of your days is endless" (line 32), but "You named us after You" (line 35). In other words, our name is linked to God's; we are part of something everlasting. What we do is not lost forever. The way we think, the way we see the world does not simply vanish when we do. It is carried on in the lives of others; it endures in holy community.

This is the *Un'taneh Tokef*'s "thin whisper of a sound" (line 7) that makes my soul shiver. It's why I sing; I still sing.

36

"How Awesome and Dreadful

God Is Enthroned and Rules with Love"

Rabbi Jonathan P. Slater, DMin

The most moving rendition of this prayer I ever heard was on Rosh Hashanah 2001. I was a stranger in a new community, having just moved to New York from California. The horror of the destruction of the World Trade Towers was fresh in everyone's minds, certainly my own, as I struggled to find my bearings in the confusion and uncertainty. I only vaguely understood that a member of the congregation was in the hospital, clinging to life, struggling to survive burns that covered his body and lungs. When the cantor came to *Un'taneh Tokef,* she could hardly sing. She choked and wavered as she came to the words "who will live and who will die"; tears filled her voice when she chanted "who by fire ... who by earthquake ... who by strangling" (lines 15–18). Everyone was stunned—not at her demeanor, but at the focus the words suddenly had been given, the reality of the questions, their immediacy.

Rabbi Jonathan P. Slater, DMin, was ordained at The Jewish Theological Seminary of America and has a doctor of ministry degree from the Pacific School of Religion. He is the author of *Mindful Jewish Living: Compassionate Practice* and codirector of programs at the Institute for Jewish Spirituality, as well as an instructor in meditation at the JCC in Manhattan and other venues.

I am sure not one congregant believed that anyone—those who died or those who survived—had been singled out by God on Rosh Hashanah (or on any other day) to die or suffer in this manner. The events of that September morning were the product of hate-filled, deluded minds and hearts. Hearing the prayer that day made it clear—to me at least—that it is not about judgment or decrees, but about life and love and responsibility. It is a prayer about God reaching out to us as much as we, then and now, confused, in pain, seek God.

What is it that makes Rosh Hashanah and Yom Kippur days of "awe and dread" (line 1)? I look to the second line, which I prefer to translate thus: "On it your kingdom will be raised up, and your throne will be made firm with love, so that You may rule from it in truth" (lines 2–3).

In the Jewish mystical tradition, the term "kingdom" (*malkhut*) is associated with the *Shekhinah*, God's presence in the world. Yet the *Shekhinah* is also that part of God that is in exile: alienated, cast down in pain, suffering with all Israel, yearning to be made whole. Thus, the *Shekhinah* is also known as *K'nesset Yisrael*, the Community of Israel, embracing all Jews (and ultimately all creation) in her being. To raise up God's kingdom, then, is to raise up the *Shekhinah*, to bring wholeness to God and to all creation, to ameliorate suffering and help all who are lost return from their personal exiles.

The elevation of the *Shekhinah* and the establishment of God's kingdom can only come about through love. When God is enthroned in love, God "reigns in truth." This truth forgets nothing: it includes all creation in its brief. It takes note of all beings as they are at this moment, surely acknowledging their past but focused on their present state. God counts, and accounts for, all beings on the basis of love. It is because we love—our fellows, the stranger, God—that God then turns to and rules the world in truth. Truth, then, is also raised up and established by us, with love.

I am reminded of this midrash (*Genesis Rabbah* 8:5) about the creation of human beings:

> Rabbi Shimon said: When the blessed Holy One came to create the first human being, the ministering angels formed themselves into groups and parties. Some of them say, "Let them be created," while others say, "Let them not be created." This is as it is written, "Love and Truth fought

together, Righteousness and Peace combated each other"
(Psalm 85:11): Love says, "Let them be created, because
they will do acts of loving-kindness"; Truth says, "Let them
not be created, because they are nothing but falsehood";
Righteousness says, "Let them be created, because they will
perform righteous deeds"; Peace says, "Let them not be
created, because they are full of strife." What did the Holy
One do? God took Truth and cast it to the ground. The
ministering angels said before the Holy One: "Sovereign of
the universe! Why do You so humiliate your Seal? Raise
Truth from the earth!"

Love and righteousness are the qualities that justify human existence;
falsehood and strife disqualify. While correct in arguing the human
propensity to falsehood, Truth is nevertheless cast to the earth. The ministering angels decry this derogation of God's primary quality. They
would have truth raised up again, set in its "rightful" place, even if this
would prevent the creation of human beings. But God knows better:

Rav Huna the Elder of Sepphoris, said: While the ministering angels were arguing and disputing with each other,
the blessed Holy One created human beings. God said to
them, "Why are you still arguing? Humans have already
been made!"

Human beings could only be created when truth was removed from the
divine realm to the human. Truth can only be redeemed, raised up, when
we human beings enact love. To do so, however, we must acknowledge
the truth of our own inner struggles, our propensity to confusion, con-
tention, and unhappiness. Facing that truth directly, without flinching or
turning away, we learn that the root of our struggle is our fear of death, of
meaninglessness. Yet mortality—loss and the end of life—is a fundamental truth of human existence. Nevertheless, we can, with wisdom, respond
with love for ourselves and for all other beings who suffer and struggle
just as we do. It is through love, true love, that we are able to raise up the
Shekhinah and truth, so that God might rule in truth, so that the world
might run in its truest form.

"Truly You are judge" (line 3)—this next phrase in our prayer is
paralleled later: "Truly you are their creator and You know their nature"

(line 25). We are to read these two passages together. Judgment here does not mean the outcome of a trial, an assessment of our worthiness. Rather, God has a constant concern for us, for our well-being. As ruler of the universe, the life force in all things, that which sustains all existence, God is constantly caring for us. God is our judge because God created us and is constantly involved in our lives. As such, judgment is constant, experienced in the unfolding of all life, in the constant, shifting allocation of life through nature and through human communities. The point of judgment is not punishment or chastisement, but more life.

We are creatures of the creator, merely "flesh and blood" (line 26). Our origin is from dust and our end is to the dust. The issue before God at this moment—in any moment—is not that we are sinful, but that we are merely mortal, fallible. Our hold on life is tenuous: it so easily passes away, "like blowing wind and like sprouting dust and like a dream that will fly away" (line 30). That God is "everlasting" (line 31) makes our lives possible. We realize that what we do matters to God, so much so that God remembers "everything that has been forgotten" (line 5)—even the good we have done. We are so important that God has "named us after [God's] name" (line 35). Indeed, this very relationship of interconnection and interdependence is key to what happens next in our prayer. We join the heavenly chorus to do that for which we are called into being: to sanctify God's name through word and deed, bringing holiness into the world, thereby raising up God's kingdom.

Reciting the *K'dushah*, however, is the product of awareness, and proper awareness is difficult. There are too many distractions. We get so caught up in what we have to do, what we want to do, what others expect of us. We lose track of where we are going. We put off what is really important and do, instead, what just *seems* urgent and immediate, yet is actually passing. Then, something interrupts the taken-for-grantedness of life's flow. We get sick, or a loved one does; we suffer a loss in business, or we know someone who does; we discover we are in exile from our families, our friends, our own hearts; we notice that we are unable to sit still in our lives, that we are dissatisfied, unhappy, confused. Or we come to synagogue and are confronted with this truth: aging, loss, sickness, dissatisfaction, unhappiness, confusion—these are happening all the time, everywhere, to someone right now and, eventually, to us. Hence the middle section of the prayer, a consideration of "who will live and who will die, ... who by fire and who by water, who by warfare and who by wildlife, who by hunger and who by thirst" (lines 15–17). This is not God's check-off list; it is the outpouring of our awareness, arising when we finally sit still long enough to pay attention to the most fundamental truth: people all around us are living and dying in all of these different ways. They are all suffering and rejoicing, finding and losing, winning and failing—always, everywhere, every day.

On Rosh Hashanah we notice; on Yom Kippur we really pay attention. On this day God sits on God's throne in truth—and we confront the truth fully. We remember that we are created in love, for love. It is through love and righteousness that God's *Shekhinah* is raised up, that wholeness is created in the world. We must not deny the truth of living and dying; there is no end, in this world, of suffering. But true love impels us to seek its end, whereby we might at least "help the hardship of the decree pass" (line 21). We sanctify God's name through repentance, prayer, and charity: acknowledging the truth to reorient our lives, speaking the truth without fear to connect with love, so that we might more freely enact love and righteousness in truth.

37

God's Hands

Rabbi Brent Chaim Spodek
and Ruth Messinger

For most American Jews, the three-letter word G-O-D inevitably conjures images of a bearded king on a throne, high up in the heavens,
perhaps with the voice of James Earl Jones booming out over the mountains. For some, this is a comforting image of a benign ruler, managing
and guiding the world in its particulars and apportioning just deserts to
the wicked and the righteous. Others recoil at the distance of the image,
finding the idea of a monarch too alienating to inform their religious lives.

Be it attractive or repulsive, for Jews who come to synagogue on the
High Holy Days, the sense that the divine is a judging God is only
heightened by the refrain that these few days *are* the days of judgment,
into which we come as peons into the hall of the mighty, judging king to
await our fate for the coming year. *Un'taneh Tokef,* arguably the definitive
poem of the period, begins by describing in some detail how God the
king is exalted on this terrible and holy day of judgment while He reigns
from his throne in truth. He alone is the judge, prosecutor, and witness
who records our deeds in a tremendous book and then renders judgment
for the coming year. The poem cultivates a frame of mind in which we
hope God judges us favorably, but if our deeds do not merit our continued existence, then, "repentance, prayer, and charity" (line 21)—we prefer the word "giving"—may remove the severity of the decree. The poem
invites us to throw ourselves at the mercy of the court.

Rabbi Brent Chaim Spodek is the rabbi in residence of American Jewish
World Service. Ruth Messinger is the president of American Jewish World
Service.

The challenge, of course, is believing that there is a master who metes out rewards to the righteous and punishments to the wicked and that this master can be placated with repentance, prayer, and giving. This Judaism of reward and punishment is the Judaism that Kohelet (Ecclesiastes), Spinoza, and close observers of humanity ever after have derided as simply false.[1] After all, if there is a master of reward and punishment, then wealthy dictators such as Robert Mugabe of Zimbabwe must be not just privileged or lucky, but very, very righteous, while the one billion humans who are suffering malnutrition, many of them dying for lack of food,[2] are not simply unlucky or victims, but very, very wicked. At some level, we take comfort in the idea of a moral system with laws as immutable as those of physics—we want to believe that the wicked are punished as surely as an apple falls from a tree—but experience tells us that isn't so.

The intellectual move of ascribing to humans ultimate responsibility for their fate, be it good or bad, allows us to preserve the image of the powerful judging God by shifting blame for misfortune to the unfortunate: if you suffer, it must be because *you* did something wrong. As Rabbi Ovadia Yosef, the former Sephardi chief rabbi of Israel put it, "The six million Holocaust victims were reincarnations of the souls of sinners, people who transgressed and did all sorts of things that should not be done. They had been reincarnated in order to atone."[3] In other words, given the fullness of time, we are all compensated for our deeds, with the righteous flourishing and the wicked being cut down by fire, water, sword, and beast. By this logic, six million Jews were murdered in the Shoah and one billion people still die of starvation in the world—as punishment for their sins. We who eat plentifully are simply being rewarded for our righteousness.

This thinking, which seems to be at the core of *Un'taneh Tokef,* is the theology of a child—"Oh God, I'll do what you say as long as you don't spank me." Worse still, it is a flight from responsible agency. It willfully ignores the acts that humans could have taken, *should* have taken, to change our fate. In the face of suffering, we should not pray for God to save the righteous—we should act ourselves. The Torah itself makes this point powerfully in telling of the Israelites' escape from Egypt. With Pharaoh's army fast on their heels and the Red Sea directly in front of them, Moses shouts, "Stand by, and witness the deliverance which Adonai will work for you today.... Adonai will battle for you!" Moses's calls for patience until the moment of Divine intervention are interrupted with a sharp rebuke from on high, "Why do you cry out to *Me*?" God says. "*You* tell the Israelites to go forward!'" (Exodus 14:13–15). When Moses needed to change some aspect of the physical world, even the Holy One knew that prayer is not the way to make that happen.

Prayer cannot change the reality of suffering, although it can ameliorate the pain of suffering. This is the claim that *Un'taneh Tokef* makes with its haunting refrain that defies any easy translation. *Ut'shuvah, ut'fillah, utz'dakah ma'avirin et ro'a hag'zerah*: "Repentance, prayer, and charity" do something, but what? The verb *ma'avirin* is usually understood to mean "cancel," as if repenting, praying, and giving can annul a negative decree. But as Rabbi Lawrence Kushner points out, it really means "to cross over."[4] It's the word that's used to describe Jacob crossing the Yabok River before wrestling with the angel (Genesis 32:23). Repentance, prayer and donating do not change the facts of life—our disbursement of blessings and curses will continue to bear little relation to our moral virtue, whether or not we pray, repent, or donate. But a heart habitually opened by repentance, prayer, and donating will cross through life's inescapable misfortunes somewhat more gently. Our road will still be bumpy, but we'll have better shock absorbers.

However, if God is not emending our fates based on the sincerity of our prayers, our repentance, or our donations, then what is God doing? Does God simply sit on the throne of judgment, aloof and indifferent to our prayers while rewarding Robert Mugabe and punishing the world's bottom billion? To understand *Un'taneh Tokef* as describing the role of prayer in making it easier to cope with inevitable human suffering might answer one question—what are we doing when we pray? However, it begs another, possibly weightier question—what is *God* doing when we pray?

For an especially powerful understanding of what God does—not just when we pray, but always—we turn to Rabbi Levi Yitzchak of Berdichev, one of the most important of the early Hasidic masters. In an audacious interpretation of the verse *Adonai tzilkha*, "God is your protection" (Psalm 121:5), Levi Yitzchak makes it painfully clear that the power to dole out justice and mercy, to bring joy into the world, and to save the innocent does not rest in Divine hands, far away from us.[5] Astoundingly, he reads *tzilkha* literally, as "your shadow," so that the words mean "God is your shadow." Just as the shadow of a person does whatever that person does, so, too, does the divine do what we do. Divinity is the shadow of human action. If we save a human life, so too does God; if we decide to end a human life, God does also. At some level, the utterly transcendent divinity is right at hand, for the divinity we hope to worship is a shadow of ourselves, our best parts and our worst. If you want to see God save the innocent, *you* need to get off the couch and save the innocent. If you want to see God feed the hungry, *you* need to feed the hungry. If you want to see God stand by while the innocent suffer, all you need to do is stand by and do nothing *yourself.*

With the acknowledgment that we are God's hands and feet on earth, the accusing question of the skeptic—how can *God* stand by when children are killed in Auschwitz, Guatemala, and Darfur?—is turned back with a penetrating fury. The question becomes, how can *we* stand by when children are killed in Auschwitz, Guatemala, and Darfur?

For Levi Yitzchak, the presence of God isn't revealed in a supernal visage of the divine hand reaching down from a sky with thunder bolts and lightning rods. God's hands are the hands of humanity, and God's face the face of us all. The divinity we seek and fear lurks in the countenance of every human being, including our own, and revelation is the moment when we recognize that the flesh and bone of humanity are traces of the divine. We pray to see God's face, but the face has already been revealed, set atop every human body, and we are better served to pray for the ability to see it.

So what then do we do on Rosh Hashanah when the cantor first intones *Un'taneh Tokef*? What do we do if we cannot join our medieval ancestors in hoping that God will requite us all according to our merits? On the day of Rosh Hashanah, we pray that because of our practices of repentance, prayer, and donating, we have the resources to cross over our own pain and suffering as gently as possible. But things do not stop there. On the very first day *after* Rosh Hashanah, we pray with our hands and our feet that all who suffer will have the resources they need—provided by the divine through our actions.

38

The Call to Turn Inward

Rabbi David A. Teutsch, PhD

Why do Jews return to the synagogue in such large throngs on the *Yamim Nora'im*? Is it a homing instinct akin to that of pigeons or of the swallows to Capistrano? Of course custom, memory, and the changing of seasons all play a role, but the relatively small attendance during Sukkot suggests there is more to it than that. In the turning of the year from the languor of summer to the busyness of fall, there is more in the air than the start of a new school term. It is a shift in the balance of things. One of the images of the *Yamim Nora'im* is *moznayim*, the balancing scales that are also a symbol of Libra, the astronomical sign for this time of year. The onset of cooler weather and of falling leaves marks the end of the growing season and the shift toward winter. That shift inevitably contains intimations of mortality. We are somehow aware of our human fragility in the face of the shortening days, and in some primordial, inchoate, largely unselfconscious way, we turn to the synagogue—a sacred space for this "tribal" gathering—for reassurance about the year ahead.

The relative security of modern life is reflected in the existence of heating and air-conditioning, supermarkets stocked year-round with fruit

Rabbi David A. Teutsch, PhD, is the Wiener Professor of Contemporary Jewish Civilization and director of the Center for Jewish Ethics at the Reconstructionist Rabbinical College, where he served as president for nearly a decade. He was editor-in-chief of the seven-volume *Kol Haneshamah* prayer book series. He is the author of *Spiritual Community: The Power to Restore Hope, Commitment and Joy* (Jewish Lights).

and vegetables, indoor plumbing, and regular garbage pickups. But there are transitional moments when we peer through the cracks in the security of our routine and glimpse its limitations. It is precisely such a moment that brings us to worship on the *Yamim Nora'im.* As we sit and stand together with our fellow worshipers, we search the *machzor* for guidance about how to deal with these glimpses of our finitude and how to deal with our hopes and fears about the year ahead. Those hopes and fears can bubble up best when we gather with our community to experience sacred time in sacred space.

From this perspective, it is easy to understand why *Un'taneh Tokef* is emotionally central to the High Holy Day experience. It begins by invoking the holiness and solemnity of the day. When the existential cracks open up, we peer anxiously through them to glimpse the under-lying whole beyond all the separate people and activities in our lives. We sense the deep unity that is usually obscured in the myriad details. At such liminal times as Rosh Hashanah and Yom Kippur—times, that is, when we are betwixt and between one year and the next—we espe-cially sense the brevity of our lives compared with eternity. It is then that we speak theologically about God and holiness and dominion. On a deeper level than our words explain, we simply feel the presence of the Holy One.

We feel the presence of judgment also. That is so for me even though I do not believe that God watches what I do or metes out individ-ual reward and punishment. Theology takes a backseat to the moment. All that we have been and done is measured now, not by everyday stan-dards but against our sense of ultimacy. The chapter that each of us has written in the book of our years confronts us. This is potentially a revela-tory moment for the collectivity of the community of *k'lal yisrael,* the Jewish people whose members together hear the sound of the shofar, and for each naked individual soul that encounters the still, small Voice or "a thin whisper of a sound" (line 7). As I tremble in this fearsome moment, it feels as if heaven and earth are trembling as well—the angels shake as they proclaim the day. This truly is the day of judgment, for out of the liminal moment, the Voice whispers its demands.

In our everyday lives, we live with an illusion of control. We guard our health by eating well, exercising, and getting regular checkups. We get ahead professionally by working hard and building effective relationships. At the liturgical moment of *Un'taneh Tokef,* we are forced to admit how profoundly our lives can be altered by random occurrences over which we have no control. A brain hemorrhage or heart attack can come out of nowhere. A drunk driver can cripple or kill. A parent can have to bury a child. An organization's sudden economic reversals can unexpectedly result in layoffs or firings. A healthy pregnancy can end with a stillbirth. A competent person can be unable to find work. A trusted marriage can collapse. In my heart of hearts I know that I have as little control as any other sheep in the flock. At the moment of *Un'taneh Tokef,* I know for a certainty that my life hangs in the balance. When these High Holy Days end, I may be lulled back into my false sense of security, the cocoon of my routine. But today I feel my exposure, sense the danger inherent in life, re-encounter my mortality. My end is dust.

But part of the future is in my control. Will I allow envy, jealousy, and enmity to occupy my days, or will I grow in maturity and self-reflection? Will I persist in egotism and grandiosity, or will I find my way toward humility and gratitude? Will I be totally possessed by my desire to get ahead, or will I remember to look out for others and act caringly? Will I learn to be happy with my lot, or will nothing truly satisfy me?

T'shuvah, t'fillah, and *tz'dakah* will mitigate the bad in the decree (line 21). I cannot control the unexpected blows that will affect my family, my job, my health. But I can control how I live with them. *T'shuvah* means returning to awareness of the One and walking the path of Torah. *T'fillah* ("prayer") can cultivate gratitude, innerness, connection to transcendent values, and spiritual depth. *Tz'dakah* is not just about giving significant amounts to charity and, thereby, cultivating personal generosity; it is also about making the pursuit of *tzedek* ("justice") a central part of life. When we concern ourselves with feeding the hungry, healing the sick, and seeking peace, the ripples of goodness move both inward and outward. *T'shuvah, t'fillah* and *tz'dakah* will not stop stock-market crashes, lung cancer, or the other blows that come our way, but they can radically transform how we are affected by those blows.

Developing our commitment to making a difference in the world, to deepening our connection to the divine, and to living harmoniously softens the blows by giving us critically important perspective about what matters most. It is true that our origin is dust and our end is dust, but there is redeeming power in the Eternal One. Our lives are lifted by our connection to the divine. We become holy by linking ourselves to the Holy One.

Each year we cycle back to this place, but the spiral of our lives means that we are different when we return. This is our opportunity to set a course that can help us be uplifted by the spiral, that can ease the return and help us look to the future with greater equanimity.

Un'taneh Tokef is not about bribing God with our repentance, nor is it about magic. It is about facing mortality and seeking the redemptive power of God's presence through lives of spiritual seriousness and moral goodness. We are capable of submitting our lives to judgment, but judgment should not be understood as an alien and arbitrary force; rather, it is the process of personal insight and inner renewal that initiates redemption of ourselves and of our world. There is reciprocity here. God calls on us, and we call on God. Our partnership puts a human face on the divine as we proclaim the awe-filled holiness of this moment.

39

Shattered Pottery— Unshattered Hope

Rabbi Gordon Tucker, PhD

The latter part of *Un'taneh Tokef* presents a series of eight similes for human life, all of them apparently "downers" in that they seem to describe the finitude, fragility, and transience of our presence on this earth: "[Human beings] are like shattered pottery, like withered grass and like a faded blossom, like a passing shadow and like a vanishing cloud ... like blowing wind and like sprouting dust and like a dream that will fly away" (lines 28–30). This part of the prayer reads as a relentlessly dark sequence of thoughts on our impermanence, and thus perhaps—one might be forgiven for sensing—on our ultimate unimportance. One might even understand this as a brutal contrast to the God whose eternality and holiness we are about to celebrate in the *K'dushah*.

A closer and more careful reading of the similes, however, reveals something far more profound. For there is an inconspicuous but crucial difference between the first of these eight images and the other seven. Let's look at the provenance of the seven that conclude the list: "withered grass," "a faded blossom," and "blowing wind" are all taken from the same biblical text—chapter 40 of the book of Isaiah. Biblical, too, are the images of "a passing shadow," "a vanishing cloud," "sprouting dust," and "a dream that will fly away" (Psalm 144:4, Job 7:9, Isaiah 5:24, and Job 20:8, respectively).

Rabbi Gordon Tucker, PhD, is senior rabbi at Temple Israel Center in White Plains, New York, and adjunct assistant professor of Jewish philosophy at The Jewish Theological Seminary of America. He is the editor and translator of *Heavenly Torah: As Refracted Through the Generations*.

It is, of course, no surprise to find a virtuoso of a liturgical poet drawing on the rich literary lode of the *Tanakh* in order to craft an evocative prayer or meditation. Isaiah, Psalms, and Job, especially, turn up repeatedly in our liturgical poetry; they repay the poets' attentions handsomely with strong and haunting images like the ones we find here. And here is an especially salient point: the poet has been true to the original context in all seven of these cases, since these phrases are metaphorical not only in our prayer, but also—and in essentially the same way, a description of human life—in the original biblical context.

But the very first item on our list, "shattered pottery" (*cheres hanishbar*), stands out. If, as seems likely and natural, the author mined the *Tanakh* for this image, then it is clear where he found it. There is only one place in the whole Bible where the word for pottery (*cheres*) is coupled with the Hebrew root for shattering (*sh.b.r.*): Leviticus 6:21, "An earthen vessel in which it [the flesh of a *chatat*—a sin offering] was boiled shall be broken." This is no metaphor. It is, rather, a very concrete prescription for how a vessel made from earth is to be treated should it become unfit for normal human use (in this case, by having been used for sacred things). What could this context possibly have to do with what the poet is trying to express at the end of *Un'taneh Tokef*?

Like other legal material in the Torah, the treatment of the problematic earthen vessel was augmented by Rabbinic tradition. According to Rabbinic interpretation, vessels of any kind can become unfit for use not only because of contact with the most holy, but also because of contact with impurity. And thus arises the question of how impure, contaminated vessels are to be made pure and usable again. Metal vessels have their own method of purification, as do wooden and glass vessels. What about earthenware? Drawing on our text in Leviticus, Rabbinic literature ruled that earthen vessels could be purified by being *broken*. In fact, both the Mishnah (Kelim 2:1) and the Tosefta (Kelim [Bava Kamma] 7:14) rule that for earthenware, brokenness is the *only* possible method of purification. This was meant quite literally—it was not just a rhetorical way to say that such pottery was now forever useless and should be broken and *discarded*. The Mishnah explicitly advocates reassembling and refusing the shards of the once impure, contaminated utensil as a means of rendering it, from that point on, pure and usable again.

Now the author of our prayer surely knew his *Tanakh* and his Mishnah. He knew full well that the very first thing we come across in the

Torah as made from the earth is the human being. We are, in other words, the primary earthen vessels in God's world. The very first simile in his list, therefore, suggests a theological truth that is as far as anything could be from a declaration of human helplessness before forces beyond our control. The deep truth embedded in the image of the broken earthenware is that hope and affirmation grow, paradoxically, out of fracture. We humans are made from the dust of the earth, it is true, and because of that, we readily take in and absorb into ourselves all sorts of impurities: values that distort us and drive out values that sustain us, addictions to the impermanent things of this world, and neglect of our souls and our sacred relationships. But because our hearts have the capacity to break when we acknowledge our existential errors, we have hope. When our hearts in fact break within us with remorse, the earthenware becomes pure again and can be re-fused into a pure and worthy vessel. It may be futile to try to control or even to resist the withering of all physical freshness with time's passing, or the evaporation of the cloud's water with the sun's shining, or the passing of the shadow with the sun's setting. But it is never futile to attend to the renewal and purification of the shards of our earthen lives.

I suspect that in placing the image of the broken earthenware at the head of the list, the author of our poem also had at least two other passages in mind: first, Psalm 51:19, which proclaims, "True sacrifice to God is a broken spirit"; and second, a beautiful midrash that appears in the fifth-century compilation of homilies known as *Pesikta D'rav Kahana* (in the section for Shabbat Shuvah): "Rabbi Alexandri said: A typical person fulfilling a task would consider it an embarrassment to have to make use of a broken implement. But the Holy One is not like that. God's work is always done with broken implements." Or—we might say—God's *very best work* is done with broken tools.

Whatever the full range of our poet's sources was, the "bottom line" of *Un'taneh Tokef* is an assurance to us of our ability to reconstruct ourselves precisely when our hearts, our cores, are broken. As such, it is an affirmation of the power of the human spirit to renew itself. It is placed liturgically precisely before we say *kadosh, kadosh, kadosh* ("holy, holy, holy"), the very moment that we prepare to reaffirm the sanctity of the God who first blew the breath of human life into clods of ordinary earth—and made us who we are.

40

Everything Has Consequences

Dr. Ellen M. Umansky

"Let us acknowledge the power of this day's holiness" (line 1): Rosh Hashanah and Yom Kippur are set apart as days of judgment, announced by blasts of the shofar that are supposed to shake us to our very core. *Un'taneh Tokef* is a frightening prayer, conjuring up images of people burned alive, drowned, strangled, stoned or stabbed to death, eaten or torn apart by wild animals, buried by an earthquake, or fatally stricken by a plague—not to mention ordinary death from thirst or hunger.

According to this prayer, such will be God's judgment against those who have sinned and not repented. It isn't that bad things simply happen to people, deservedly or not. Such occurrences are the just punishments of a just God, proper recompense for one's past actions. We are accountable for ourselves: for who we've been, who we are, and who we will become. Certain things, however (repentance, prayer, and charity, according to the poem), can have an impact on the decree.

There are several ways to understand the Hebrew that defines that impact: *ma'avirin et ro'a hag'zerah* (line 21). Do the recommended actions actually avert the decree or, at least, lessen its severity? Or, as the translation here suggests ("help the hardship of the decree pass"), do

Dr. Ellen M. Umansky is the Carl and Dorothy Bennett Professor of Judaic Studies at Fairfield University in Fairfield, Connecticut. She is currently working on a book focusing on Judaism, liberalism, feminism, and God.

they, perhaps, just help us better understand or endure it? However we interpret these words, *Un'taneh Tokef* maintains that our destiny is not a matter of chance. It is the will of God, who, from Rosh Hashanah to Yom Kippur, stands in judgment of our actions, deciding who will live and who will die.

Some contemporary reconstructions of this prayer attempt to take these death threats less literally. They emphasize the fact that in the very nature of the universe, everything has consequences; sin too must have its necessary outcome, some form or other of spiritual or physical punishment. Inner reflection, or prayer, helps us to understand how difficult, if not impossible, it is to be at peace with one's self if we have hardened our hearts to those who've wronged us and asked our forgiveness or if we refuse to seek others' forgiveness for wrongs that we have done to them. Anger and hate eat away at us. These feelings don't just agitate us; they can make us physically ill. Perhaps we've arrogantly claimed that we have no need of anything or anyone other than ourselves—no supernatural being, no natural power, and no human help either. Denying all weakness and fragility, convinced that we're invincible, we spend more time building a fortune than we do building a relationship and find no reason to fast on Yom Kippur, bow our heads, or prostrate ourselves in prayer.

Yet, as the proverb insightfully maintains, "Pride goes before ruin, and arrogance before failure" (Proverbs 16:18). We need only pick up a newspaper or listen to the evening news to understand the truth of this claim. As author Tom Wolfe so memorably reminds us in his novel *Bonfire of the Vanities*, we are not "Masters of the Universe." Greed, corruption, and murder come with a price. Acts of *tz'dakah* cannot make up for investing someone's life savings in a Ponzi scheme or selling a kidney to the highest bidder, but they can, if done with regularity and sincerity, lead to self-transformation.

There are two major images of God in *Un'taneh Tokef* that, in my view, cannot easily be reconciled. The first is an all-seeing, all-knowing, and all-powerful God—a prosecutor, witness, and judge who resides above us, remembering our deeds and recording them each year. Those who are truly repentant will live (and be sealed in the "book of life"), while those who refuse to repent and change will die a painful, premature death. The second imagines God as a shepherd who seeks out his flock and, having found them, makes them pass under his staff. He, too, is a judge who decides the destiny of each sheep. Yet, presumably, none will be drowned, stoned, deliberately starved to death, or permanently denied water. It is left to our imagination how the shepherd will cut short the lives of some of the flock. When the shepherd does this, however, he will not be invisible to them. The sheep will see him, *panim el panim*, "face to face," and because the shepherd knows this, I imagine that he (or she, as I sometimes envision her) will try to bring as little pain to the sheep as possible. This is a God of compassion and mercy. We all are judged and sometimes found wanting. Yet God can exercise his/her power without frightening us to death. One can approach God with awe but, despite the double meaning of the Hebrew, should not feel terror.

I once questioned the image of God as shepherd, finding it to be both personally irrelevant and theologically troubling. Having spent my life in an urban or suburban setting, I found it difficult to make a personal connection to the pastoral images of shepherd and sheep (much as I find it difficult connecting to God as either lord or king). Still, realizing that one cannot always find relevance in prayers written hundreds if not thousands of years ago, I remained willing to recite some that lacked personal meaning. I was not, however, willing to say, or chant, those that actually led me *away* from a possible divine encounter. I found the passivity of the sheep, that is, those who silently follow the shepherd wherever he/she leads them, to be antithetical to my own understanding of the covenantal nature of the human/divine encounter. Indeed, I *still* find it difficult to recite psalms and other liturgical prayers that conjure up images of silent, dutiful lambs. Years of travel have made this image less foreign to me, but not less troublesome as a metaphor for God.

In the *Un'taneh Tokef*, however, this pastoral image takes on a new dimension. Here, the shepherd actively searches out the sheep and, finding them, has them pass under his/her staff one by one, judging each of them individually. If we carry the metaphor to its logical conclusion, we may say that the sheep are humbled, but not cowed into submission; they know, as we do, that there are consequences for one's actions, although they do not yet know what those consequences will be.

Even if we refuse to believe, as I do, that natural disasters are divine punishments, we can still find meaning in the *Un'taneh Tokef*. This day is indeed holy. Awakened by the shofar and soberly reminded of our mortality, we can no longer hide or make excuses for our actions. It is a time of *cheshbon hanefesh*—a taking stock of ourselves, acknowledging our shortcomings, and truly resolving to change.

41

The Seven Questions You're Asked in Heaven

Dr. Ron Wolfson

Ever since I was a kid in Omaha, the most moving prayer of the High Holy Day liturgy for me has been the *Un'taneh Tokef.* The hazzan and choir would offer a somber musical rendition of the Hebrew, while my eyes would drift to the English translation. The notion of "a thin whisper of a sound" (line 7; I learned it as a "still, small voice") resonated with my lifelong fascination with "self-talk," the constant conversation going on in my head ... and in my heart. The call to judgment felt like a summons to a trial, an invitation to enter the courtroom of the Almighty—the all-seeing, all-knowing Judge.

Perhaps it was the popularity of television shows like *Perry Mason*—courtroom dramas featuring articulate prosecutors, indefatigable defense attorneys, and wise judges—that set the stage for my encounters with *Un'taneh Tokef.* Even after I began to understand the metaphoric meaning

Dr. Ron Wolfson is Fingerhut Professor of Education at American Jewish University in Los Angeles and a cofounder of Synagogue 3000. He is author of *The Seven Questions You're Asked in Heaven: Reviewing and Renewing Your Life on Earth; God's To-Do List: 103 Ways to Be an Angel and Do God's Work on Earth;* the three volumes *Hanukkah, Passover,* and *Shabbat,* all family guides to spiritual celebrations; *The Spirituality of Welcoming: How to Transform Your Congregation into a Sacred Community; A Time to Mourn, a Time to Comfort: A Guide to Jewish Bereavement and Comfort;* and, with Rabbi Lawrence A. Hoffman, *What You Will See Inside a Synagogue* (all Jewish Lights).

of the prayer, the literal idea of a heavenly tribunal continued to haunt my imagination. What if I were on trial for my life? What questions would I be asked? How would I answer?

I have learned that I am not alone in imagining such questions. The Rabbis themselves tried compiling a list of them.

So, what are the questions we'll be asked in heaven about our lives on earth?

Over the course of a year, I asked this question about questions to many family members, friends, and colleagues. Here's what I got:

> Were you a good person?
> Were you successful?
> Were you popular?
> Were you a good parent, spouse, sibling, daughter, or son?
> Did you make a lot of money?
> Did you make a contribution to society?
> Did you give to charity?
> Did you believe in God?
> Why do you deserve to be here?
> Whom do you want to reassure that you are in a good place?
> What are the biggest insights of your life?
> Whom would you want to have with you here in heaven?

All interesting questions, to be sure. But I went back to the sources I love from Jewish tradition to see what great rabbis of the past thought the questions might be. I found seven in all: five from the Talmud and two from more modern sources. Frankly, they are surprising. Unexpected.

The fourth-century Talmudic sage Rava said (Shabbat 31a):

> When a human being is led in for judgment, they ask:
> Did you conduct your business honestly?
> Did you set times to study Torah?
> Did you engage in procreation?
> Did you hope for deliverance?
> Did you seek wisdom and discern one thing from another?

1. "Did you conduct your business honestly?" When I first read this, I was in shock.

The very first question asked upon reaching heaven is "Were you honest in your business?"! Not "Did you believe in God?" Not "Did you observe the commandments?" Not "Did you repair the world?"

Yet, upon further reflection, I saw that the question is not just about business. It is about honesty, integrity, faithfulness. If you are not honest in your business dealings, can you be trusted to be honest in other relationships? If you are not honest with others, can you be honest with yourself? If you are not faithful with others, can your faith in God be trusted?

2. "Did you set times to study Torah?" As a Jewish educator, I was thrilled with this question—a call for lifelong adult learning. One of my favorite texts of all time is also found in Tractate Shabbat (127a):

> These are the commandments that yield immediate fruit and continue to yield fruit in the world to come: honoring parents; doing deeds of loving-kindness; attending the house of study punctually, morning and evening; providing hospitality; visiting the sick; helping the needy bride; attending the dead; devotion in prayer; and making peace between people. But, *talmud Torah k'neged kulam*—the study of Torah is basic to them all.

Louis Finkelstein famously said, "Prayer is the way we talk to God; study is the way God talks to us." Study leads us to a life of meaning and purpose through the mitzvot.

3. "Did you engage in procreation?" Rava's third question is tough. Approximately ten percent of couples cannot conceive a child, and yet having children in one's life is of paramount Jewish value. The question, I suggest, has this deeper meaning: "Did you leave a legacy?" My teacher, Rabbi Harold Schulweis, has eloquently taught that children offer "the immortality of influence." This is the call to be an ancestor, either by giving birth to children, adopting and raising children, or mentoring them.

4. "Did you hope for deliverance?" To the Jewish mind, the fourth question is another shocker. "Deliverance," "salvation"—aren't these Christian terms? No. They were Jewish concepts long before Christianity appropriated and reshaped them for its own ends. Our liturgy is replete with references to deliverance—the opening line of the *Havdalah* ceremony begins with Isaiah 12:2–3, *Hinei, El y'shu'ati*, "Behold, God of my salvation." I reframe the "deliverance" question as "Did you have hope?"

It is the notion of hope that has sustained the Jewish people through tragedies, displacements, even genocide.

5. "Did you seek wisdom and discern one thing from another?" Rava's last query is a double-header: did you seek wisdom, and could you distinguish one thing from another? It relies on the difference between *chokhmah* (wisdom from experience) and *binah* (analytic ability). The fifth question asks if you were able to combine your analytical abilities with your hard-won experience to make good choices. Could you tell what was really important … and what was not? Did you learn to prioritize? Did you get your priorities straight?

6. The sixth question comes from Rabbi Samson Raphael Hirsch (1805–88), the intellectual founder of modern Orthodoxy. It is reported that on his deathbed, he turned to his students and demanded to be taken to nearby Switzerland. When his disciples objected, he offered his reason (my paraphrase): "When I stand shortly before the Almighty, I will be answerable to many questions, but what will I say when I'm asked, and I will surely be asked: "Did you see my Alps?"

This is the question based on the instruction from the Jerusalem Talmud (Kiddushin 4:12)—Rabbi Chizkiyah quoted Rabbi Kohen in the name of Rav: "A human being will have to give account for all that his eye beheld and he did not eat." This sixth question is not about what you *did*, but about what you *did not do*. It is the "bucket list" question: Have you enjoyed everything permitted to you in this life? Did you take advantage of the enormous beauty and joys in God's creation?

7. The seventh question is perhaps the best known of all. Martin Buber (*Tales of the Hasidim*) calls it "the Query of All Queries":

> Rabbi Zusya said, "In the coming world, they will not ask me, 'Why were you not Moses?' They will ask me, 'Why were you not Zusya?'"

Here is the great insight of Zusya: You are not someone else. You are you. If you are only expected to be you, you do not have to be someone else. That means you can take risks, fall down, come up short. The question underneath the question is "Are you the best 'you' you can be? How can you go about becoming a better you?"

Un'taneh Tokef offers us a good start on how to become a better person. The entire prayer is a three-part drama. The first two paragraphs set the scene, telling us that God will judge every creature in the universe. Then, we hear the litany of questions: Who shall live and who shall die? Who by fire and who by water? And so on. And, then, we are told that the severity of the judgment can be ameliorated through three acts: *t'shu-vah* ("repentance"), *t'fillah* ("prayer"), and *tz'dakah* ("charity"). Three ways to be a better *you*.

This is "in-your-face" Judaism. So much of our educational energy is devoted to inspiring children and adults to do the work popularly known as *tikkun olam*, "the repair of the world." The idea comes from the mystical notion that in the course of its creation, the world was shattered into billions of pieces, leaving it to human beings to work toward repairing the "brokenness." *Tikkun* is often translated as "repair," and the call for *tikkun olam* applies to social justice efforts, community organizing, and communal philanthropy.

But there is another translation of *tikkun*: not repairing, but *perfecting*. And there is another kind of *tikkun: tikkun atzmi*, "the perfecting of the self." *Un'taneh Tokef* brings us face-to-face with our time-limited journey on this earth, reminding us of the questions we will have to answer when we die, having tried to be the best person we can be. Perfec*tion* is not the goal. Perfect*ing* is—"perfecting the self" and "perfecting the world" around us. How do you go about perfecting either?

Un'taneh Tokef answers that question with its three powerful directives of "repentance, prayer, and charity"—a yearly rehearsal for the heavenly tribunal we will face some day. Our ongoing work of perfecting prepares us to take that stairway to heaven, where we will answer the seven questions with a resounding "Yes!" and take our rightful place among the angels.

Notes

Un'taneh Tokef as Poetry and Legend
by Rabbi Lawrence A. Hoffman, PhD

1. The literature on *Un'taneh Tokef* is vast. While the nature of this series prohibits detailed footnotes, it would be improper to omit the names of at least a few of the most important works that have informed this analysis, in expectation that some readers may wish to read further on this fascinating topic. Much of the literature is in Hebrew and German; I include only English language sources. Eric Werner's pioneer observations were made in *The Sacred Bridge* (New York: Schocken Books, 1953), 252–255. A parallel *Kontakion* by Romanus is translated from the Greek in Marjorie Carpenter, *Kontakia of Romanus, Byzantine Melodist* (Columbia: University of Missouri Press, 1973), 372–80. The attribution of *Un'taneh Tokef* to Yannai is conveniently summarized by Yosef Yahalom in the English language edition of *Ha'aretz*, August 10, 2009. Robert Chazan discusses Rabbi Ephraim of Bonn's account in "Rabbi Ephraim of Bonn's Sefer Zechirah," *Révue des Études Juives* 132 (1973): 119–26. Yehezkel Hovav provides the historical reconstruction of an Amnon from Italy, but only in Hebrew. Of the many fine literary analyses of the Amnon legend, most are in Hebrew, but see Ivan G. Marcus, "A Pious Community and Doubt: *Qiddush Hashem* in Ashkenaz and the Story of Rabbi Amnon of Mainz," in Julius Carlebach, *Festschrift, Studien zur jüdischen Geschichte und Soziologie* (Heidelberg: Carl Winter University Publication, 1992), 97–113. The literature as a whole is surveyed and discussed by Lucia Raspe—again, in German—but she touches on some of the issues in her "Jewish Saints in Medieval Ashkenaz," *Frankfurt Jewish Studies Bulletin* 31 (2004): 75–90.

Un'taneh Tokef: Behind the Translation

1. For detail, see Joel M. Hoffman, *And God Said: How Translations Conceal the Bible's Original Meaning* (New York: Thomas Dunne, 2010), chapter 5.

1. The Exodus and the Elephant by Rabbi Tony Bayfield, DD

1. *Forms of Prayer*, 7th ed. (Oxford: Oxford University Press), 4:74. The service ends with the return of the scrolls to the ark.
2. The 1950s saw the foundation of many Reform synagogues in Britain. The Southwest Essex Reform Synagogue in Northeast London was founded in 1956 and used the local town hall for High Holy Day services.

3. My father's name is actually Ronald David, and my Hebrew name is Avraham ben David u'Malka, not Avraham ben Canute!

4. *Forms of Prayer,* 8th ed., vol. 3 (London: The Reform Synagogues of Great Britain, 1985).

5. Ibid., 517. See Franz Rosenzweig, *The Star of Redemption,* trans. William W. Hallo (London: Routledge and Kegan Paul, 1971), 424.

6. *Forms of Prayer,* 8th ed., vol. 1 (London: The Movement for Reform Judaism, 2008).

7. See Dow Marmur, "My Absentee Mentor Emil Fackenheim," *Manna* 105 (Autumn 2009).

8. *Forms of Prayer,* 8th ed., vol. 3 (London: The Reform Synagogues of Great Britain, 1985), 459.

2. Aw-full Thoughts on Words a Melody Cannot Save by Rabbi Andrew Goldstein, PhD

1. Throughout this essay, rather than the translation used here, we include the version referred to by the author, since he refers to the specific *machzor* that he has edited.

5. A Rationalist's View by Rabbi Charles H. Middleburgh, PhD

1. Herman Kieval, *The Holy Days: A Commentary on the Prayerbook of Rosh Hashanah and Yom Kippur* (New York: Burning Bush Press, 1959), 143.

2. Eric L. Friedland, *Were Our Mouths Filled with Song* (Cincinnati: Hebrew Union College Press, 1997), 38 (referring to 1896 translation of the German original). Transliterations of *Un'taneh Tokef* have been altered to reflect the transliteration used in this book.

3. *Liberal Jewish Prayer Book* (*LJPB*) vol. 2, ed. Rabbi Israel Mattuck (1937) 186–88.

6. Universalism versus Martyrdom: *Un'taneh Tokef* and Its Frame Narrative by Rabbi Marc Saperstein, PhD

1. Marc Saperstein "Inscribed for Life or Death?" *Journal of Reform Judaism* 28 (1983): 18–26; reprinted in Marc Saperstein, *"Your Voice Like a Ram's Horn": Themes and Texts in Traditional Jewish Preaching* (Cincinnati: HUC Press, 1996), 37–44.

2. Max Arzt, *Justice and Mercy: Commentary on the Liturgy of the New Year and the Day of Atonement* (New York: Holt, Rinehart and Winston, 1963).

3. See, e.g., the first scholar to reflect this understanding, Eric Werner, *The Sacred Bridge: The Interdependence of Liturgy and Music in Synagogue and Church During the First Millennium* (New York: Columbia University Press, 1959), 252–55.

4. A Rabbinic midrash on Job 37:7 (*Sifrei D'varim* 307) is the source of the image that all human beings must sign and seal the account of their deeds, but this occurs at the time of their death—an intermediate position between the eschatology of the Christian texts and the annual occurrence in the liturgical poem. See Daniel Goldschmidt, *Machzor Layamim Hanora'im,* 2 vols., 1:169; *Sifre: A Tannaitic*

Commentary on the Book of Deuteronomy, trans. and ed. Reuven Hammer (New Haven: Yale University Press, 1986), 312.

5. Shlomo Eidelberg, "*Bin'tivei Ashkenaz,*" *Medieval Ashkenazic History: Studies on German Jewry in the Middle Ages,* vol. 2, (Brooklyn: Sepher-Hermon Press, 1999–2001), 23 (the article was originally published in *Hadoar* in 1974).

6. For an accessible translation of the full text, see S. Y. Agnon, *Days of Awe* (New York: Schocken, 1965), 83–85.

7. See Shlomo Eidelberg, *The Jews and the Crusaders: The Hebrew Chronicles of the First and Second Crusades* (Madison: University of Wisconsin Press, 1977), 101: "The Bishop then took some of the burghers and cut off their hands, for he was a righteous man among the Gentiles." See also Robert Chazan, *European Jewry and the First Crusade* (Berkeley: University of California Press, 1987), 227.

8. "When the Crusaders saw that they would not accept baptism ... then the enemy leaped upon them and struck them with axes and blows. There the pious ones were killed for the sanctification of the Name" (Chazan, *European Jewry and the First Crusade,* 266, see also 271).

9. In Worms, the Crusaders dragged a Jew through the city with a rope around neck, offering to save him if he converted; he refused, and they killed him by cutting off his head (ibid., 230–31). In an unspecified town, the Crusaders are said to have tortured the Jews with "terrible tortures and wounded them repeatedly, so that they would believe in their abomination" (ibid., 277).

10. Ibid., 292–94.

11. See, for example, the passage from Ephraim of Bonn about the 1171 ritual murder accusation at Blois, in Jacob Rader Marcus, *The Jew in the Medieval World,* rev. ed. (Cincinnati: HUC Press, 1999), 145.

12. These are weasel words that I would omit from serious Jewish discourse; their failure to provide even a clue of where, when, and by whom it was said strikes me as a way of avoiding any responsibility for what follows, and often of concealing ignorance of the source. Similarly, "The story is told that...."

13. *Gates of Repentance: The New Union Prayerbook for the Days of Awe* (New York: Central Conference of American Rabbis, 1978), 106.

14. See the recent review of these problems by Daniel Plotkin, "Giving Meaning to Our Days: Reimagining *Un'taneh Tokef:* A Survey of Selected Sermons," *CCAR Journal* 66: 2 (Spring 2009): 6–15.

13. Death without Dying by Rabbi Lawrence Kushner

1. Adin Steinsaltz, *The Thirteen Petalled Rose* (New York: Basic Books, 1980), 129.
2. Abraham Joshua Heschel, *Man's Quest for God* (New York: Scribner's, 1954), xiii, 7.
3. *Maggid D'varav L'ya'akov,* ed. Rivka Schatz-Uffenheimer, 184, no. 106.
4. *Yosher Divrei Emet* (Munkacz, 1905), f.15b.
5. Talmud, Ketubot 5a.
6. *Maggid D'varav L'ya'akov,* 24, no. 9.
7. *The Book of Job,* trans. Stephen Mitchell (San Francisco: North Point Press, 1987), xxviii.

14. Laminated in the Book of Life? by Rabbi Ruth Langer, PhD

1. *Union Prayer Book*, newly rev. ed., vol. 2, (Cincinnati: Central Conference of American Rabbis, 1945), 256 in English, continuing onto 259 in Hebrew.
2. *Gates of Repentance* (New York: Central Conference of American Rabbis, 1978), Rosh Hashanah Morning Service I: 106–110, II: 175–179; Yom Kippur Morning Service: 311–15. Note that in the traditional liturgy, this is the function of *Un'taneh Tokef*, but in *Musaf.* There is no *Musaf* service in American Reform liturgies.
3. "A Young Man's Viewpoint," *Conference on the Perpetuation of Judaism, Thirtieth Council, Union of American Hebrew Congregations, Cleveland 1927* (Cincinnati: Union of American Hebrew Congregations, 1927), 45.
4. Present in the 1925 rev. ed., 238. They are not present in the 1893 original edition (excerpts from the prayer, 198–99), and this recent change may well have generated this discussion, though the Rodef Shalom archives did not yield support for this supposition.

17. Meditations on the Poetry of *Un'taneh Tokef* by Rabbi Margaret Moers Wenig, DD

1. Many of these reflections first appeared in Margaret Moers Wenig, "The Poetry and Power of Paradox," *CCAR Journal: The Reform Jewish Quarterly*, vol. 51:2, Spring 2009, 52–74.
2. The connection between the *ro'eh* in *Un'taneh Tokef* and the *ro'eh* in Psalm 23 was made apparent to me by Professor/Rabbi Raymond Scheindlin one Rosh Hashanah, years ago. At the words, *k'vakarat ro'eh edro, ma'avir tzono tachat shivto*, he segued seamlessly into a well-known melody for Psalm 23.
3. For reflections on "How many will pass on and how many will be created … who by fire and who by water …" see Wenig, "The Poetry and Power of Paradox," 68–69, n11.
4. For my understanding of *t'shuvah*, *t'fillah*, and *tz'dakah*, see Margaret Moers Wenig, "Feeling Like a Bowling Pin," in *I Am the Lord Who Heals You: Reflections on Healing, Wholeness, and Restoration*, ed. G. Scott Morris (Nashville: Abingdon Press, 2004), 67–76.
5. See Wenig, "The Poetry and Power of Paradox," 62.
6. "Sources XV," in *Adrienne Rich's Poetry and Prose: A Norton Critical Edition*, ed. Barbara Charlesworth Gelpi and Albert Gelpi (New York: Norton, 1993), 108.

18. Who by Fire: Contemporary Personal and Literary Reflections by Dr. Wendy Zierler

1. Diana Spechler, *Who by Fire* (New York: Harper Perennial, 2008), 158.
2. My thanks go out to Eran Tzelgov, for providing explanatory notes for his poem, which was published as the lead poem in the collection *Latzeit!* (2009), protesting the war in Gaza. See http://www.etgar.info/he/article__311.
3. Editor's note: 1948—the year of Israel's War of Independence.
4. A pun on 1956 and 5.56 caliber bullets. [Editor's note: 1956—the year of the Sinai Campaign, when Israel joined England and France in crossing the Sinai desert to remove the Egyptian blockade of its southern port, Eilat.]

5. *P'ulot Tagmul,* the retributive acts of Israeli unit 101, under General Ariel Sharon (later Prime Minister Sharon), which supported the Christian Lebanese militia's massacre of Muslims in the refugee camps of Sabra and Shatilla. In the Hebrew original, the words *p'ulot tagmul* are elided into one word, a rhetorical move that underscores how language and rhetoric enable swift, in some cases, unthinking action, leading to regrettable results.

6. Referring to an order by Yitzchak Rabin (minister of defense and then prime minister) to break the arms and legs of every stone thrower.

7. An Israeli who, posing as a soldier on duty, shot and killed seven Arabs in Rishon L'tzion after checking their identity cards and confirming they were Arab.

8. The year the poet first voted.

9. Qana, a village in southern Lebanon, known for two incidents in which civilians died as a result of Israeli Defense Force operations. The first incident alluded to here occurred on April 18, 1996. During heavy fighting between the Israel Defense Forces and Hezbollah fighters, the Israelis shelled a Fijian UNIFIL compound, resulting in civilian casualties.

10. Euphemism for using snipers to shoot suspects from afar.

11. Refers to the "targeted prevention" killing of a terrorist using huge bombs, resulting in fourteen more civilian deaths, including his wife and children.

12. This alludes to the second incident in Qana. On July 30, 2006, during the war in Lebanon, Israeli planes bombed an apartment building, resulting in the death of civilians, some of them children.

13. Bombs forbidden by the Geneva accords because of their cruelty.

14. The name of the operation in Gaza and also a line in a children's Chanukah song by Chaim Hachman Bialik, which begins with the line, "My father gave me a dreidel, a dreidel made of cast lead. Do you know what it was in honor of? In honor of Chanukah."

15. In an e-mail exchange I had with the poet, he related the following:

> I am often asked two questions when I read/perform this poem:
>
> How come you don't recount all the Palestinians' deeds (terror attacks, qassam rocket attacks, suicide bombings, and so on and so forth)?
>
> Why do you use a High Holiday prayer for your poem?
>
> I see these two questions as related and this is how I answer: I am not religious and never was, however, I was always told that there is one principle that is very important, that is, fix yourself, or correct yourself, before you come and preach to others. By this I feel, I follow Y. H. Brenner advice in *Ha'arachat Atzmenu* (Evaluation of Ourselves) a piece of advice which applies to all fields of life, and not literature alone: "Our mission now is specifically to recognize and admit our lack of pedigree from ancient times until today, our defective nature—and to rise above it and begun everything anew. We are not of distinguished lineage, broth-

ers of Israel, O! How undistinguished we are! But there is still room to fix ourselves, and 'he who confesses and abandons [his sin], is granted mercy.'"

For the full text of Brenner's essay see http://benyehuda.org/ brenner/haaraxat_atzmenu.html.

At the Edge of the Abyss by Rabbi Sharon Brous

1. Joan Didion, *The Year of Magical Thinking* (New York: Vintage, 2007).

21. The Answer Is "Me!" by Rabbi Edward Feinstein

1. See *Goldschmidt Machzor*, Yom Kippur, 170n21.

25. A Text in Context by Rabbi Jonathan Magonet, PhD

1. *Forms of Prayer for Jewish Worship I Daily, Sabbath and Occasional Prayers,* 7th ed., ed. Assembly of Rabbis (Reform Synagogues of Great Britain, London, 1977).
2. *Forms of Prayer for Jewish Worship III Prayers for the High Holydays,* 8th ed., ed. Assembly of Rabbis (Reform Synagogues of Great Britain, London, 1985).
3. Ibid., 459.
4. Ibid.
5. Ibid.

27. Mortal Matters: The Faith of *Un'taneh Tokef* by Rabbi David Stern

1. Viktor Frankl, *Man's Search for Meaning* (New York: Pocket Books, 1963), 104.
2. Ibid., 205.
3. Samuel Karff, "The Soul of the Rav," in *The Soul of the Rav: Sermons, Lectures, and Essays* (Austin: Eakin Press, 1999), 289.

28. Turning Fate into Destiny by Rabbi Avraham Weiss

1. Maimonides, *Mishneh Torah, Hilkhot T'shuvah* 3:1–2. Maimonides adds that this assessment is qualitative and can only be made by God. One good deed may outweigh all the evil ones—and vice versa.
2. *Tosafot,* Rosh Hashanah 16b, s.v. *v'nechtamin.*
3. Ravad on Maimonides' *Mishneh Torah Hilkhot T'shuvah* 3:3.
4. Rabbi Joseph B. Soloveitchik, Kol Dodi Dofek, *Listen—My Beloved Knocks.* Trans. by David Z. Gordon. (Jersey City: KTAV, 2006), 5–6.
5. Yeshiva University 1995 Commencement Address, delivered by Esther Wachsman. The transcript was published by Yeshiva University.

34. The Eternal and the Ephemeral: The Stark Contrasts of *Un'taneh Tokef* by Rabbi Aaron Panken, PhD

1. Claude Levi-Strauss, *Structural Anthropology* (Basic Books: New York, 1963), 279.

2. Philip Birnbaum, *High Holyday Prayer Book* (Hebrew Publishing Company: New York, 1979), 362.

3. Eugene B. Borowitz, *Renewing the Covenant* (Philadelphia: Jewish Publication Society, 1991), 289.

35. Theology or Anthropology? by Rabbi Sandy Eisenberg Sasso

1. The poem is included in Yehuda Amichai, *Yehuda Amichai: A Life of Poetry 1948–1994*, trans. Benjamin and Narbara Harshav (New York: HarperCollins, 1994).

37. God's Hands by Rabbi Brent Chaim Spodek and Ruth Messinger

1. Baruch Spinoza, *Theologico-Political Treatise*, 2nd ed., trans. and ed. Samuel Shirley and Seymour Feldman, (Indianapolis: Hacket Publishing Company, 1991), 154.

2. World Food Programme, "Number of World's Hungry Tops a Billion," June 19, 2009, http://www.wfp.org/stories/number-world-hungry-tops-billion (accessed January 1, 2010).

3. Jack Katzenell, "Rabbi says Holocaust Victims Were Reincarnations of Sinners" *The London Independent*, August 6, 2000.

4. Rabbi Lawrence Kushner, "Everything All at Once; Just One Thing at a Time," (speech given at the 92nd Street "Y", October 20, 2002).

5. *Kedushat Levi, M'tzora*. Thanks to Rabbi Jonah Steinberg for bringing this text to our attention.

Glossary

The following glossary presents names and Hebrew words used regularly throughout this volume and provides the way they are pronounced. Sometimes two pronunciations are common, in which case the first is the way the word is sounded in Hebrew, and the second is the way it is sometimes heard in common speech, under the influence of Yiddish, the folk language of Jews in northern and eastern Europe (a combination, mostly, of Hebrew and German). Our goal is to provide the way that many Jews actually use these words, not just the technically correct version.

- The pronunciations are divided into syllables by dashes.
- The accented syllable is written in capital letters.
- "Kh" represents a guttural sound, similar to the German (as in "sprach").
- The most common vowel is "a" as in "father," which appears here as "ah."
- The short "e" (as in "get") is written as either "e" (when it is in the middle of a syllable) or "eh" (when it ends a syllable).
- Similarly, the short "i" (as in "tin") is written as either "i" (when it is in the middle of a syllable) or "ih" (when it ends a syllable).
- A long "o" (as in "Moses") is written as "oe" (as in the word "toe") or "oh" (as in the word "Oh!").

Adonai (pronounced ah-doh-NA'I): The pronunciation for the tetragrammaton. See **Tetragrammaton**.

Alenu (pronounced ah-LAY-noo): The first word and, therefore, the title of a major prayer compiled in the second or third century as part of the New Year (Rosh Hashanah) service, but from about the fourteenth century on, used also as part of the concluding section of every daily service. *Alenu* means "it is incumbent upon us …" and introduces the prayer's theme: our duty to praise God. The Great *Alenu* is the version of *Alenu* encountered on Rosh Hashanah at *Musaf*. It is sung to a particularly majestic melody.

247

Al kiddush hashem (pronounced ahl kee-DOOSH hah-SHEM): Literally, "for the sake of the sanctity of the name [of God]," a term used to describe martyrdom.

Amidah (pronounced either ah-mee-DAH or, commonly, ah-MEE-dah): One of three commonly used titles for the second of two central units in the worship service, the first being The *Sh'ma* and Its Blessings. It is composed of a series of blessings, many of which are petitionary, except on Sabbaths and holidays, when the petitions are removed out of deference to the holiness of the day. Also called *T'fillah* and *Sh'moneh Esreh*. *Amidah* means "standing" and refers to the fact that the prayer is said standing up.

Ashkenazi (pronounced ahsh-k'-nah-ZEE or, commonly, ahsh'k'-NAH-zee): From the Hebrew word *Ashkenaz*, meaning the geographic area of northern and eastern Europe. Ashkenazi is the adjective, describing the liturgical rituals and customs practiced there, as opposed to *Sephardi*, meaning the liturgical rituals and customs that are derived from *Sefarad*, Spain (see **Sephardi**).

Birkat Hamazon (pronounced beer-KAHT hah-mah-ZOHN): Literally, "blessing over food," but actually a set of four blessings said together after eating, the equivalent of a Jewish Grace after Meals.

Chuppah (pronounced khoo-PAH, but, commonly, chu-PAH): The wedding canopy, or just a word for "wedding" proper.

Daven (pronounced DAH-v'n): The Yiddish word describing the traditionalist mode of prayer by which congregants recite each prayer (or part of a prayer) privately and, more or less, silently—after which the cantor chants out loud the end of what was said.

Gaon (pronounced gah-OHN; plural: *Geonim*, pronounced g'-oh-NEEM): Title for the leading Rabbis in Babylon (present-day Iraq) from about 750 to 1038. From a biblical word meaning "glory," which is equivalent in the title to saying "Your Excellence."

Great *Alenu*: See **Alenu**.

Havdalah (pronounced hahv-dah-LAH): Literally, "separation"; hence, the set of prayers that mark the separation between Shabbat or holy days and the day following. One version is inserted into the *Amidah* of the evening service that concludes the sacred day in question; another is recited at home that evening.

Hallel (pronounced hah-LAYL or, commonly, HAH-layl): A Hebrew word meaning "praise" and, by extension, the name given to sets of psalms that are recited liturgically in praise of God: Psalms 145–150, the Daily *Hallel*, are recited each morning; Psalm 136, the Great *Hallel*, is recited on Shabbat and holidays and is part of the Passover Seder. Psalms 113–118, the best-known *Hallel*, known more fully as the Egyptian *Hallel*, are recited on holidays and get their name from Psalm 114:1, which celebrates the moment "when Israel left Egypt."

Kabbalah (pronounced kah-bah-LAH or, commonly, kah-BAH-lah): A general term for Jewish mysticism, but used properly for a specific mystical doctrine that began in western Europe in the eleventh or twelfth century; was recorded in the *Zohar* in the thirteenth century; and was further elaborated, especially in the Land of Israel (in Safed), in the sixteenth century. From a Hebrew word meaning "to receive" or "to welcome" and, secondarily, "tradition," implying the receiving of tradition from one's past.

K'dushah (pronounced k'-doo-SHAH or, commonly, k'-DOO-shah): From the Hebrew word meaning "holy," and therefore one of several prayers from the first or second century occurring in several places and versions, all of which have in common the citing of Isaiah 6:3—*Kadosh, kadosh, kadosh ...*, "Holy, holy, holy is the Lord of hosts. The whole earth is full of his glory." Among other places, it appears in the third blessing of the *Amidah*. *Un'taneh Tokef* is a poem (*piyyut*) inserted into this *Amidah* form of the *K'dushah*.

K'dushat hashem (pronounced k'-doo-SHAHT hah-SHEM) or **kiddush hashem** (pronounced kee-DOOSH hah-SHEM): Literally, "sanctification of the name [of God]," a term used to describe dying for the sanctification of God's name—that is, martyrdom.

K'dushat hayom (pronounced k'-doo-SHAHT hah-YOHM): Literally, "the holiness of the day;" hence, the technical name of prayers that express the presence of a sacred day (Shabbat or holidays). There are three instances: the *Kiddush* that inaugurates the day either at the dinner table or at the opening evening (*Ma'ariv*) service; the fourth benediction of the Shabbat or holiday *Amidah*; and the final benediction after the *haftarah* is recited.

K'dushta (pronounced k'-doosh-TAH or, commonly, k'-DOOSH-tah): The most famous genre of liturgical poem in antiquity. It had nine parts inserted throughout the first three blessings of the Shabbat or holiday *Amidah*; the last seven were placed within the third benediction, allowing the poem to reach its climax there.

Kittel (pronounced KIH-t'l): The Yiddish word denoting a white garment worn on the High Holy Days, but in which people may also be buried. White connotes purity and, hence, the forgiveness of sin.

Kol Nidre (pronounced kohl need-RAY, or, commonly, kohl NID-ray): Literally, "all vows ..." the first words of the most famous prayer inaugurating the evening service for Yom Kippur and, by extension, not just the name of the prayer, but a common way of referring to that service in its entirety.

Kotel (pronounced KOH-tehl): literally, "wall," the Western Wall, still standing from the destruction of the Temple by the Romans in 70 CE.

K'rovah (pronounced k'-roh-VAH; plural, *k'rovot*, pronounced k'-roh-VOHT): From the Hebrew root *k.r.v.*, "to approach, to draw close," alluding to the act of worship whereby we draw close to God. The same root gives us *korban* (pronounced kohr-BAHN), "sacrifice," as the gift with which our ancestors approached God during the days of the ancient Temple cult. *K'rovah* is thus the name of a particular form of poetic addition (*piyyut*) that is inserted into the *Amidah* as a verbal offering to God.

Mazal (pronounced mah-ZAHL or, commonly, MAH-z'l), originally the word for "constellation," and hence, "luck" or "chance." The common expression *mazal tov* (MAH-z'l tohv), "congratulations," comes from the original meaning of "a good constellation."

Midrash (pronounced meed-RAHSH or, commonly, MID-rahsh): From a Hebrew word meaning "to ferret out the meaning of a text," and therefore, a Rabbinic interpretation of a biblical word or verse. By extension, a body of Rabbinic literature that offers classical interpretations of the Bible.

Mishnah (pronounced mish-NAH or, commonly, MISH-nah): The name of the definitive six-volume statement of Jewish law from the Land of Israel, c. 200 CE, that culminates the era called "tannaitic" (after the title we give the Rabbis to that point; see **Tannaim**). But equally, the name applied to any particular teaching in that statement, for which the plural, *mishnayot* (pronounced mish-nah-YOHT), exists also (more than one such teaching).

Mitzvah (pronounced meetz-VAH or, commonly, MITZ-vah; plural: mitzvot, pronounced meetz-VOTE): A Hebrew word used commonly to mean "good deed" but, in the more technical sense, denoting any commandment from God and therefore, by extension, what God wants us to do. Reciting the *Sh'ma* morning and evening, for instance, is a mitzvah.

Musaf (pronounced moo-SAHF or, commonly, MOO-sahf): The Hebrew word meaning "extra" or "added" and, therefore, the title of the additional sacrifice that was offered in the Temple on Shabbat and holy days. It is now the name given to an additional service of worship appended to the morning service on those days.

N'ilah (pronounced n'-ee-LAH, or, commonly NEE-lah): Literally "closing [of the gates]"; hence, the name of the final service for Yom Kippur, based on the memory of the Temple's gates that were closed as the Day of Atonement came to an end.

Payyetanim (pronounced pah-y'-tah-NEEM; singular, *payyetan*, pronounced pah-y'-TAN): Literally, "poets"; the word applied, in the context of this book, to the writers of liturgical poetry (*piyyutim*).

Pirkei Avot (pronounced pihr-KAY ah-VOHT, or, commonly, PIHR-kay ah-VOHT): Literally, "chapters of the fathers"; hence, the title of a tractate in the *Mishnah*, a rabbinic compilation dating from the end of the second century CE. Unlike the rest of the Mishnah, which is legal in nature, *Pirkei Avot* relates sayings, adages, and proverbial advice offered by the Rabbinic authorities whom the Mishnah cites.

Piyyut (pronounced pee-YOOT; plural: *piyyutim*, pronounced pee-yoo-TEEM): Literally, "a poem," but used technically to mean liturgical poems composed in classical and medieval times and inserted into the standard prayers on special occasions.

Sefer hachayim (pronounced SAY-fehr hah-chah-YEEM): Literally, "book of life," a reference to the image of God, recording our names "for life" on the High Holy Days. That fate is said to be written on Rosh Hashanah and sealed on Yom Kippur.

Sephardi (pronounced s'-fahr-DEE or, commonly, s'-FAHR-dee): From the Hebrew word *Sefarad* (pronounced s'-fah-RAHD), meaning the geographic area of modern-day Spain and Portugal. "Sephardi" is the adjective, describing the liturgical rituals and customs that are derived from *Sefarad* prior to the expulsion of Jews from there at the end of the fifteenth century, as opposed to "Ashkenazi" (see **Ashkenazi**), meaning the liturgical rituals and customs common to northern and eastern Europe. Nowadays "Sephardi" refers also to the customs of Jews from North Africa and Arab lands, whose ancestors came from Spain.

Shabbat (pronounced shah-BAHT; plural, Shabbatot, pronounced shah-bah-TOHT): The Hebrew word for "Sabbath," from a word meaning "to rest."

Shacharit (pronounced shah-khah-REET or, commonly, SHAH-khah-reet): The name given to the morning worship service; from the Hebrew word *shachar* (SHAH-khar), meaning "morning."

Sh'liach tzibbur (pronounced sh'-LEE-ahkh tsee-BOOR): Literally, the "agent of the congregation" and, therefore, the name given to the person who leads the prayer service.

Shul (pronounced SHOOL): The Yiddish word for "synagogue."

Siddur (pronounced see-DOOR or, commonly, SIH-d'r): From the Hebrew word *seder*, meaning "order," and therefore, by extension, the name given to the "order of prayers," or prayer book.

Silluk (pronounced see-LOOK or, commonly, SEE-look): The climactic and final part of the genre of liturgical poem known as *K'dushta* (see **K'dushta**), occurring in the third benediction of the *Amidah*.

S'lichah (pronounced s'-lee-KHAH; plural, *s'lichot*, pronounced, s'-lee-KHOHT): From the root *s.l.ch.*, "to forgive"; hence, a liturgical poem requesting divine forgiveness. The singular, *s'lichah*, is also the name given to a blessing in the daily *Amidah* requesting forgiveness. The plural, *s'lichot*, is also, by extension, the title given to penitential services held on Saturday night prior to Rosh Hashanah (or, if Rosh Hashanah falls in the first half of the week following, the Saturday before that).

S'lichot: See **s'lichah**.

Talmud (pronounced tahl-MOOD or, more commonly, TAHL-m'd): The name given to each of two great compendia of Jewish law and lore compiled over several centuries and, ever since, the literary core of the Rabbinic heritage. The *Talmud Yerushalmi* (pronounced y'-roo-SHAHL-mee), the "Jerusalem Talmud," is earlier, a product of the Land of Israel generally dated about 400 CE. The better-known *Talmud Bavli* (pronounced BAHV-lee), or "Babylonian Talmud," took shape in Babylonia (present-day Iraq) and is traditionally dated about 550 CE. When people say "the Talmud" without specifying which one they mean, they are referring to the Babylonian version. *Talmud* means "teaching."

Tannaim (pronounced tah-nah-EEM or, commonly, tah-NAH-yim): Authorities in the time of the Mishnah, that is, prior to the third century. Singular: Tanna (pronounced TAH-nah).

Tetragrammaton: The technical term for the four-letter name of God that appears in the Bible. Treating it as sacred, Jews stopped pronouncing it centuries ago, so that the actual pronunciation has been lost; instead of reading it according to its letters, it is replaced in speech by the alternative name of God, Adonai (pronounced ah-doh-NA'I).

T'fillah (pronounced t'-fee-LAH or, commonly, t'-FEE-lah): A Hebrew word meaning "prayer" but also used technically to mean a specific prayer, namely, the second of the two main units in the worship service. It is known also as the *Amidah* or the *Sh'moneh Esreh* (see ***Amidah***). Also the title of the sixteenth blessing of the *Amidah*, a petition for God to accept our prayer.

Tikkun olam (pronounced tee-KOON oh-LAHM, or, commonly, TEE-koon oh-LAHM): Literally, "repair of the world"; originally a mystical term, but now used commonly to denote charitable work designed to make the world a better place.

T'shuvah (pronounced t'shoo-VAH or, commonly, t'SHOO-vah): From the Hebrew root *sh.u.v.*, "to return"; hence, "repentance." Also used technically as the title of the fifth blessing in the daily *Amidah,* a petition by worshipers that they successfully turn to God in heartfelt repentance.

Tz'dakah (pronounced ts-dah-KAH, or, commonly ts'DAH-kah): From the Hebrew root *tz.d.k.*, "righteous"; hence, "charity."

Un'taneh Tokef (pronounced oo-n'-TAH-neh TOH-kehf): A *piyyut* (liturgical poem) for the High Holy Days emphasizing the awesome nature of these days when we stand before God for judgment; but originally, the ninth part (see ***Silluk***) of a longer poem for the *Amidah* called *K'dushta* (see ***K'dushta***). Although widely connected with a legend of Jewish martyrdom in medieval Germany, the poem more likely derives from a Byzantine poet, circa sixth century. It is known for its climactic insistence that: "penitence, prayer, and charity help the hardship of the decree pass."

Yamim Nora'im (pronounced yah-MEEM noh-rah-EEM): Literally, "awesome days"; hence, the Hebrew for "Days of Awe," the High Holy Days of Rosh Hashanah and Yom Kippur.

Yontif (pronounced YOHN-tihf): Yiddish form of the Hebrew *yom tov* (pronounced yohm TOHV), literally, "good day," meaning a Jewish holiday.

Bible Study / Midrash

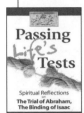

Passing Life's Tests: Spiritual Reflections on the Trial of Abraham, the Binding of Isaac *By Rabbi Bradley Shavit Artson, DHL*
Invites us to use this powerful tale as a tool for our own soul wrestling, to confront our existential sacrifices and enable us to face—and surmount—life's tests.
6 x 9, 176 pp, Quality PB, 978-1-58023-631-7 **$18.99**

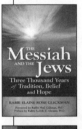

The Messiah and the Jews: Three Thousand Years of Tradition, Belief and Hope *By Rabbi Elaine Rose Glickman; Foreword by Rabbi Neil Gillman, PhD; Preface by Rabbi Judith Z. Abrams, PhD*
Explores and explains an astonishing range of primary and secondary sources, infusing them with new meaning for the modern reader.
6 x 9, 192 pp, Quality PB, 978-1-58023-690-4 **$16.99**

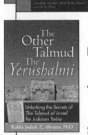

Speaking Torah: Spiritual Teachings from around the Maggid's Table—in Two Volumes *By Arthur Green, with Ebn Leader, Ariel Evan Mayse and Or N. Rose*
The most powerful Hasidic teachings made accessible—from some of the world's preeminent authorities on Jewish thought and spirituality.
Volume 1—6 x 9, 512 pp, Hardcover, 978-1-58023-668-3 **$34.99**
Volume 2—6 x 9, 448 pp, Hardcover, 978-1-58023-694-2 **$34.99**

Masking and Unmasking Ourselves: Interpreting Biblical Texts on Clothing & Identity *By Dr. Norman J. Cohen*
Presents ten Bible stories that involve clothing in an essential way, as a means of learning about the text, its characters and their interactions.
6 x 9, 240 pp, HC, 978-1-58023-461-0 **$24.99**

The Genesis of Leadership: What the Bible Teaches Us about Vision, Values and Leading Change *By Rabbi Nathan Laufer; Foreword by Senator Joseph I. Lieberman*
6 x 9, 288 pp, Quality PB, 978-1-58023-352-1 **$18.99**

Hineini in Our Lives: Learning How to Respond to Others through 14 Biblical Texts and Personal Stories *By Rabbi Norman J. Cohen, PhD* 6 x 9, 240 pp, Quality PB, 978-1-58023-274-6 **$16.99**

The Modern Men's Torah Commentary: New Insights from Jewish Men on the 54 Weekly Torah Portions *Edited by Rabbi Jeffrey K. Salkin*
6 x 9, 368 pp, HC, 978-1-58023-395-8 **$24.99**

Moses and the Journey to Leadership: Timeless Lessons of Effective Management from the Bible and Today's Leaders *By Rabbi Norman J. Cohen, PhD*
6 x 9, 240 pp, Quality PB, 978-1-58023-351-4 **$18.99**; HC, 978-1-58023-227-2 **$21.99**

The Other Talmud—The Yerushalmi: Unlocking the Secrets of The Talmud of Israel for Judaism Today *By Rabbi Judith Z. Abrams, PhD*
6 x 9, 256 pp, HC, 978-1-58023-463-4 **$24.99**

Sage Tales: Wisdom and Wonder from the Rabbis of the Talmud
By Rabbi Burton L. Visotzky 6 x 9, 256 pp, HC, 978-1-58023-456-6 **$24.99**

The Torah Revolution: Fourteen Truths That Changed the World
By Rabbi Reuven Hammer, PhD 6 x 9, 240 pp, HC, 978-1-58023-457-3 **$24.99**

The Wisdom of Judaism: An Introduction to the Values of the Talmud
By Rabbi Dov Peretz Elkins 6 x 9, 192 pp, Quality PB, 978-1-58023-327-9 **$16.99**

Congregation Resources

Jewish Megatrends: Charting the Course of the American Jewish Future
By Rabbi Sidney Schwarz; Foreword by Ambassador Stuart E. Eizenstat
Visionary solutions for a community ripe for transformational change—from
fourteen leading innovators of Jewish life.
6 x 9, 288 pp, HC, 978-1-58023-667-6 **$24.99**

Relational Judaism: Using the Power of Relationships to Transform the
Jewish Community *By Dr. Ron Wolfson*
How to transform the model of twentieth-century Jewish institutions into twenty-first-
century relational communities offering meaning and purpose, belonging and blessing.
6 x 9, 288 pp, HC, 978-1-58023-666-9 **$24.99**

Revolution of Jewish Spirit: How to Revive *Ruakh* in Your Spiritual
Life, Transform Your Synagogue & Inspire Your Jewish Community
By Rabbi Baruch HaLevi, DMin, and Ellen Frankel, LCSW; Foreword by Dr. Ron Wolfson
A practical and engaging guide to reinvigorating Jewish life. Offers strategies for
sustaining and expanding transformation, impassioned leadership, inspired pro-
gramming and inviting sacred spaces.
6 x 9, 224 pp, Quality PB Original, 978-1-58023-625-6 **$19.99**

Building a Successful Volunteer Culture: Finding Meaning in Service in the Jewish
Community *By Rabbi Charles Simon; Foreword by Shelley Lindauer; Preface by Dr. Ron Wolfson*
6 x 9, 192 pp, Quality PB, 978-1-58023-408-5 **$16.99**

The Case for Jewish Peoplehood: Can We Be One?
By Dr. Erica Brown and Dr. Misha Galperin; Foreword by Rabbi Joseph Telushkin
6 x 9, 224 pp, HC, 978-1-58023-401-6 **$21.99**

Empowered Judaism: What Independent Minyanim Can Teach Us about Building
Vibrant Jewish Communities *By Rabbi Elie Kaunfer; Foreword by Prof. Jonathan D. Sarna*
6 x 9, 224 pp, Quality PB, 978-1-58023-412-2 **$18.99**

Finding a Spiritual Home: How a New Generation of Jews Can Transform the
American Synagogue *By Rabbi Sidney Schwarz*
6 x 9, 352 pp, Quality PB, 978-1-58023-185-5 **$19.95**

Inspired Jewish Leadership: Practical Approaches to Building Strong Communities
By Dr. Erica Brown 6 x 9, 256 pp, HC, 978-1-58023-361-3 **$27.99**

Jewish Pastoral Care, 2nd Edition: A Practical Handbook from Traditional &
Contemporary Sources *Edited by Rabbi Dayle A. Friedman, MSW, MAJCS, BCC*
6 x 9, 528 pp, Quality PB, 978-1-58023-427-6 **$35.00**

Jewish Spiritual Direction: An Innovative Guide from Traditional and
Contemporary Sources
Edited by Rabbi Howard A. Addison, PhD, and Barbara Eve Breitman, MSW
6 x 9, 368 pp, HC, 978-1-58023-230-2 **$30.00**

A Practical Guide to Rabbinic Counseling
Edited by Rabbi Yisrael N. Levitz, PhD, and Rabbi Abraham J. Twerski, MD
6 x 9, 432 pp, HC, 978-1-58023-562-4 **$40.00**

Professional Spiritual & Pastoral Care: A Practical Clergy and Chaplain's Handbook
Edited by Rabbi Stephen B. Roberts, MBA, MHL, BCJC
6 x 9, 480 pp, HC, 978-1-59473-312-3 **$50.00**

Reimagining Leadership in Jewish Organizations: Ten Practical Lessons to
Help You Implement Change and Achieve Your Goals *By Dr. Misha Galperin*
6 x 9, 192 pp, Quality PB, 978-1-58023-492-4 **$16.99**

Rethinking Synagogues: A New Vocabulary for Congregational Life
By Rabbi Lawrence A. Hoffman, PhD 6 x 9, 240 pp, Quality PB, 978-1-58023-248-7 **$19.99**

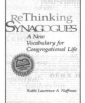

Spiritual Community: The Power to Restore Hope, Commitment and Joy
By Rabbi David A. Teutsch, PhD
5½ x 8½, 144 pp, HC, 978-1-58023-270-8 **$19.99**

Spiritual Boredom: Rediscovering the Wonder of Judaism *By Dr. Erica Brown*
6 x 9, 208 pp, HC, 978-1-58023-405-4 **$21.99**

The Spirituality of Welcoming: How to Transform Your Congregation into a
Sacred Community *By Dr. Ron Wolfson* 6 x 9, 224 pp, Quality PB, 978-1-58023-244-9 **$19.99**

Social Justice

Where Justice Dwells
A Hands-On Guide to Doing Social Justice in Your Jewish Community
By Rabbi Jill Jacobs; Foreword by Rabbi David Saperstein
Provides ways to envision and act on your own ideals of social justice.
7 x 9, 288 pp, Quality PB Original, 978-1-58023-453-5 **$24.99**

There Shall Be No Needy
Pursuing Social Justice through Jewish Law and Tradition
By Rabbi Jill Jacobs; Foreword by Rabbi Elliot N. Dorff, PhD; Preface by Simon Greer
Confronts the most pressing issues of twenty-first-century America from a deeply Jewish perspective. 6 x 9, 288 pp, Quality PB, 978-1-58023-425-2 **$16.99**

There Shall Be No Needy Teacher's Guide 8½ x 11, 56 pp, PB, 978-1-58023-429-0 **$8.99**

Conscience
The Duty to Obey and the Duty to Disobey
By Rabbi Harold M. Schulweis
Examines the idea of conscience and the role conscience plays in our relationships to government, law, ethics, religion, human nature, God—and to each other.
6 x 9, 160 pp, Quality PB, 978-1-58023-419-1 **$16.99**; HC, 978-1-58023-375-0 **$19.99**

Judaism and Justice
The Jewish Passion to Repair the World
By Rabbi Sidney Schwarz; Foreword by Ruth Messinger
Explores the relationship between Judaism, social justice and the Jewish identity of American Jews. 6 x 9, 352 pp, Quality PB, 978-1-58023-353-8 **$19.99**

Spirituality / Women's Interest

New Jewish Feminism
Probing the Past, Forging the Future
Edited by Rabbi Elyse Goldstein; Foreword by Anita Diamant
Looks at the growth and accomplishments of Jewish feminism and what they mean for Jewish women today and tomorrow.
6 x 9, 480 pp, HC, 978-1-58023-359-0 **$24.99**

The Divine Feminine in Biblical Wisdom Literature
Selections Annotated & Explained
Translation & Annotation by Rabbi Rami Shapiro
5½ x 8½, 240 pp, Quality PB, 978-1-59473-109-9 **$16.99**
(A book from SkyLight Paths, Jewish Lights' sister imprint)

The Quotable Jewish Woman
Wisdom, Inspiration & Humor from the Mind & Heart
Edited by Elaine Bernstein Partnow
6 x 9, 496 pp, Quality PB, 978-1-58023-236-4 **$19.99**

The Women's Haftarah Commentary
New Insights from Women Rabbis on the 54 Weekly Haftarah Portions, the 5 Megillot & Special Shabbatot
Edited by Rabbi Elyse Goldstein
Illuminates the historical significance of female portrayals in the Haftarah and the Five Megillot. 6 x 9, 560 pp, Quality PB, 978-1-58023-371-2 **$19.99**

The Women's Torah Commentary
New Insights from Women Rabbis on the 54 Weekly Torah Portions
Edited by Rabbi Elyse Goldstein
Over fifty women rabbis offer inspiring insights on the Torah, in a week-by-week format.
6 x 9, 496 pp, Quality PB, 978-1-58023-370-5 **$19.99**; HC, 978-1-58023-076-6 **$34.95**

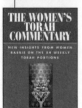

See Passover for *The Women's Passover Companion: Women's Reflections on the Festival of Freedom* and *The Women's Seder Sourcebook: Rituals & Readings for Use at the Passover Seder.*

Meditation

The Magic of Hebrew Chant: Healing the Spirit, Transforming the
Mind, Deepening Love
By Rabbi Shefa Gold; Foreword by Sylvia Boorstein
Introduces this transformative spiritual practice as a way to unlock the power
of sacred texts and make prayer and meditation the delight of your life. Includes
musical notations. 6 x 9, 352 pp, Quality PB, 978-1-58023-671-3 **$24.99**

The Magic of Hebrew Chant Companion—The Big Book of Musical Notations
and Incantations
8½ x 11, 154 pp, PB, 978-1-58023-722-2 **$19.99**

Jewish Meditation Practices for Everyday Life
Awakening Your Heart, Connecting with God
By Rabbi Jeff Roth
Offers a fresh take on meditation that draws on life experience and living life with
greater clarity as opposed to the traditional method of rigorous study.
6 x 9, 224 pp, Quality PB, 978-1-58023-397-2 **$18.99**

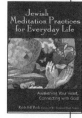

Discovering Jewish Meditation, 2nd Edition
Instruction & Guidance for Learning an Ancient Spiritual Practice
By Nan Fink Gefen, PhD 6 x 9, 208 pp, Quality PB, 978-1-58023-462-7 **$16.99**

The Handbook of Jewish Meditation Practices
A Guide for Enriching the Sabbath and Other Days of Your Life
By Rabbi David A. Cooper 6 x 9, 208 pp, Quality PB, 978-1-58023-102-2 **$16.95**

Meditation from the Heart of Judaism
Today's Teachers Share Their Practices, Techniques, and Faith
Edited by Avram Davis 6 x 9, 256 pp, Quality PB, 978-1-58023-049-0 **$16.95**

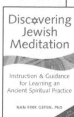

Ritual / Sacred Practices

God in Your Body: Kabbalah, Mindfulness and Embodied Spiritual Practice
By Jay Michaelson
The first comprehensive treatment of the body in Jewish spiritual practice and an
essential guide to the sacred. 6 x 9, 272 pp, Quality PB, 978-1-58023-304-0 **$18.99**

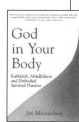

The Book of Jewish Sacred Practices: CLAL's Guide to Everyday &
Holiday Rituals & Blessings *Edited by Rabbi Irwin Kula and Vanessa L. Ochs, PhD*
6 x 9, 368 pp, Quality PB, 978-1-58023-152-7 **$18.95**

The Jewish Dream Book: The Key to Opening the Inner Meaning of Your Dreams
By Vanessa L. Ochs, PhD, with Elizabeth Ochs; Illus. by Kristina Swarner
8 x 8, 128 pp, Full-color illus., Deluxe PB w/ flaps, 978-1-58023-132-9 $16.95

Jewish Ritual: A Brief Introduction for Christians
By Rabbi Kerry M. Olitzky and Rabbi Daniel Judson
5½ x 8½, 144 pp, Quality PB, 978-1-58023-210-4 **$14.99**

The Rituals & Practices of a Jewish Life: A Handbook for Personal Spiritual
Renewal *Edited by Rabbi Kerry M. Olitzky and Rabbi Daniel Judson*
6 x 9, 272 pp, Illus., Quality PB, 978-1-58023-169-5 **$18.95**

The Sacred Art of Lovingkindness: Preparing to Practice
By Rabbi Rami Shapiro 5½ x 8½, 176 pp, Quality PB, 978-1-59473-151-8 **$16.99**
(A book from SkyLight Paths, Jewish Lights' sister imprint)

Mystery & Detective Fiction

Criminal Kabbalah: An Intriguing Anthology of Jewish Mystery &
Detective Fiction *Edited by Lawrence W. Raphael; Foreword by Laurie R. King*
All-new stories from twelve of today's masters of mystery and detective fiction—
sure to delight mystery buffs of all faith traditions.
6 x 9, 256 pp, Quality PB, 978-1-58023-109-1 **$16.95**

Mystery Midrash: An Anthology of Jewish Mystery & Detective Fiction
Edited by Lawrence W. Raphael; Preface by Joel Siegel
6 x 9, 304 pp, Quality PB, 978-1-58023-055-1 **$16.95**

Spirituality

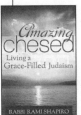

Amazing Chesed: Living a Grace-Filled Judaism
By Rabbi Rami Shapiro
Drawing from ancient and contemporary, traditional and non-traditional Jewish wisdom, reclaims the idea of grace in Judaism.
6 x 9, 176 pp, Quality PB, 978-1-58023-624-9 **$16.99**

Jewish with Feeling: A Guide to Meaningful Jewish Practice
By Rabbi Zalman Schachter-Shalomi with Joel Segel
Takes off from basic questions like "Why be Jewish?" and whether the word God still speaks to us today and lays out a vision for a whole-person Judaism.
5½ x 8½, 288 pp, Quality PB, 978-1-58023-691-1 **$19.99**

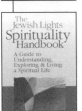

The Jewish Lights Spirituality Handbook: A Guide to Understanding, Exploring & Living a Spiritual Life *Edited by Stuart M. Matlins*
What exactly is "Jewish" about spirituality? How do I make it a part of my life? Fifty of today's foremost spiritual leaders share their ideas and experience with us.
6 x 9, 456 pp, Quality PB, 978-1-58023-093-3 **$19.99**

Aleph-Bet Yoga: Embodying the Hebrew Letters for Physical and Spiritual Well-Being
By Steven A. Rapp; Foreword by Tamar Frankiel, PhD, and Judy Greenfeld; Preface by Hart Lazer
7 x 10, 128 pp, b/w photos, Quality PB, Lay-flat binding, 978-1-58023-162-6 **$16.95**

A Book of Life: Embracing Judaism as a Spiritual Practice
By Rabbi Michael Strassfeld 6 x 9, 544 pp, Quality PB, 978-1-58023-247-0 **$19.99**

Bringing the Psalms to Life: How to Understand and Use the Book of Psalms
By Rabbi Daniel F. Polish, PhD 6 x 9, 208 pp, Quality PB, 978-1-58023-157-2 **$16.95**

Does the Soul Survive? A Jewish Journey to Belief in Afterlife, Past Lives & Living with Purpose *By Rabbi Elie Kaplan Spitz; Foreword by Brian L. Weiss, MD*
6 x 9, 288 pp, Quality PB, 978-1-58023-165-7 **$18.99**

Entering the Temple of Dreams: Jewish Prayers, Movements and Meditations for the End of the Day *By Tamar Frankiel, PhD, and Judy Greenfeld*
7 x 10, 192 pp, illus., Quality PB, 978-1-58023-079-7 **$16.95**

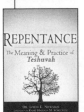

First Steps to a New Jewish Spirit: Reb Zalman's Guide to Recapturing the Intimacy & Ecstasy in Your Relationship with God *By Rabbi Zalman M. Schachter-Shalomi with Donald Gropman* 6 x 9, 144 pp, Quality PB, 978-1-58023-182-4 **$16.95**

Foundations of Sephardic Spirituality: The Inner Life of Jews of the Ottoman Empire
By Rabbi Marc D. Angel, PhD 6 x 9, 224 pp, Quality PB, 978-1-58023-341-5 **$18.99**

God & the Big Bang: Discovering Harmony between Science & Spirituality
By Dr. Daniel C. Matt 6 x 9, 216 pp, Quality PB, 978-1-879045-89-7 **$18.99**

God in Our Relationships: Spirituality between People from the Teachings of Martin Buber *By Rabbi Dennis S. Ross* 5½ x 8½, 160 pp, Quality PB, 978-1-58023-147-3 **$16.95**

Judaism, Physics and God: Searching for Sacred Metaphors in a Post-Einstein World
By Rabbi David W. Nelson 6 x 9, 352 pp, Quality PB, inc. reader's discussion guide,
978-1-58023-306-4 **$18.99**; HC, 352 pp, 978-1-58023-252-4 **$24.99**

Meaning & Mitzvah: Daily Practices for Reclaiming Judaism through Prayer, God, Torah, Hebrew, Mitzvot and Peoplehood *By Rabbi Goldie Milgram*
7 x 9, 336 pp, Quality PB, 978-1-58023-256-2 **$19.99**

Repentance: The Meaning and Practice of Teshuvah
By Dr. Louis E. Newman; Foreword by Rabbi Harold M. Schulweis; Preface by Rabbi Karyn D. Kedar
6 x 9, 256 pp, HC, 978-1-58023-426-9 **$24.99** Quality PB, 978-1-58023-718-5 **$18.99**

The Sabbath Soul: Mystical Reflections on the Transformative Power of Holy Time
Selection, Translation and Commentary by Eitan Fishbane, PhD
6 x 9, 208 pp, Quality PB, 978-1-58023-459-7 **$18.99**

Tanya, the Masterpiece of Hasidic Wisdom: Selections Annotated & Explained
Translation & Annotation by Rabbi Rami Shapiro; Foreword by Rabbi Zalman M. Schachter-Shalomi
5½ x 8½, 240 pp, Quality PB, 978-1-59473-275-1 **$16.99**

These Are the Words, 2nd Edition: A Vocabulary of Jewish Spiritual Life
By Rabbi Arthur Green, PhD 6 x 9, 320 pp, Quality PB, 978-1-58023-494-8 **$19.99**

Inspiration

Saying No and Letting Go: Jewish Wisdom on Making Room for What Matters Most
By Rabbi Edwin Goldberg, DHL; Foreword by Rabbi Naomi Levy
Taps into timeless Jewish wisdom that teaches how to "hold on tightly" to the things that matter most while learning to "let go lightly" of the demands and worries that do not ultimately matter. 6 x 9, 192 pp, Quality PB, 978-1-58023-670-6 **$16.99**

The Magic of Hebrew Chant: Healing the Spirit, Transforming the Mind, Deepening Love *By Rabbi Shefa Gold; Foreword by Sylvia Boorstein*
Introduces this transformative spiritual practice as a way to unlock the power of sacred texts and make prayer and meditation the delight of your life. Includes musical notations. 6 x 9, 352 pp, Quality PB, 978-1-58023-671-3 **$24.99**

The Bridge to Forgiveness: Stories and Prayers for Finding God and Restoring Wholeness *By Rabbi Karyn D. Kedar* 6 x 9, 176 pp, Quality PB, 978-1-58023-451-1 **$16.99**

The Empty Chair: Finding Hope and Joy—Timeless Wisdom from a Hasidic Master, Rebbe Nachman of Breslov *Adapted by Moshe Mykoff and the Breslov Research Institute*
4 x 6, 128 pp, Deluxe PB w/ flaps, 978-1-879045-67-5 **$9.99**

A Formula for Proper Living: Practical Lessons from Life and Torah
By Rabbi Abraham J. Twerski, MD 6 x 9, 144 pp, HC, 978-1-58023-402-3 **$19.99**

The Gentle Weapon: Prayers for Everyday and Not-So-Everyday Moments—Timeless Wisdom from the Teachings of the Hasidic Master, Rebbe Nachman of Breslov *Adapted by Moshe Mykoff and S. C. Mizrahi, together with the Breslov Research Institute*
4 x 6, 144 pp, Deluxe PB w/ flaps, 978-1-58023-022-3 **$9.99**

The God Upgrade: Finding Your 21st-Century Spirituality in Judaism's 5,000-Year-Old Tradition *By Rabbi Jamie Korngold; Foreword by Rabbi Harold M. Schulweis*
6 x 9, 176 pp, Quality PB, 978-1-58023-443-6 $15.99

God Whispers: Stories of the Soul, Lessons of the Heart *By Rabbi Karyn D. Kedar*
6 x 9, 176 pp, Quality PB, 978-1-58023-088-9 **$15.95**

God's To-Do List: 103 Ways to Be an Angel and Do God's Work on Earth
By Dr. Ron Wolfson 6 x 9, 144 pp, Quality PB, 978-1-58023-301-9 **$16.99**

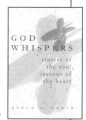

Happiness and the Human Spirit: The Spirituality of Becoming the Best You Can Be
By Rabbi Abraham J. Twerski, MD
6 x 9, 176 pp, Quality PB, 978-1-58023-404-7 **$16.99**; HC, 978-1-58023-343-9 **$19.99**

Life's Daily Blessings: Inspiring Reflections on Gratitude and Joy for Every Day, Based on Jewish Wisdom *By Rabbi Kerry M. Olitzky* 4½ x 6½, 368 pp, Quality PB, 978-1-58023-396-5 **$16.99**

Restful Reflections: Nighttime Inspiration to Calm the Soul, Based on Jewish Wisdom
By Rabbi Kerry M. Olitzky and Rabbi Lori Forman-Jacobi 5 x 8, 352 pp, Quality PB, 978-1-58023-091-9 **$16.99**

Sacred Intentions: Morning Inspiration to Strengthen the Spirit, Based on Jewish Wisdom
By Rabbi Kerry M. Olitzky and Rabbi Lori Forman-Jacobi 4½ x 6½, 448 pp, Quality PB, 978-1-58023-061-2 **$16.99**

The Seven Questions You're Asked in Heaven: Reviewing and Renewing Your Life on Earth *By Dr. Ron Wolfson* 6 x 9, 176 pp, Quality PB, 978-1-58023-407-8 **$16.99**

Kabbalah / Mysticism

Jewish Mysticism and the Spiritual Life: Classical Texts, Contemporary Reflections *Edited by Dr. Lawrence Fine, Dr. Eitan Fishbane and Rabbi Or N. Rose*
Inspirational and thought-provoking materials for contemplation, discussion and action. 6 x 9, 256 pp, HC, 978-1-58023-434-4 **$24.99** Quality PB, 978-1-58023-719-2 **$18.99**

Ehyeh: A Kabbalah for Tomorrow
By Rabbi Arthur Green, PhD 6 x 9, 224 pp, Quality PB, 978-1-58023-213-5 **$18.99**

The Gift of Kabbalah: Discovering the Secrets of Heaven, Renewing Your Life on Earth
By Tamar Frankiel, PhD 6 x 9, 256 pp, Quality PB, 978-1-58023-141-1 **$16.95**

Seek My Face: A Jewish Mystical Theology *By Rabbi Arthur Green, PhD*
6 x 9, 304 pp, Quality PB, 978-1-58023-130-5 **$19.95**

Zohar: Annotated & Explained *Translation & Annotation by Dr. Daniel C. Matt; Foreword by Andrew Harvey* 5½ x 8½, 176 pp, Quality PB, 978-1-893361-51-5 **$16.99**
(A book from SkyLight Paths, Jewish Lights' sister imprint)

See also *The Way Into Jewish Mystical Tradition* in The Way Into… Series.

Theology / Philosophy / The Way Into... Series

The Way Into... series offers an accessible and highly usable "guided tour" of the Jewish faith, people, history and beliefs—in total, an introduction to Judaism that will enable you to understand and interact with the sacred texts of the Jewish tradition. Each volume is written by a leading contemporary scholar and teacher, and explores one key aspect of Judaism. The Way Into... series enables all readers to achieve a real sense of Jewish cultural literacy through guided study.

The Way Into Encountering God in Judaism
By Rabbi Neil Gillman, PhD
For everyone who wants to understand how Jews have encountered God throughout history and today.
6 x 9, 240 pp, Quality PB, 978-1-58023-199-2 **$18.99**; HC, 978-1-58023-025-4 **$21.95**
Also Available: **The Jewish Approach to God:** A Brief Introduction for Christians
By Rabbi Neil Gillman, PhD
5½ x 8½, 192 pp, Quality PB, 978-1-58023-190-9 **$16.95**

The Way Into Jewish Mystical Tradition
By Rabbi Lawrence Kushner
Allows readers to interact directly with the sacred mystical texts of the Jewish tradition. An accessible introduction to the concepts of Jewish mysticism, their religious and spiritual significance, and how they relate to life today.
6 x 9, 224 pp, Quality PB, 978-1-58023-200-5 **$18.99**

The Way Into Jewish Prayer
By Rabbi Lawrence A. Hoffman, PhD
Opens the door to 3,000 years of Jewish prayer, making anyone feel at home in the Jewish way of communicating with God.
6 x 9, 208 pp, Quality PB, 978-1-58023-201-2 **$18.99**

The Way Into Jewish Prayer Teacher's Guide
By Rabbi Jennifer Ossakow Goldsmith
8½ x 11, 42 pp, PB, 978-1-58023-345-3 **$8.99**
Download a free copy at www.jewishlights.com.

The Way Into Judaism and the Environment
By Jeremy Benstein, PhD
Explores the ways in which Judaism contributes to contemporary social-environmental issues, the extent to which Judaism is part of the problem and how it can be part of the solution.
6 x 9, 288 pp, Quality PB, 978-1-58023-368-2 **$18.99**; HC, 978-1-58023-268-5 **$24.99**

The Way Into Tikkun Olam (Repairing the World)
By Rabbi Elliot N. Dorff, PhD
An accessible introduction to the Jewish concept of the individual's responsibility to care for others and repair the world.
6 x 9, 304 pp, Quality PB, 978-1-58023-328-6 **$18.99**

The Way Into Torah
By Rabbi Norman J. Cohen, PhD
Helps guide you in the exploration of the origins and development of Torah, explains why it should be studied and how to do it.
6 x 9, 176 pp, Quality PB, 978-1-58023-198-5 **$16.99**

The Way Into the Varieties of Jewishness
By Sylvia Barack Fishman, PhD
Explores the religious and historical understanding of what it has meant to be Jewish from ancient times to the present controversy over "Who is a Jew?"
6 x 9, 288 pp, Quality PB, 978-1-58023-367-5 **$18.99**; HC, 978-1-58023-030-8 **$24.99**

Theology / Philosophy

From Defender to Critic: The Search for a New Jewish Self
By Dr. David Hartman
A daring self-examination of Hartman's goals, which were not to strip halakha of its authority but to create a space for questioning and critique that allows for the traditionally religious Jew to act out a moral life in tune with modern experience.
6 x 9, 336 pp, HC, 978-1-58023-515-0 **$35.00**

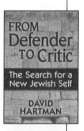

The God Who Hates Lies: Confronting & Rethinking Jewish Tradition
A deeply personal look at the struggle between commitment to Jewish religious tradition and personal morality.
By Dr. David Hartman with Charlie Buckholtz 6 x 9, 208 pp, HC, 978-1-58023-455-9 **$24.99**

Our Religious Brains: What Cognitive Science Reveals about Belief, Morality, Community and Our Relationship with God
By Rabbi Ralph D. Mecklenburger; Foreword by Dr. Howard Kelfer; Preface by Dr. Neil Gillman
This is a groundbreaking, accessible look at the implications of cognitive science for religion and theology, intended for laypeople. 6 x 9, 224 pp, HC, 978-1-58023-508-2 **$24.99**

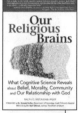

The Other Talmud—*The Yerushalmi*: Unlocking the Secrets of The Talmud of Israel for Judaism Today *By Rabbi Judith Z. Abrams, PhD*
A fascinating—and stimulating—look at "the other Talmud" and the possibilities for Jewish life reflected there. 6 x 9, 256 pp, HC, 978-1-58023-463-4 **$24.99**

The Way of Man: According to Hasidic Teaching
By Martin Buber; New Translation and Introduction by Rabbi Bernard H. Mehlman and Dr. Gabriel E. Padawer; Foreword by Paul Mendes-Flohr
An accessible and engaging new translation of Buber's classic work—*available as an e-book only.* E-book, 978-1-58023-601-0 Digital List Price **$14.99**

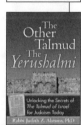

The Death of Death: Resurrection and Immortality in Jewish Thought
By Rabbi Neil Gillman, PhD 6 x 9, 336 pp, Quality PB, 978-1-58023-081-0 **$18.95**

Doing Jewish Theology: God, Torah & Israel in Modern Judaism *By Rabbi Neil Gillman, PhD*
6 x 9, 304 pp, Quality PB, 978-1-58023-439-9 **$18.99**; HC, 978-1-58023-322-4 **$24.99**

A Heart of Many Rooms: Celebrating the Many Voices within Judaism
By Dr. David Hartman 6 x 9, 352 pp, Quality PB, 978-1-58023-156-5 **$19.95**

Jewish Theology in Our Time: A New Generation Explores the Foundations and Future of Jewish Belief *Edited by Rabbi Elliot J. Cosgrove, PhD; Foreword by Rabbi David J. Wolpe; Preface by Rabbi Carole B. Balin, PhD* 6 x 9, 240 pp, Quality PB, 978-1-58023-630-1, **$19.99**; HC, 978-1-58023-413-9 **$24.99**

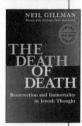

Maimonides—Essential Teachings on Jewish Faith & Ethics: The Book of Knowledge & the Thirteen Principles of Faith—Annotated & Explained
Translation and Annotation by Rabbi Marc D. Angel, PhD
5½ x 8½, 224 pp, Quality PB Original, 978-1-59473-311-6 **$18.99***

Maimonides, Spinoza and Us: Toward an Intellectually Vibrant Judaism
By Rabbi Marc D. Angel, PhD 6 x 9, 224 pp, HC, 978-1-58023-411-5 **$24.99**

Your Word Is Fire: The Hasidic Masters on Contemplative Prayer
Edited and translated by Rabbi Arthur Green, PhD, and Barry W. Holtz
6 x 9, 160 pp, Quality PB, 978-1-879045-25-5 **$16.99**

I Am Jewish
Personal Reflections Inspired by the Last Words of Daniel Pearl
Almost 150 Jews—both famous and not—from all walks of life, from all around the world, write about many aspects of their Judaism.
Edited by Judea and Ruth Pearl 6 x 9, 304 pp, Deluxe PB w/ flaps, 978-1-58023-259-3 **$19.99**
Download a free copy of the *I Am Jewish Teacher's Guide* at www.jewishlights.com.

Hannah Senesh: Her Life and Diary, The First Complete Edition
By Hannah Senesh; Foreword by Marge Piercy; Preface by Eitan Senesh; Afterword by Roberta Grossman
6 x 9, 368 pp, b/w photos, Quality PB, 978-1-58023-342-2 **$19.99**

*A book from SkyLight Paths, Jewish Lights' sister imprint

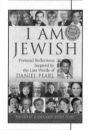

Spirituality / Prayer

Davening: A Guide to Meaningful Jewish Prayer
By Rabbi Zalman Schachter-Shalomi with Joel Segel; Foreword by Rabbi Lawrence Kushner
A fresh approach to prayer for all who wish to appreciate the power of prayer's poetry, song and ritual, and to join the age-old conversation that Jews have had with God. 6 x 9, 240 pp, Quality PB, 978-1-58023-627-0 **$18.99**

Jewish Men Pray: Words of Yearning, Praise, Petition, Gratitude and Wonder from Traditional and Contemporary Sources
Edited by Rabbi Kerry M. Olitzky and Stuart M. Matlins; Foreword by Rabbi Bradley Shavit Artson, DHL
A celebration of Jewish men's voices in prayer—to strengthen, heal, comfort, and inspire—from the ancient world up to our own day.
5 x 7¼, 400 pp, HC, 978-1-58023-628-7 **$19.99**

Making Prayer Real: Leading Jewish Spiritual Voices on Why Prayer Is Difficult and What to Do about It *By Rabbi Mike Comins* 6 x 9, 320 pp, Quality PB, 978-1-58023-417-7 **$18.99**

Witnesses to the One: The Spiritual History of the *Sh'ma*
By Rabbi Joseph B. Meszler; Foreword by Rabbi Elyse Goldstein
6 x 9, 176 pp, Quality PB, 978-1-58023-400-9 **$16.99**; HC, 978-1-58023-309-5 **$19.99**

My People's Prayer Book Series: Traditional Prayers, Modern Commentaries *Edited by Rabbi Lawrence A. Hoffman, PhD*
Provides diverse and exciting commentary to the traditional liturgy. Will help you find new wisdom in Jewish prayer, and bring liturgy into your life. Each book includes Hebrew text, modern translations and commentaries from all perspectives of the Jewish world.

Vol. 1—The *Sh'ma* and Its Blessings
  7 x 10, 168 pp, HC, 978-1-879045-79-8 **$29.99**
Vol. 2—The *Amidah* 7 x 10, 240 pp, HC, 978-1-879045-80-4 **$24.95**
Vol. 3—*P'sukei D'zimrah* (Morning Psalms)
  7 x 10, 240 pp, HC, 978-1-879045-81-1 **$29.99**
Vol. 4—*Seder K'riat Hatorah* (The Torah Service)
  7 x 10, 264 pp, HC, 978-1-879045-82-8 **$29.99**
Vol. 5—*Birkhot Hashachar* (Morning Blessings)
  7 x 10, 240 pp, HC, 978-1-879045-83-5 **$24.95**
Vol. 6—*Tachanun* and Concluding Prayers
  7 x 10, 240 pp, HC, 978-1-879045-84-2 **$24.95**
Vol. 7—*Shabbat at Home* 7 x 10, 240 pp, HC, 978-1-879045-85-9 **$24.95**
Vol. 8—*Kabbalat Shabbat* (Welcoming Shabbat in the Synagogue)
  7 x 10, 240 pp, HC, 978-1-58023-121-3 **$24.99**
Vol. 9—Welcoming the Night: *Minchah* and *Ma'ariv* (Afternoon and Evening Prayer) 7 x 10, 272 pp, HC, 978-1-58023-262-3 **$24.99**
Vol. 10—Shabbat Morning: *Shacharit* and *Musaf* (Morning and Additional Services) 7 x 10, 240 pp, HC, 978-1-58023-240-1 **$29.99**

Spirituality / Lawrence Kushner

I'm God; You're Not: Observations on Organized Religion & Other Disguises of the Ego
6 x 9, 256 pp, Quality PB, 978-1-58023-513-6 **$18.99**; HC, 978-1-58023-441-2 **$21.99**

The Book of Letters: A Mystical Hebrew Alphabet
Popular HC Edition, 6 x 9, 80 pp, 2-color text, 978-1-879045-00-2 **$24.95**
Collector's Limited Edition, 9 x 12, 80 pp, gold-foil-embossed pages, w/ limited-edition silkscreened print, 978-1-879045-04-0 **$349.00**

The Book of Miracles: A Young Person's Guide to Jewish Spiritual Awareness
6 x 9, 96 pp, 2-color illus., HC, 978-1-879045-78-1 **$16.95** *For ages 9–13*

God Was in This Place & I, i Did Not Know: Finding Self, Spirituality and Ultimate Meaning 6 x 9, 192 pp, Quality PB, 978-1-879045-33-0 **$16.95**

Honey from the Rock: An Introduction to Jewish Mysticism
6 x 9, 176 pp, Quality PB, 978-1-58023-073-5 **$16.95**

Invisible Lines of Connection: Sacred Stories of the Ordinary
5½ x 8½, 160 pp, Quality PB, 978-1-879045-98-9 **$16.99**

The Way Into Jewish Mystical Tradition
6 x 9, 224 pp, Quality PB, 978-1-58023-200-5 **$18.99**; HC, 978-1-58023-029-2 **$21.95**

Holidays / Holy Days

Prayers of Awe Series

An exciting new series that examines the High Holy Day liturgy to enrich the praying experience of everyone—whether experienced worshipers or guests who encounter Jewish prayer for the very first time.

We Have Sinned—Sin and Confession in Judaism: Ashamnu and Al Chet
Edited by Rabbi Lawrence A. Hoffman, PhD
A varied and fascinating look at sin, confession and pardon in Judaism, as suggested by the centrality of *Ashamnu* and *Al Chet*, two prayers that people know so well, though understand so little.   6 x 9, 304 pp, HC, 978-1-58023-612-6 **$24.99**

Who by Fire, Who by Water—Un'taneh Tokef
Edited by Rabbi Lawrence A. Hoffman, PhD 6 x 9, 272 pp, HC, 978-1-58023-424-5 **$24.99**

All These Vows—Kol Nidre
Edited by Rabbi Lawrence A. Hoffman, PhD 6 x 9, 288 pp, HC, 978-1-58023-430-6 **$24.99**

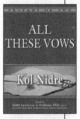

Rosh Hashanah Readings: Inspiration, Information and Contemplation
Yom Kippur Readings: Inspiration, Information and Contemplation
Edited by Rabbi Dov Peretz Elkins; Section Introductions from Arthur Green's These Are the Words
Rosh Hashanah: 6 x 9, 400 pp, Quality PB, 978-1-58023-437-5 **$19.99**
Yom Kippur: 6 x 9, 368 pp, Quality PB, 978-1-58023-438-2 **$19.99**; HC, 978-1-58023-271-5 **$24.99**

Reclaiming Judaism as a Spiritual Practice: Holy Days and Shabbat
By Rabbi Goldie Milgram 7 x 9, 272 pp, Quality PB, 978-1-58023-205-0 **$19.99**

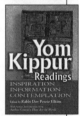

The Sabbath Soul: Mystical Reflections on the Transformative Power of Holy Time
Selection, Translation and Commentary by Eitan Fishbane, PhD
6 x 9, 208 pp, Quality PB, 978-1-58023-459-7 **$18.99**

Shabbat, 2nd Edition: The Family Guide to Preparing for and Celebrating the Sabbath
By Dr. Ron Wolfson 7 x 9, 320 pp, Illus., Quality PB, 978-1-58023-164-0 **$19.99**

Hanukkah, 2nd Edition: The Family Guide to Spiritual Celebration
By Dr. Ron Wolfson 7 x 9, 240 pp, Illus., Quality PB, 978-1-58023-122-0 **$18.95**

Passover

My People's Passover Haggadah
Traditional Texts, Modern Commentaries
Edited by Rabbi Lawrence A. Hoffman, PhD, and David Arnow, PhD
A diverse and exciting collection of commentaries on the traditional Passover Haggadah—in two volumes!
Vol. 1: 7 x 10, 304 pp, HC, 978-1-58023-354-5 **$24.99**
Vol. 2: 7 x 10, 320 pp, HC, 978-1-58023-346-0 **$24.99**

Freedom Journeys: The Tale of Exodus and Wilderness across Millennia
By Rabbi Arthur O. Waskow and Rabbi Phyllis O. Berman
Explores how the story of Exodus echoes in our own time, calling us to relearn and rethink the Passover story through social-justice, ecological, feminist and interfaith perspectives.   6 x 9, 288 pp, HC, 978-1-58023-445-0 **$24.99**

Leading the Passover Journey: The Seder's Meaning Revealed,
the Haggadah's Story Retold *By Rabbi Nathan Laufer*
Uncovers the hidden meaning of the Seder's rituals and customs.
6 x 9, 224 pp, Quality PB, 978-1-58023-399-6 **$18.99**

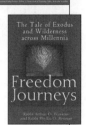

Creating Lively Passover Seders, 2nd Edition: A Sourcebook of Engaging Tales,
Texts & Activities *By David Arnow, PhD* 7 x 9, 464 pp, Quality PB, 978-1-58023-444-3 **$24.99**

Passover, 2nd Edition: The Family Guide to Spiritual Celebration
By Dr. Ron Wolfson with Joel Lurie Grishaver 7 x 9, 416 pp, Quality PB, 978-1-58023-174-9 **$19.95**

The Women's Passover Companion: Women's Reflections on the Festival of Freedom
Edited by Rabbi Sharon Cohen Anisfeld, Tara Mohr and Catherine Spector; Foreword by Paula E. Hyman
6 x 9, 352 pp, Quality PB, 978-1-58023-231-9 **$19.99**; HC, 978-1-58023-128-2 **$24.95**

The Women's Seder Sourcebook: Rituals & Readings for Use at the Passover Seder
Edited by Rabbi Sharon Cohen Anisfeld, Tara Mohr and Catherine Spector
6 x 9, 384 pp, Quality PB, 978-1-58023-232-6 **$19.99**

About Jewish Lights

People of all faiths and backgrounds yearn for books that attract, engage, educate, and spiritually inspire.

Our principal goal is to stimulate thought and help all people learn about who the Jewish People are, where they come from, and what the future can be made to hold. While people of our diverse Jewish heritage are the primary audience, our books speak to people in the Christian world as well and will broaden their understanding of Judaism and the roots of their own faith.

We bring to you authors who are at the forefront of spiritual thought and experience. While each has something different to say, they all say it in a voice that you can hear.

Our books are designed to welcome you and then to engage, stimulate, and inspire. We judge our success not only by whether or not our books are beautiful and commercially successful, but by whether or not they make a difference in your life.

For your information and convenience, at the back of this book we have provided a list of other Jewish Lights books you might find interesting and useful. They cover all the categories of your life:

Bar/Bat Mitzvah	Life Cycle
Bible Study / Midrash	Meditation
Children's Books	Men's Interest
Congregation Resources	Parenting
Current Events / History	Prayer / Ritual / Sacred Practice
Ecology / Environment	Social Justice
Fiction: Mystery, Science Fiction	Spirituality
Grief / Healing	Theology / Philosophy
Holidays / Holy Days	Travel
Inspiration	Twelve Steps
Kabbalah / Mysticism / Enneagram	Women's Interest

Stuart M. Matlins, Publisher

Or phone, fax, mail or e-mail to: **JEWISH LIGHTS Publishing**
Sunset Farm Offices, Route 4 • P.O. Box 237 • Woodstock, Vermont 05091
Tel: (802) 457-4000 • Fax: (802) 457-4004 • www.jewishlights.com
Credit card orders: (800) 962-4544 (8:30AM–5:30PM EST Monday–Friday)
Generous discounts on quantity orders. SATISFACTION GUARANTEED. Prices subject to change.

For more information about each book, visit our website at www.jewishlights.com